The Pump House Gang

TOM

WOLFE

by Tom Wolfe

The Pump House Gang

FARRAR, STRAUS & GIROUX
New York

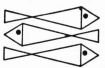

To my father and mother

Published in Canada by Collins Publishers, Toronto
Printed in the United States of America

Acknowledgments

The following chapters were first published, in slightly different form, in the London *Weekend Telegraph:* "The Noonday Underground," "The Life & Hard Times of a Teenage London Society Girl," "The Private Game," and "The Mid-Atlantic Man." All the other chapters first appeared in *New York*, the Sunday magazine section of the New York *World Journal Tribune*. Many of these have been substantially revised, and several appeared under different titles: "The Hair Boys" appeared as "Happy Mass Fop"; "Tom Wolfe's New Book of Etiquette" appeared as "New Manners for New York"; and "Bob and Spike" as "Upward with the Arts."

Illustrations by the author

Contents

x : *Contents*

The Pump House Gang

Introduction

I WROTE all but two* of these stories in one ten-month stretch after the publication of my first book, *The Kandy-Kolored Tangerine-Flake Streamline Baby*. It was a strange time for me. Many rogue volts of euphoria. I went from one side of this country to the other and then from one side of England to the other. The people I met—the things they did—I was entranced. I met Carol Doda. She blew up her breasts with emulsified silicone, the main ingredient in Silly Putty, and became the greatest resource of the San Francisco tourist industry. I met a group of surfers, the Pump House Gang. They attended the Watts riot as if it were the Rose Bowl game in Pasadena. They came to watch "the drunk niggers" and were reprimanded by the same for their rowdiness. In London I met a competitive 17-year-old named Nicki who got one-up on her schoolgirl chums by taking a Kurdish clubfoot lover. I met a £9-a-week office boy named Larry Lynch. He spent his lunch hour every day with hundreds of other child laborers in the crazed pitchblack innards of a noonday nightclub called Tiles. All of them *in ecstasis* from the frug, the rock 'n' roll, and God

* "The Automated Hotel" and "Tom Wolfe's New Book of Etiquette."

knows what else, for an hour—then back to work. In
Chicago I met Hugh Hefner. He revolved on his bed,
offering scenic notes as his head floated by—

Now, about Hefner. I was heading for California from
New York and I happened to stop off in Chicago. I was
walking down North Michigan Avenue when I ran into a
man from the Playboy organization, Lee Gottlieb. Something he said made me assume that Hefner was out of town.

"Out of town?" said Gottlieb. "Hef never leaves his
house."

"Never?"

Never, said Gottlieb. At least not for months at a time,
and even then only long enough to get in a limousine and
go to the airport and fly to New York for a TV show or to
some place or other for the opening of a new Playboy
Club. This fascinated me, the idea that Hefner, the Main
Playboy himself, was now a recluse. The next afternoon I
went to the Playboy offices on East Ohio Street to see
about getting in to see him. In the office they kept track of
Hefner's physical posture in his Mansion, which was over
on North State Parkway, as if by play-by-play Telex. He
was flat out in bed asleep, they told me, and wouldn't be
awake until around midnight. That night I was killing time
in a dive in downtown Chicago when a courier materialized
and told me Hefner was now on his feet and could see me.

Hefner's Playboy Mansion had a TV eye at the front
portals and huge black guards or major-domos inside.
Nubian slaves, I kept saying to myself. One of the blacks
led me up a grand staircase covered in red wall-to-wall, to a
massive carved-wood doorway bearing the inscription,
Si Non Oscillas, Noli Tintinnare, "If you don't swing, don't
ring." Inside were Hefner's private chambers. Hefner came
charging out of a pair of glass doors within. He was wound
up and ready to go. "Look at this!" he said. "Isn't this fantastic!" It was an issue of *Ramparts* magazine that had just

come. It had a glossy foldout, like the one in *Playboy*. Only this one had a picture of Hefner. In the picture he was wearing a suit and smoking a pipe. "Isn't this fantastic!" Hefner kept saying. Right now he was wearing silk pajamas, a bathrobe, and a pair of slippers with what looked like embroidered wolf heads on them. This was not, however, because he had just gotten up. It was his standard wear for the day, this day, every day, the uniform of the contemporary recluse.

There were several people in attendance at the midnight hour. The *dame d'honneur* of the palace, who was named Michele; Gottlieb; a couple of other Playboy personnel; the blacks: they were all dressed, however. Hefner showed me through his chambers. The place was kept completely draped and shuttered. The only light, day or night, was electric. It would be impossible to keep track of the days in there. And presently Hefner jumped onto . . . the center of his world, the bed in his bedroom. Aimed at the bed was a TV camera he was very proud of. Later on *Playboy* ran a cartoon showing a nude man and woman in a huge bed with a TV set facing them, and the man is saying, "And now, darling, how about an instant replay." Hefner hit a dial and the bed started revolving . . .

All I could think of at that moment was Jay Gatsby in the Fitzgerald novel. Both were scramblers who came up from out of nowhere to make their fortunes and build their palaces and ended up in regal isolation. But there was a major difference between Hefner and Gatsby. Hefner no longer dreamed, if he ever did, of making the big social leap to East Egg. It was at least plausible for Gatsby to hope to make it into Society. But Hefner? He has made a fortune, created an empire, and the Playboy Beacon shines out over the city and the Great Lakes. But socially Hefner is still a man who runs a tit magazine and a string of clubs that recall the parlor floor—not the upper floors but the parlor floor—of a red-flock whorehouse. There is no Society in Chicago for Hugh Hefner.

So he has gone them one better. He has started his own league. He has created his own world, in his own palace. He has created his own statusphere. The outside world comes to him, including the talented and the celebrated. Jules Feiffer stays awhile in his scarlet guest suite. Norman Mailer skinnydips in his Playboy swimming pool. He has his courtiers, his girls, and his Nubian slaves. Not even God's own diurnal light rhythm intrudes upon the order that Hefner has founded inside.

What a marvelous idea! After all, the community has never been one great happy family for all men. In fact, I would say the opposite has been true. Community status systems have been games with few winners and many who feel like losers. What an intriguing thought—for a man to take his new riches and free time and his machines and *split* from *communitas* and start his own league. He will still have status competition—but he invents the rules.

Why has no one ever done it before? Well, of course, people have. Robin Hood did it. Spades, homosexuals, artists, and street gangs have done it. All sorts of outlaws, and outcasts, by necessity or choice. The intriguing thing today, I was to find, is that so many Americans and Englishmen of middle and lower incomes are now doing the same thing. Not out of "rebellion" or "alienation"— they just want to be happy winners for a change.

What is a California electronics worker making $18,000 a year supposed to do with his new riches? Set about getting his son into Culver Military and himself and the wife into the Doral Beach Country Club? Socially, he is a glorified mechanic. Why not, à la Hefner, put it all into turning his home into a palace of technological glories— and extend that abroad in the land with a Buick Estate Wagon and a Pontiac GTO—and upon the seas with an

Evinrude cruiser and even into the air with a Cessna 172? Why not surround the palace with my favorite piece of landscaping of the happy worker suburbs of the American West, the Home Moat. It is about three feet wide and a foot and a half deep. Instructions for placing rocks, flowers, and shrubs are available. The Home Moat is a psychological safeguard against the intrusion of the outside world. The Home Moat guards against the fear that *It* is going to creep up in the night and press its nose against your picture window.

Southern California, I found, is a veritable paradise of statuspheres. For example, the move to age segregation. There are old people's housing developments, private developments, in which no one under 50 may buy a home. There are apartment developments for single persons 20 to 30 only. The Sunset Strip in Los Angeles has become the exclusive hangout of the 16 to 25 set. In 1966 they came close to street warfare to keep it that way, against the police who moved in to "clean up."

And . . . the Pump House Gang. Here was a group of boys and girls who had banded together in a way that superficially resembled a street gang's. They had very little of the street gang's motivation, however. They came from middle-class and upper-middle-class homes in perhaps the most high-class beach community in California, La Jolla. They had very little sense of resentment toward their parents or "society" and weren't rebels. Their only "alienation" was the usual hassle of the adolescent, the feeling that he is being prodded into adulthood on somebody else's terms. So they did the latest thing. They split off—*to the beach! into the garages!*—and started their own league, based on the esoterica of surfing. They didn't resent the older people around them; they came to pity the old bastards because they couldn't partake of this esoteric statusphere.

The day I met the Pump House Gang, a group of them had just been thrown out of "Tom Coman's garage," as it was known. The next summer they moved up from the garage life to a group of apartments near the beach, a complex they named "La Colonia Tijuana." By this time some were shifting from the surfing life to the advance guard of something else—the psychedelic *head* world of California. That is another story. But even the *hippies*, as the heads came to be known, did not develop *sui generis*. Their so-called "dropping out" was nothing more than a still further elaboration of the kind of worlds that the surfers and the car kids I met—"The Hair Boys"—had been creating the decade before.

The Pump House Gang lived as though age segregation were a permanent state, as if it were inconceivable that any of them would ever grow old, i.e., 25. I foresaw the day when the California coastline would be littered with the bodies of aged and abandoned *Surferkinder*, like so many beached whales.

In fact, however, many of these kids seem to be able to bring the mental atmosphere of the surfer life forward with them into adulthood—even into the adult world where you have to make a living. I remember going to the motorcycle races at Gardena, California, which is just south of Watts, with a surfer who is now about 30 and has developed a large water-sport equipment business. This was a month after the Watts riots. We were sitting in the stands at Gardena. The motorcycles were roaring around the half-mile track below and flashing under the lights. Just beyond the track from where we sat were Watts and Compton.

"Tom," he said to me, "you should have been here last month."

"Why?"

"The riots," he said. "You should have been here. We were all sitting here right where we are now and the bikes

were going around down below here. And over here"—
over to the left you could look over the edge of the stands
and see the highway—"the National Guard units were
pulling and jumping off the trucks and getting into forma-
tion and everything with the bayonets and all. It was
terrific. And then, there"—and his gaze and his voice got a
far-off quality, going beyond the track and toward
Watts—"and there, there in the distance, was Los Angeles
. . . *burning!*"

A few minutes later ten motorcycles came into the first
turn, right in front of where we were sitting. Five went
down in a pile-up. Bodies shot through the air every which
way. I saw one, a rider in black and white racing leathers,
get hit in midair by one motorcycle and run over by the
one behind it. This was a kid named Clemmie Jackson. He
was dead. Everybody could see that. His neck was broken
like a stick. Two other riders were seriously injured. The
p.a. announcer didn't mention those who were lying there,
however. He only mentioned those who got up. "There's
No. 353, Rog Rogarogarog, he's up and his bike looks
O.K. . . ." As soon as the bodies were removed, the race
resumed. Luckily they hadn't had to take both the ambulances. They have two ambulances at the track, and if both
have to leave, the races have to stop until one returns. They
were able to get the three worst bodies into one ambulance.
The ambulance, a big white Cadillac, left very quietly. It
didn't even flash a light. About three minutes later you
could hear the siren start up, way down the highway. Off
in the distance, as they say. It was a freaking ghastly sound,
under the circumstances. Within seconds, however, the
race was on again, with five bikes instead of ten, and all was
forgotten. As usual, there were only a couple of paragraphs
in the papers about the death.

I don't think that is a very morbid incident, taken in
context. The half-mile racers are the wildest and most

suicidal crowd in the motorcycle life, but all the motorcycle crowds get a lot of their juice out of the luxury of
risking their necks. The motorcycle life has been perfect as
a statusphere. It is dangerous and therefore daring. It is as
esoteric as surfing. It can liberate you physically from the
communitas.

When you mention the motorcycle life, people tend to
think—again—of outlaws. Namely, the Hell's Angels. The
Angels and other motorcycle outlaws, however, make up
only a small part of the people who have started their own
league with their bikes. I'll never forget the Harley-
Davidson agency in Columbus, Ohio. A guy came in the
back there dragging a big Harley. It was all bent and
mashed, the spokes, the headers, the cylinder heads, the
sprocket, the drive chain. Everybody said, You had a
wreck! The guy said, Naw, it was my wife. Everybody
said, Was she hurt bad! The guy said, Naw, she took a
block of cement about this big and she—well, it seems she
had smashed the hell out of it. He had first bought the
Harley just for a little recreation away from the wife and
kids. Then he had discovered hundreds of motorcyclists
around Columbus—all drifting away from the wife and
kids. Pretty soon he was meeting the boys every day after
work at a place called Gully's and they would drink beer
and ride up to Lake Erie before coming home, a mere 200-
mile trip. By and by they had a whole new life for themselves—blissful liberation!—based on the motorcycle. Until
his wife decided to sort that little situation out . . .

Columbus is the world capital of the motorcycle life.
This statement, I find, comes as a surprise and an annoy-
ance—the damnable Hell's Angels again—to a lot of people
in Columbus, despite the fact that the American Motorcycle Association has its headquarters there. On the surface, Columbus could not be more conservative and
traditional. A few big property-owning families seem to

control everything. Well, they don't control the motor-cycle life, which has proliferated in and around the town over the past ten years in full rich variety, from half-mile racing daredevils to Honda touring clubs. They also have a local version of the Hell's Angels, the Road Rogues. The vast majority of Columbus motorcyclists, however, are perfectly law-abiding citizens who happen to have found an infinitely richer existence than being a standard wage-mule for whoever does run Columbus.

The two great motorcyclists of Columbus are Dick Klamforth, a former half-mile racing champion and now owner of the Honda agency there, the biggest in the country, and Tom Reiser. Reiser is truly one of the greats. He built "Tom's Bomb." He achieved an ultimate. He flew through the air of the American Midwest, astride a 300-horsepower Chevrolet V-8 engine . . . riding bare-back . . .

Now, this is not exactly what the great Utopian thinkers of the nineteenth century, the Saint-Simons, the Fouriers, and the Owens, had in mind when they envisioned a world of the future in which the ordinary working man would have the time and the money to extend his God-given potential to the fullest. The old Utopians believed in indus-trialism. In fact, it was Saint-Simon who coined the word. Yet the worker paradise industrialism would make possible was to take a somewhat more pastoral form. They saw it as a kind of Rousseauvian happy-primitive village with mod-ern conveniences. In short, a community, with everyone, great and small, knit together forever after, grateful as spaniels. More recently, in the 1920's and 1930's, the vision was amended. It now put the happy workers into neat lead-white blocks of Bauhaus apartments and added Culture. Every night, in this vision, the family would gather around the hearth and listen to Dad read from John Strachey or

Mayakovsky while WQXR droned in the background. The high point of the week would be Saturday afternoon, when Dad would put on his electric-blue suit—slightly gauche, you understand, but neat and clean and pressed, "touching," as it were—and the whole family would hold hands and walk up to the Culture Center to watch the Shock Workers of the Dance do a ballet called "Factory." Well, today, in the 1960's, the Culture Centers have sprouted up, sure enough. We have them in most of the metropolises of America. But where have all the happy workers gone? These temples to breeding and taste are usually constructed at great cost, in the name of "the people." But the people, the happy people, have left them to the cultivated, educated classes, the "diploma elite," who created them.

And even the cultivated classes—the term "upper classes" no longer works—are in a state of rather amusing confusion on the subject. When great fame—the certification of status—is available without great property, it is very bad news for the old idea of a class structure. In New York, for example, it is done for, but no one has bothered to announce its death. As a result, New York "Society" is now made up of a number of statuspheres—all busily raiding the old class order for trappings to make their fame look genuine. Business and other corporate statuspheres have been so busy cannibalizing the old aristocratic modes, I have had to write an entire new gull's handbook on the subject ("Tom Wolfe's New Book of Etiquette"). The great hotel corporations now advertise Luxury (equals "class") to the same crowd who used to go to those durable second-raters, the commercial or businessman's hotel. It is a pretty amusing invention, this second-class *class*, unless you happen to stay at The Automated Hotel without knowing the name of the game. Meanwhile, individual climbers are busy moving into separate little preserves that once made up the happy monolith of "the upper class"—such as charities and *Yes!* Culture—and I offer the golden example of Bob and Spike Scull for those who want to make it *Now*, without having to wait three generations, as old-fashioned sorts, such as the Kennedy family, had to do. Of course, with so many statuspheres now in operation, and so many short cuts available, there is a chronic chaos in Society. People are now reaching the top without quite knowing what on earth they have reached the top of. They don't know whether they have reached *The* Top or whether they have just had a wonderful fast ride up the service elevator. But as Bob Scull himself says: "Enjoy!"

What struck me throughout America and England was that so many people have found such novel ways of doing just that, *enjoying*, extending their egos way out on the best terms available, namely, their own. It is curious how many serious thinkers—and politicians—resist this rather obvious fact. Sheer ego extension—especially if attempted by all those rancid proles and suburban petty burghers—is a perplexing prospect. Even scary, one might say. Intellectuals and politicians currently exhibit a vast gummy nostalgia for the old restraints, the old limits, of the ancient ego-crusher: *Calamity*. Historically, calamity has been the one serious concern of serious people. War, Pestilence—Apocalypse! I was impressed by the profound relief with which intellectuals and politicians discovered poverty in America in 1963, courtesy of Michael Harrington's book *The Other America*. And, as I say, it was *discovered*. Eureka! We have found it again! We thought we had lost it! That was the spirit of the enterprise. When the race riots erupted—and when the war in Vietnam grew into a good-sized hell—intellectuals welcomed all that with a ghastly embrace, too. War! Poverty! Insurrection! Alienation! O Four Horsemen, you have not deserted us entirely. The game can go on.

One night, in the very middle of the period when I was writing these stories, I put on *my* electric-blue suit—it is truly electric blue—and took part in a symposium at Princeton with Günter Grass, Allen Ginsberg, and Gregory Markopoulos, who is an "underground" film-maker, before 1,200 students. The subject was "The Style of the Sixties." Paul Krassner was the moderator, and Krassner has a sense of humor, but the Horsemen charged on. Very soon the entire discussion was centered on police repression, Gestapo tactics, the knock on the door, the Triumph of the Knout. I couldn't believe what was happening, but there it was.

"What are you talking about?" I said. "We're in the middle of a . . . Happiness Explosion!" But I didn't know where to begin. I might as well have said let's talk about the Fisher King. Happiness, said Saint-Just a century ago, is a new concept in Europe. Apparently it was new here, un-heard-of almost. Ah, *philosophes!*—if we want to be *serious*, let us discuss the real apocalyptic future and things truly scary: ego extension, the politics of pleasure, the self-realization racket, the pharmacology of Overjoy . . .

But why discuss it now. I, for one, will be content merely to watch the faces of our leaders, political and intellectual, the day they wake up and look over their shoulders and catch the first glimpse of their erstwhile followers—streaking—*happy workers!*—in precisely the opposite direction, through God's own American ozone—*apocalyptic riders!*—astride their own custom versions—*enjoy!*—of the 300-horsepower Chevrolet V-8 engines of this world . . . riding bareback . . .

Part One

1 *The Pump House Gang*

OUR BOYS never hair out. The black panther has black feet. Black feet on the crumbling black panther. Pan-thuh. Mee-dah. Pam Stacy, 16 years old, a cute girl here in La Jolla, California, with a pair of orange bell-bottom hip-huggers on, sits on a step about four steps down the stairway to the beach and she can see a pair of revolting black feet without lifting her head. So she says it out loud, "The black panther."

Somebody farther down the stairs, one of the boys with the *major* hair and khaki shorts, says, "The black feet of the black panther."

"Mee-dah," says another kid. This happens to be the cry of a, well, *underground* society known as the Mac Meda Destruction Company.

"The pan-thuh."

"The poon-thuh."

All these kids, seventeen of them, members of the Pump House crowd, are lollygagging around the stairs down to Windansea Beach, La Jolla, California, about 11 a.m., and they all look at the black feet, which are a woman's pair of black street shoes, out of which stick a pair of old veiny white ankles, which lead up like a senile cone to a fudge of tallowy, edematous flesh, her thighs, squeezing out of her bathing suit, with old faded yellow bruises on them, which she probably got from running eight feet to catch a bus or something. She is standing with her old work-a-hubby, who has on *san*dals: you know, a pair of navy-blue anklet socks and these sandals with big, wide, new-smelling tan straps going this way and that, *for keeps.* Man, they look like orthopedic sandals, if one can imagine that. Obviously, these people come from Tucson or Albuquerque or one of those hincty adobe towns. All these hincty, crumbling black feet come to La Jolla-by-the-sea from the adobe towns for the weekend. They even drive in cars all full of thermos bottles and mayonnaisey sandwiches and some kind of latticework wooden-back support for the old crock who drives and Venetian blinds on the back window.

"The black panther."

"Pan-thuh."

"Poon-thuh."

"Mee-dah."

Nobody says it to the two old crocks directly. God, they must be practically 50 years old. Naturally, they're carrying every piece of garbage imaginable: the folding aluminum chairs, the newspapers, the lending-library book with the clear plastic wrapper on it, the sunglasses, the sun ointment, about a vat of goo—

It is a Mexican standoff. In a Mexican standoff, both parties narrow their eyes and glare but nobody throws a punch. Of course, nobody in the Pump House crowd would ever even jostle these people or say anything right to them; they are too cool for that.

Everybody in the Pump House crowd looks over, even Tom Coman, who is a cool person. Tom Coman, 16 years old, got thrown out of his garage last night. He is sitting up on top of the railing, near the stairs, up over the beach, with his legs apart. Some nice long willowy girl in yellow slacks is standing on the sidewalk but leaning into him with her arms around his body, just resting. Neale Jones, 16, a boy with great lank perfect surfer's hair, is standing nearby with a Band-Aid on his upper lip, where the sun has burnt it raw. Little Vicki Ballard is up on the sidewalk. Her older sister, Liz, is down the stairs by the Pump House itself, a concrete block, 15 feet high, full of machinery for the La Jolla water system. Liz is wearing her great "Liz" styles, a hulking rabbit-fur vest and black-leather boots over her Levis, even though it is about 85 out here and the sun is plugged in up there like God's own dentist lamp and the Pacific is heaving in with some fair-to-middling surf. Kit Tilden is lollygagging around, and Tom Jones, Connie Carter, Roger Johnson, Sharon Sandquist, Mary Beth White, Rupert Fellows, Glenn Jackson, Dan Watson from San Diego, they are all out here, and everybody takes a look at the panthers.

The old guy, one means, you know, he must be practically 50 years old, he says to his wife, "Come on, let's go farther up," and he takes her by her fat upper arm as if to wheel her around and aim her away from here.

But she says, "No! We have just as much right to be here as they do."

"That's *not the point—*"

"Are you going to—"

"*Mrs. Roberts,*" the work-a-hubby says, calling his own wife by her official married name, as if to say she took a vow once and his word is law, even if he is not testing it with the blond kids here—"farther up, *Mrs. Roberts.*"

They start to walk up the sidewalk, but one kid won't move his feet, and, oh, god, her work-a-hubby breaks into a terrible shaking Jello smile as she steps over them, as if to say, Excuse me, sir, I don't mean to make trouble, please, and don't you and your colleagues rise up and jump me, screaming *Gotcha*—

Mee-dah!

But exactly! This beach *is* verboten for people practically 50 years old. This is a segregated beach. They can look down on Windansea Beach and see nothing but lean tan kids. It is posted "no swimming" (for safety reasons), meaning surfing only. In effect, it is segregated by age. From Los Angeles on down the California coast, this is an era of age segregation. People have always tended to segregate themselves by age, teenagers hanging around with teenagers, old people with old people, like the old men who sit on the benches up near the Bronx Zoo and smoke black cigars. But before, age segregation has gone on within a larger community. Sooner or later during the day everybody has melted back into the old community network that embraces practically everyone, all ages.

But in California today surfers, not to mention rock 'n' roll kids and the hot-rodders or Hair Boys, named for their fanciful pompadours—all sorts of sets of kids—they don't merely hang around together. They establish whole little societies for themselves. In some cases they live with one another for months at a time. The "Sunset Strip" on Sunset Boulevard used to be a kind of Times Square for Hollywood hot dogs of all ages, anyone who wanted to promenade in his version of the high life. Today "The Strip" is almost completely the preserve of kids from about 16 to 25. It is lined with go-go clubs. One of them, a place called It's Boss, is set up for people 16 to 25 and won't let in anybody over 25, and there are some terrible I'm-dying-a-thousand-deaths scenes when a girl comes up with her boyfriend and the guy at the door at It's Boss doesn't think she looks under 25 and tells her she will have to produce some identification proving she is young enough to come in here and live The Strip kind of life and—she's *had* it, because she can't get up the I.D. and nothing in the world is going to make a woman look stupider than to stand around trying to argue *I'm younger than I look, I'm younger than I look.* So she practically shrivels up like a Peruvian shrunken head in front of her boyfriend and he trundles her off, looking for some place you can get an old doll like this into. One of the few remaining clubs for "older people," curiously, is the Playboy Club. There are apartment houses for people 20 to 30 only, such as the Sheri Plaza in Hollywood and the E'Questre Inn in Burbank. There are whole suburban housing developments, mostly private developments, where only people over 45 or 50 can buy a house. Whole towns, meantime, have become identified as "young": Venice, Newport Beach, Balboa—or "old": Pasadena, Riverside, Coronado Island.

Behind much of it—especially something like a whole nightclub district of a major city, "The Strip," going teenage—is, simply, money. World War II and the prosperity that followed pumped incredible amounts of money into the population, the white population at least, at every class level. All of a sudden here is an area with thousands of people from 16 to 25 who can get their hands on enough money to support a whole nightclub belt and to have the cars to get there and to set up autonomous worlds of their own in a fairly posh resort community like La Jolla—

—Tom Coman's garage. Some old bastard took Tom Coman's garage away from him, and that means eight or nine surfers are out of a place to stay.

"I went by there this morning, you ought to see the guy," Tom Coman says. Yellow Stretch Pants doesn't move. She has him around the waist. "He was out there painting and he had this brush and about a thousand gallons of ammonia. He was really going to scrub me out of there."

"What did he do with the furniture?"

"I don't know. He threw it out."

"What are you going to do?"

"I don't know."

"Where are you going to stay?"

"I don't know. I'll stay on the beach. It wouldn't be the first time. I haven't had a place to stay for three years, so I'm not going to start worrying now."

Everybody thinks that over awhile. Yellow Stretch just hangs on and smiles. Tom Coman, 16 years old, piping fate again. One of the girls says, "You can stay at my place, Tom."

"Um. Who's got a cigarette?"

Pam Stacy says, "You can have these."

Tom Coman lights a cigarette and says, "Let's have a destructo." A destructo is what can happen in a garage after eight or 10 surfers are kicked out of it.

"Mee-dah!"

"Wouldn't that be bitchen?" says Tom Coman. Bitchen is a surfer's term that means "great," usually.

"Bitchen!"

"Mee-dah!"

It's incredible—that old guy out there trying to scour the whole surfing life out of that garage. He's a pathetic figure. His shoulders are hunched over and he's dousing and scrubbing away and the sun doesn't give him a tan, it gives him these . . . *mottles* on the back of his neck. But never mind! The hell with destructo. One only has a destructo spontaneously, a Dionysian . . . *bursting out*, like those holes through the wall during the Mac Meda Destruction Company Convention at Manhattan Beach— Mee-dah!

Something will pan out. It's a magic economy—yes!—all up and down the coast from Los Angeles to Baja California kids can go to one of these beach towns and live the complete surfing life. They take off from home and get to the beach, and if they need a place to stay, well, somebody rents a garage for twenty bucks a month and everybody moves in, girls and boys. Furniture—it's like, one means, you know, one *appropriates* furniture from here and there. It's like the Volkswagen buses a lot of kids now use as beach wagons instead of woodies. Woodies are old station wagons, usually Fords, with wooden bodies, from back before 1953. One of the great things about a Volkswagen bus is that one can . . . *exchange* motors in about three minutes. A good VW motor exchanger can go up to a parked Volkswagen, and a few ratchets of the old wrench here and it's up and out and he has a new motor. There must be a few nice old black panthers around wondering why their nice hubby-mommy VWs don't run so good anymore—but—then—they—are—probably—puzzled—about —a—lot of things. Yes.

Cash—it's practically in the air. Around the beach in La Jolla a guy can walk right out in the street and stand there, stop cars and make the candid move. Mister, I've got a quarter, how about 50 cents so I can get a *large* draft. Or, I need some after-ski boots. And the panthers give one a Jello smile and hand it over. Or a guy who knows how to do it can get $40 from a single night digging clams, and it's nice out there. Or he can go around and take up a collection for a keg party, a keg of beer. Man, anybody who won't kick in a quarter for a keg is a jerk. A couple of good keg collections—that's a trip to Hawaii, which is the surfer's version of a trip to Europe: there is a great surf and great everything there. Neale spent three weeks in Hawaii last year. He got $30 from a girl friend, he scrounged a little here and there and got $70 more and he headed off for Hawaii with $100.02, that being the exact plane fare, and borrowed 25 cents when he got there to . . . blast the place up. He spent the 25 cents in a photo booth, showed

the photos to the people on the set of *Hawaii* and got a job
in the movie. What's the big orgy about money? It's warm,
nobody even wears shoes, nobody is starving.

All right, Mother gets worried about all this, but it is
limited worry, as John Shine says. Mainly, Mother says,
Sayonara, you all, and you head off for the beach.

The thing is, everybody, practically everybody, comes
from a good family. Everyone has been . . . *reared well*,
as they say. Everybody is very upper-middle, if you want
to bring it down to that. It's just that this is a new order.
Why hang around in the hubby-mommy household with
everybody getting neurotic hang-ups with each other and
slamming doors and saying, Why can't they have some
privacy? Or, it doesn't mean anything that I have to work
for a living, does it? It doesn't mean a thing to you. All of
you just lie around here sitting in the big orange easy chair
smoking cigarettes. I'd hate for you to have to smoke standing up, you'd probably get phlebitis from it—Listen to me,
Sarah—

—why go through all that? It's a good life out here.
Nobody is mugging everybody for money and affection.
There are a lot of bright people out here, and there are a
lot of interesting things. One night there was a toga party
in a garage, and everybody dressed in sheets, like togas,
boys and girls and they put on the appropriated television
set to an old Deanna Durbin movie and turned off the
sound and put on Rolling Stones records, and you should
have seen Deanna Durbin opening her puckered kumquat
mouth with Mick Jagger's voice bawling out, *I ain't got no
satisfaction*. Of course, finally everybody started pulling
the togas off each other, but that is another thing. And one
time they had a keg party down on the beach in Mission
Bay and the lights from the amusement park were reflected
all over the water and that, the whole design of the thing,
those nutty lights, that was part of the party. Liz put out

the fire throwing a "sand potion" or something on it. One can laugh at Liz and her potions, her necromancy and everything, but there is a lot of thought going into it, a lot of, well, mysticism.

You can even laugh at mysticism if you want to, but there is a kid like Larry Alderson, who spent two years with a monk, and he learned a lot of stuff, and Artie Nelander is going to spend next summer with some Outer Mongolian tribe; he really means to do that. Maybe the "mysterioso" stuff is a lot of garbage, but still, it is interesting. The surfers around the Pump House use that word, mysterioso, quite a lot. It refers to the mystery of the Oh Mighty Hulking Pacific Ocean and everything. Sometimes a guy will stare at the surf and say, "Mysterioso." They keep telling the story of Bob Simmons' wipeout, and somebody will say "mysterioso."

Simmons was a fantastic surfer. He was fantastic even though he had a bad leg. He rode the really big waves. One day he got wiped out at Windansea. When a big wave overtakes a surfer, it drives him right to the bottom. The board came in but he never came up and they never found his body. Very mysterioso. The black panthers all talked about what happened to "the Simmons boy." But the mysterioso thing was how he could have died at all. If he had been one of the old pan-thuhs, hell, sure he could have got killed. But Simmons was, well, one's own age, he was the kind of guy who could have been in the Pump House gang, he was . . . *immune*, he was plugged into the whole pattern, he could feel the whole Oh Mighty Hulking Sea, he didn't have to think it out step by step. But he got wiped out and killed. Very mysterioso.

Immune! If one is in the Pump House gang and really keyed in to this whole thing, it's—well, one is . . . *immune*, one is not full of black pan-thuh panic. Two kids, a 14-year-old girl and a 16-year-old boy, go out to Windansea at dawn, in the middle of winter, cold as hell, and take on 12-foot waves all by themselves. The girl, Jackie Haddad, daughter of a certified public accountant, wrote a composition about it, just for herself, called "My Ultimate Journey":

"It was six o'clock in the morning, damp, foggy and cold. We could feel the bitter air biting at our cheeks. The night before, my friend Tommy and I had seen one of the greatest surf films, *Surf Classics*. The film had excited us so much we made up our minds to go surfing the following morning. That is what brought us down on the cold, wet, soggy sand of Windansea early on a December morning.

"We were the first surfers on the beach. The sets were rolling in at eight to 10, filled with occasional 12-footers. We waxed up and waited for a break in the waves. The break came, neither of us said a word, but instantly grabbed our boards and ran into the water. The paddle out was difficult, not being used to the freezing water.

"We barely made it over the first wave of the set, a large set. Suddenly Tommy put on a burst of speed and shot past me. He cleared the biggest wave of the set. It didn't hit me hard as I rolled under it. It dragged me almost 20 yards before exhausting its strength. I climbed on my board gasping for air. I paddled out to where Tommy was resting. He laughed at me for being wet already. I almost hit him but I began laughing, too. We rested a few minutes and then lined up our position with a well known spot on the shore.

"I took off first. I bottom-turned hard and started climbing up the wave. A radical cut-back caught me off balance and I fell, barely hanging onto my board. I recovered in time to see Tommy go straight over the falls on a 10-footer. His board shot nearly 30 feet in the air. Luckily, I could get it before the next set came in, so Tommy didn't have to make the long swim in. I pushed it to him and then laughed. All of a sudden Tommy yelled, 'Outside!'

"Both of us paddled furiously. We barely made it up to the last wave, it was a monster. In precision timing we wheeled around and I took off. I cut left in reverse stance, then cut back, driving hard toward the famous Windansea bowl. As I crouched, a huge wall of energy came down over me, covering me up. I moved toward the nose to gain more speed and shot out of the fast-flowing suction just in time to kick out as the wave closed out.

"As I turned around I saw Tommy make a beautiful drop-in, then the wave peaked and fell all at once. Miraculously he beat the suction. He cut back and did a spinner, which followed with a reverse kick-up.

"Our last wave was the biggest. When we got to shore, we rested, neither of us saying a word, but each lost in his own private world of thoughts. After we had rested, we began to walk home. We were about half way and the rain came pouring down. That night we both had bad colds, but we agreed it was worth having them after the thrill and satisfaction of an extra good day of surfing."

John Shine and Artie Nelander are out there right now. They are just "outside," about one fifth of a mile out from the shore, beyond where the waves start breaking. They are straddling their surfboards with their backs to the shore, looking out toward the horizon, waiting for a good set. Their backs look like some kind of salmon-colored porcelain shells, a couple of tiny shells bobbing up and down as the swells roll under them, staring out to sea like Phrygian sacristans looking for a sign.

John and Artie! They are—they are what one means when one talks about the surfing life. It's like, you know, one means, they have this life all of their own; it's like a glass-bottom boat, and it floats over the "real" world, or the square world or whatever one wants to call it. They are not exactly off in a world of their own, they are and they aren't. What it is, they float right through the real world, but it can't touch them. They do these things, like the time they went to Malibu, and there was this party in some guy's apartment, and there wasn't enough *legal* parking space for everybody, and so somebody went out and painted the red curbs white and everybody parked. Then the cops came. Everybody ran out. Artie and John took an airport bus to the Los Angeles Airport, just like they were going to take a plane, in khaki shorts and T-shirts with Mac Meda Destruction Company stenciled on them. Then they took a helicopter to Disneyland. At Disneyland crazy Ditch had his big raincoat on and a lot of flasks strapped onto his body underneath, Scotch, bourbon, all kinds of stuff. He had plastic tubes from the flasks sticking out of the flyfront of his raincoat and everybody was sipping whiskey through the tubes—

—Ooooo-eeee—Mee-dah! They chant this chant, Mee-dah, in a real fakey deep voice, and it *really bugs people*. They don't know what the hell it is. It is the cry of the Mac Meda Destruction Company. The Mac Meda Destruction Company is . . . an *underground* society that started in La Jolla about three years ago. Nobody can remember exactly how; they have arguments about it. Anyhow, it is mainly something to *bug* people with and organize huge beer orgies with. They have their own complete, bogus phone number in La Jolla. They have Mac Meda Destruction Company decals. They stick them on phone booths, on cars, any place. Some mommy-hubby will come out of the shopping plaza and walk up to his Mustang, which is supposed to make him a hell of a tiger now, and he'll see a sticker on the side of it saying, "Mac Meda Destruction Company," and for about two days or something he'll think the sky is going to fall in.

But the big thing is the parties, the "conventions." Anybody can join, any kid, anybody can come, as long as they've heard about it, and they can only hear about it by word of mouth. One was in the Sorrento Valley, in the gulches and arroyos, and the fuzz came, and so the older guys put the young ones and the basket cases, the ones just too stoned out of their gourds, into the tule grass, and the cops shined their searchlights and all they saw was tule grass, while the basket cases moaned scarlet and oozed on their bellies like reptiles and everybody else ran down the arroyos, yelling Mee-dah.

The last one was at Manhattan Beach, inside somebody's poor hulking house. The party got *very Dionysian* that night and somebody put a hole through one wall, and everybody else decided to see if they could make it bigger. Everybody was stoned out of their hulking gourds, and it got to be about 3:30 a.m. and everybody decided to go see the riots. These were the riots in Watts. The Los Angeles *Times* and the San Diego *Union* were all saying, WATTS NO-MAN'S LAND and STAY WAY FROM WATTS YOU GET YO' SE'F KILLED, but naturally nobody believed that. Watts was a blast, and the Pump House gang was immune to the trembling gourd panic rattles of the L. A. *Times* black pan-thuhs. Immune!

So John Shine, Artie Nelander and Jerry Sterncorb got in John's VW bus, known as the Hog of Steel, and they went to Watts. Gary Wickham and some other guys ran into an old man at a bar who said he owned a house in Watts and had been driven out by the drunk niggers. So they drove in a car to save the old guy's house from the drunk niggers. Artie and John had a tape recorder and decided they were going to make a record called "Random Sounds from the Watts Riots." They drove right into Watts in the Hog of Steel and there was blood on the streets and roofs blowing off the stores and all these apricot flames and drunk Negroes falling through the busted plate glass of the liquor stores. Artie got a nice recording of a lot of Negroes chanting "Burn, baby, burn." They all got out and talked to some Negro kids in a gang going into a furniture store, and the Negro kids didn't say Kill Whitey or Geed'um or any of that. They just said, Come on, man, it's a party and it's free. After they had been in there for about three hours talking to Negroes and watching drunks collapse in the liquor stores, some cop with a helmet on came roaring up and said, "Get the hell out of here, you kids, we cannot and will not provide protection."

Meantime, Gary Wickham and his friends drove in in a car with the old guy, and a car full of Negroes *did* stop them and say, Whitey, Geed'um, and all that stuff, but one of the guys in Gary's car just draped a pistol he had out the window and the colored guys drove off. Gary and everybody drove the old guy to his house and they all walked in and had a great raunchy time drinking beer and raising hell. A couple of Negroes, the old guy's neighbors, came over and told the old guy to cut out the racket. There were flames in the sky and ashes coming down with little rims of fire on them, like apricot crescents. The old guy got very cocky about all his "protection" and went out on the front porch about dawn and started yelling at some Negroes across the street, telling them "No more drunk niggers in Watts" and a lot of other unwise slogans. So Gary Wickham got up and everybody left. They were there about four hours altogether and when they drove out, they had to go through a National Guard checkpoint, and a lieutenant from the San Fernando Valley told them he could not and would not provide protection.

But exactly! Watts just happened to be what was going on at the time, as far as the netherworld of La Jolla surfing was concerned, and so one goes there and sees what is happening and comes back and tells everybody about it and laughs at the L.A. *Times.* That is what makes it so weird when all these black pan-thuhs come around to pick up "surfing styles," like the clothing manufacturers. They don't know what any of it means. It's like archaeologists discovering hieroglyphics or something, and they say, god, that's neat—Egypt!—but they don't know what the hell it is. They don't know anything about . . . *The Life.* It's great to think of a lot of old emphysematous pan-thuhs in the Garment District in New York City struggling in off the street against a gummy 15-mile-an-hour wind full of soot and coffee-brown snow and gasping in the elevator to clear their old nicotine-phlegm tubes on the way upstairs to make out the invoices on a lot of surfer stuff for 1966, the big nylon windbreakers with the wide, white horizontal competition stripes, nylon swimming trunks with competition stripes, bell-bottom slacks for girls, the big hairy sleeveless jackets, vests, the blue "tennies," meaning tennis shoes, and the . . . *look,* the Major Hair, all this long lank blond hair, the plain face kind of tanned and bleached out at the same time, but with big eyes. It all starts in a few places, a few strategic groups, the Pump House gang being one of them, and then it moves up the beach, to places like Newport Beach and as far up as Malibu.

Well, actually there is a kind of back-and-forth thing with some of the older guys, the old heroes of surfing, like Bruce Brown, John Severson, Hobie Alter and Phil Edwards. Bruce Brown will do one of those incredible surfing movies and he is out in the surf himself filming Phil Edwards coming down a 20-footer in Hawaii, and Phil has on a pair of nylon swimming trunks, which he has had made in Hawaii, because they dry out fast—and it is like a grapevine. Everybody's got to have a pair of nylon swimming trunks, and then the manufacturers move in, and everybody's making nylon swimming trunks, boxer trunk style, and pretty soon every kid in Utica, N.Y., is buying a pair of them, with the competition stripe and the whole thing, and they never heard of Phil Edwards. So it works back and forth—but so what? Phil Edwards is part of it. He may be an old guy, he is 28 years old, but he and Bruce Brown, who is even older, 30, and John Severson, 32, and Hobie Alter, 29, never haired out to the square world even though they make thousands. Hair refers to courage. A guy who "has a lot of hair" is courageous; a guy who "hairs out" is yellow.

Bruce Brown and Severson and Alter are known as the "surfing millionaires." They are not millionaires, actually, but they must be among the top businessmen south of Los Angeles. Brown grossed something around $500,000 in 1965 even before his movie *Endless Summer* became a hit nationally; and he has only about three people working for him. He goes out on a surfboard with a camera encased in a plastic shell and takes his own movies and edits them himself and goes around showing them himself and narrating them at places like the Santa Monica Civic Auditorium, where 24,000 came in eight days once, at $1.50 a person, and all he has to pay is for developing the film and hiring the hall. John Severson has the big surfing magazine, *Surfer.* Hobie Alter is the biggest surfboard manufacturer, all hand-made boards. He made 5,000 boards in 1965 at $140 a board. He also designed the "Hobie" skate boards and gets 25 cents for every one sold. He grossed between $900,000 and $1 million in 1964.

God, if only everybody could grow up like these guys and know that crossing the horror dividing line, 25 years old, won't be the end of everything. One means, keep on living *The Life* and not get sucked into the ticky-tacky life with some insurance salesman sitting forward in your stuffed chair on your wall-to-wall telling you that life is like a football game and you sit there and take that stuff.

The hell with that! Bruce Brown has the money and *The Life*. He has a great house on a cliff about 60 feet above the beach at Dana Point. He is married and has two children, but it is not that hubby-mommy you're-breaking-my-gourd scene. His office is only two blocks from his house and he doesn't even have to go on the streets to get there. He gets on his Triumph scrambling motorcycle and cuts straight across a couple of vacant lots and one can see him . . . *bounding* to work over the vacant lots. The Triumph hits ruts and hummocks and things and Bruce Brown bounces into the air with the motor—*thragggggh*—moaning away, and when he gets to the curbing in front of his office, he just leans back and pulls up the front wheel and hops it and gets off and walks into the office barefooted. *Barefooted;* why not? He wears the same things now that he did when he was doing nothing but surfing. He has on a faded gray sweatshirt with the sleeves cut off just above the elbows and a pair of faded corduroys. His hair is the lightest corn yellow imaginable, towheaded, practically white, from the sun. Even his eyes seem to be bleached. He has a rain-barrel old-apple-tree Tom-Sawyer little-boy roughneck look about him, like Bobby Kennedy.

Sometimes he carries on his business right there at the house. He has a dugout room built into the side of the cliff, about 15 feet down from the level of the house. It is like a big pale green box set into the side of the cliff, and inside is a kind of upholstered bench or settee you can lie down on if you want to and look out at the Pacific. The surf is crashing like a maniac on the rocks down below. He has a telephone in there. Sometimes it will ring, and Bruce Brown says hello, and the surf is crashing away down below, roaring like mad, and the guy on the other end, maybe one of the TV networks calling from New York or some movie hair-out from Los Angeles, says:

"What is all that noise? It sounds like you're sitting out in the surf."

"That's right," says Bruce Brown, "I have my desk out on the beach now. It's nice out here."

The guy on the other end doesn't know what to think. He is another Mr. Efficiency who just got back from bloating his colon up at a three-hour executive lunch somewhere and now he is Mr.-Big-Time-Let's-Get-This-Show-on-the-Road.

"On the beach?"

"Yeah. It's cooler down here. And it's good for you, but it's not so great for the desk. You know what I have now? A warped leg."

"A warped leg?"

"Yeah, and this is an $800 desk."

Those nutball California kids—and he will still be muttering that five days after Bruce Brown delivers his film, on time, and Mr. Efficiency is still going through memo thickets or heaving his way into the bar car to Darien—in the very moment that Bruce Brown and Hobie Alter are both on their motorcycles out on the vacant lot in Dana Point. Hobie Alter left his surfboard plant about two in the afternoon because the wind was up and it would be good catamaranning and he wanted to go out and see how far he could tip his new catamaran without going over, and he did tip it over, about half a mile out in high swells and it was hell getting the thing right side up again. But he did, and he got back in time to go scrambling on the lot with Bruce Brown. They are out there, roaring over the ruts, bouncing up in the air, and every now and then they roar up the embankment so they can . . . fly, going up in the air about six feet off the ground as they come up off the embankment—*thraaagggggh*—all these people in the houses around there come to the door and look out. These two

. . . nuts are at it again. Well, they can only fool around there for 20 minutes, because that is about how long it takes the cops to get there if anybody gets burned up enough and calls, and what efficient business magnate wants to get hauled off by the Dana Point cops for scrambling on his motorcycle in a vacant lot.

Bruce Brown has it figured out so no one in the whole rubber-bloated black pan-thuh world can trap him, though. He bought a forest in the Sierras. There is nothing on it but trees. His own wilds: no house, no nothing, just Bruce Brown's forest. Beautiful things happen up there. One day, right after he bought it, he was on the edge of his forest, where the road comes into it, and one of these big rancher king motheroos with the broad belly and the $70 lisle Safari shirt comes tooling up in a Pontiac convertible with a funnel of dust pouring out behind. He gravels it to a great flashy stop and yells:

"Hey! You!"

Of course, what he sees is some towheaded barefooted kid in a torn-off sweatshirt fooling around the edge of the road.

"Hey! You!"

"Yeah?" says Bruce Brown.

"Don't you know this is private property?"

"Yeah," says Bruce Brown.

"Well, then, why don't you get your ass off it?"

"Because it's mine, it's my private property," says Bruce Brown. "Now you get *yours* off it."

And Safari gets a few rays from that old apple-tree rainbarrel don't-cross-that-line look and doesn't say anything and roars off, slipping gravel, the dumb crumbling pan-thuh.

But . . . perfect! It is like, one means, you know, poetic justice for all the nights Bruce Brown slept out on the beach at San Onofre and such places in the old surfing days

and would wake up with some old crock's black feet standing beside his head and some phlegmy black rubber voice
saying:

"All right, kid, don't you know this is private property?"

And he would prop his head up and out there would be
the Pacific Ocean, a kind of shadowy magenta-mauve, and
one thing, *that* was nobody's private property—

But how many Bruce Browns can there be? There is a
built-in trouble with age segregation. Eventually one *does*
reach the horror age of 25, the horror dividing line.
Surfing and the surfing life have been going big since
1958, and already there are kids who—well, who aren't
kids anymore, they are pushing 30, and they are stagnating
on the beach. Pretty soon the California littoral will be
littered with these guys, stroked out on the beach like
beached white whales, and girls, too, who can't give up the
mystique, the mysterioso mystique, Oh Mighty Hulking
Sea, who can't *conceive* of living any other life. It is
pathetic when they are edged out of groups like the Pump
House gang. Already there are some guys who hang
around with the older crowd around the Shack who are
stagnating on the beach. Some of the older guys, like Gary
Wickham, who is 24, are still in *The Life*, they still have it,
but even Gary Wickham will be 25 one day and then 26
and then. . . . and then even pan-thuh age. Is one really
going to be pan-thuh age one day? Watch those black feet
go. And Tom Coman still snuggles with Yellow Slacks,
and Liz still roosts moodily in her rabbit fur at the bottom
of the Pump House and Pam still sits on the steps con-
templating the mysterioso mysteries of Pump House ascension and John and Artie still bob, tiny pink porcelain shells,
way out there waiting for godsown bitchen *set*, and godsown sun is still turned on like a dentist's lamp and so far—

—the panthers scrape on up the sidewalk. They are at just about the point Leonard Anderson and Donna Blanchard got that day, December 6, 1964, when Leonard said, Pipe it, and fired two shots, one at her and one at himself. Leonard was 18 and Donna was 21—21!—god, for a girl in the Pump House gang that is almost the horror line right there. But it was all so mysterioso. Leonard was just lying down on the beach at the foot of the Pump House, near the stairs, just talking to John K. Weldon down there, and then Donna appeared at the top of the stairs and Leonard got up and went up the stairs to meet her, and they didn't say anything, they weren't *angry* over anything, they never had been, although the police said they had, they just turned and went a few feet down the sidewalk, away from the Pump House and—blam blam!—these two shots. Leonard fell dead on the sidewalk and Donna died that afternoon in Scripps Memorial Hospital. Nobody knew what to think. But one thing it seemed like—well, it seemed like Donna and Leonard thought they had lived *The Life* as far as it would go and now it was running out. All that was left to do was—but that is an *insane* idea. It can't be like that, *The Life* can't run out, people can't change all that much just because godsown chronometer runs on and the body packing starts deteriorating and the fudgy tallow shows up at the thighs where they squeeze out of the bathing suit—

Tom, boy! John, boy! Gary, boy! Neale, boy! Artie, boy! Pam, Liz, Vicki, Jackie Haddad! After all this—just a pair of bitchen black panther bunions inching down the sidewalk away from the old Pump House stairs?

2 The Mid-Atlantic Man

Roger! Have you met George? Cyril! Have you met George? Keith! Have you met George? Brian! Have you met George? Tony! Have you met George? Nigel! Have you—

—oh god, he's doing a hell of a job of it, introducing everybody by their first names, first-naming the hell out of everybody, introducing them to George, who just arrived from New York: George is an American and the key man in the Fabrilex account. A hell of a job of introductions he is doing. He has everybody from the firm, plus a lot of other people, English and American, all calculated to impress and flatter American George, all piled into this sort of library-reception room upstairs at the —— Club amid the lyre-splat chairs, bullion-fringe curtains, old blacky Raeburn-style portraits, fabulously junky glass-and-ormolu chandeliers, paw-foot chiffoniers, teapoys, ingenious library steps leading resolutely up into thin air, a wonderful dark world of dark wood, dark rugs, candy-box covings, moldings, flutings, pilasters, all red as table wine, brown as boots, made to look like it has been steeped a hundred years in expensive tobacco, roast beef, horse-radish sauce and dim puddings.

The Americans really lap this Club stuff up, but that is not the point, the point is that—christ, Americans are childish in many ways and about as subtle as a Wimpy bender: but in the long run it doesn't make any difference. They just turn on the power. They have the power, they just move in and take it, introducing people by their first names as they go, people they've never laid eyes on, *pals*, and who gives a damn. They didn't go to Cambridge and learn to envy people who belonged to the Pitt Club and commit the incredible gaffe of walking into the Pitt Club with a Cambridge scarf on. They just turn on the money or whatever it takes, and they take it, and the grinning first names shall inherit the earth, their lie-down crewcuts as firm and pure as Fabrilex—and—

—he has had a couple of highballs. Highballs! That is what they call whisky-and-sodas. And now he is exhilarated with the absolute *baldness* of putting on his glistening ceramic grin and introducing all of these faces to George by their first names, good old George, cleaned-and-pressed old George, big-blucher-shoed old George, popped-out-of-the-Fabrilex-mold old George—the delicious baldness of it!—

Karl! Have you met George? Alec! Have you met George? John! Have you met George? George, predictably, has a super-ingratiating and deferential grin on his face, shaking hands, pumping away, even with people who don't put their hands out at first—Mark! shake hands with George, he wants to say—and as George shakes hands he always lowers his head slightly and grins in panic and looks up from under his eyebrows, deferentially, this kind of unconscious deference because he . . . is meeting *Englishmen* . . .

Still! Why should George give a damn? He can throw away points like this right and left. That's the way Americans are. They can make the wrong gesture, make the most horrible malapropisms, use so many wrong forks it drives the waiter up the wall; demonstrate themselves to be, palpably, social hydrocephalics, total casualties of gaucherie and humiliation—and yet afterwards they don't give a damn. They are right back the next morning as if nothing had happened, smashing on, good-humored, hard-grabbing, winning, taking, clutching. George can scrape and bobble his eyeballs under his eyebrows all day and he will still make his £20,000 a year and buy and sell every bastard in this room—

Nicholas! Have you met George?

Harold! Have you met George?

Freddie! Have you met George?

"Pe-t-e-r . . ."

. . . Oh Christ . . . the second syllable of the name just dribbles off his lips.

With Peter—suddenly he can't go through with it. He can't do the first name thing with Peter, he can't hail him over and introduce him to this American—Peter!— George!—as if of course they're pals, *pals*. Peter? A pal? Peter is on precisely his level in the hierarchy of the firm, the same age, 33, yet . . . in another hierarchy—class, to call it by its right name—

Peter's fine yet languid face, his casual yet inviolate wavy thatchy hair—that old, ancient thing, class, now has him and he can't introduce Peter by his first name. It is as if into the room has burst the policeman, the arresting officer, from . . . that world, the entire world of nannies, *cottages ornées* in Devonshire, honeysuckle iron balustrades, sailor suits, hoops and sticks, lolly Eton collars, deb parties, introductions to rich old men, clubs, cliques, horn-handled cigar cutters—in short, the ancient, ineradicable anxiety of class in England—and he knows already the look of patient, tolerant disgust that will begin to slide over Peter's face within the next half second as he looks at him and his American friends and his ceramic grin and his euphoria and his *highballs.* In that instant, confronted by the power of the future on the one hand—George's eyeballs begin to bobble under the eyebrows—and the power of the past on the other—Peter's lips begin to curdle—he realizes what has happened to himself. He has become a Mid-Atlantic Man.

Mid-Atlantic Men. He meets them all the time in London now. They are Englishmen who have reversed the usual process and . . . gone American. The usual process has been that Americans have gone to England and . . . gone English. Woodrow Wilson appoints Walter Hines Page ambassador to the Court of St. James's and tells him: "Just one word of advice, don't become an Englishman." Page says, "Sure, O.K.," but, of course, he does, he becomes so much an Englishman he can't see straight. The usual pattern is, he begins using his knife and fork Continental style, holding the fork in the left hand. He goes to a tailor who puts that nice English belly into the lapels of his coat and builds up suits made of marvelous and arcane layers and layers of worsted, welts, darts, pleats, double-stitches, linings, buttons, pockets, incredible numbers of pockets, and so many buttons to button and unbutton, and he combs his hair into wings over the ears, and he puts a certain nice drag in his voice and learns to walk like he is recovering from a broken back. But one knows about all that. The American has always gone English in order to endow himself with the mystique of the English upper classes. The Englishman today goes American, becomes a Mid-Atlantic Man, to achieve the opposite. He wants to get out from under the domination of the English upper classes by . . . going classless. And he goes classless by taking on the style of life, or part of the style of life, of a foreigner who cannot be fitted into the English class system, the modern, successful, powerful American.

The most obvious example of the Mid-Atlantic Man is

the young English show-business figure, a singer, musician, manager, producer, impresario, who goes American in a big way. A singer, for example, sings American rhythm and blues songs, in an American accent, becomes a . . . *pal* of American entertainers, studs his conversation with American slang, like, I mean you know, man, that's where it's at, baby, and, finally, begins to talk with an American accent in an attempt to remove the curse of a working-class accent. But the typical Mid-Atlantic Man is middle class and works in one of the newer industries, advertising, public relations, chemical engineering, consulting for this and that, television, credit cards, agentry, industrial design, commercial art, motion pictures, the whole world of brokerage, persuasion, savantry and shows that has grown up beyond the ancient divisions of landowning, money-lending and the production of dry goods.

He is vaguely aware—he may try to keep it out of his mind—that his background is irrevocably middle class and that everybody in England is immediately aware of it and that this has held him back. This may even be why he has gravitated into one of the newer fields, but still the ancient drag of class in England drags him, drags him, drags him.
. . .

They happen to be watching television one night and some perfectly urbane and polished person like Kenneth Allsop comes on the screen and after three or four sentences somebody has to observe, poor Kenneth Allsop, listen to the way he says practically, he will never get the Midlands out of his voice, he breaks it all up, into prac-ti-cally . . . and he laughs, but grimly, because he knows there must be at least fifty things like that to mark him as hopelessly middle class and he has none of Allsop's fame to take the curse off.

He first began to understand all this as far back as his first month at Cambridge. Cambridge!—which was supposed to turn him into one of those inviolate, superior persons who rule England and destiny. Cambridge was going to be a kind of finishing school. His parents had a very definite idea of it that way, a picture of him serving sherry to some smart friends in his chambers, wearing a jacket that seems to have worn and mellowed like a 90-year-old Persian rug. Even he himself had a vague notion of how Cambridge was going to transform him from a bright and mousy comprehensive schoolboy into one of those young men with spread collars and pale silk ties who just . . . *assumes* he is in control, at restaurants, in clubs, at parties, with women, in careers, in life, on rural weekends, and thereby is.

And then the very first month this thing happened with the Pitt Club and the Cambridge scarf. His first move on the road to having smart people over to his chambers for sherry, and Cuban tobacco—Cuban tobacco was also included in this vision—was to buy a Cambridge scarf, a nice long thing with confident colors that would wrap around the neck and the lower tip of his chin and flow in the wind. So he would put on his scarf and amble around the streets, by the colleges, peeking in at the Indian restaurants, which always seemed to be closed, and thinking, Well, here I am, a Cambridge man.

One day he came upon this place and a glow came from inside, red as wine, brown as boots, smart people, sherry-sherry, and so he stepped inside—and suddenly a lot of white faces turned his way, like a universe erupting with eggs Benedict, faces in the foyer, faces from the dining tables farther in. A porter with chipped-beef jowls stepped up and looked him up and down once, dubious as hell, and said:

"Are you a member, sir?"

Such a voice! It was obvious that he knew immediately

that he was not a member and the question was merely, witheringly, rhetorical and really said, Why does a hopeless little nit like you insist on wandering in where you don't belong, and all the eggs Benedict faces turned toward him were an echo of the same thing. They all knew immediately! And it was as if their eyes had fastened immediately upon his jugular vein—no!—upon the Cambridge scarf.

He mumbled and turned his head . . . there in the ancient woody brown of the place was a long coat rack, and hanging on it was every kind of undergraduate garment a *right* mind could think of, greatcoats, riding macs, cloaks, capes, gowns, mantles, even ponchos, mufflers, checked mufflers, Danish mufflers, camel-tan mufflers, ratty old aunt-knitty mufflers—everything and anything in the whole woofy English goddamn universe of cotton, wool, rubber and leather . . . except for a Cambridge scarf. This place turned out to be the Pitt Club, watering trough of the incomparables, the Cambridge elite. Wearing a Cambridge scarf in here was far, far worse than having no insignia at all. In a complex Cambridge hierarchy of colleges and clubs—if all one had was an insignia that said merely that one had been admitted to the university—that was as much as saying, well, he's here and that's all one can say about him, other than that he is a hopeless fool.

He did not throw the Cambridge scarf away, strangely enough. He folded it up into a square and tucked it way back in the bottom of his bottom drawer, along with the family Bible his grandfather had given him. From that day on he was possessed by the feeling that there were two worlds, the eggs Benedict faces and his, and never, in four years, did he invite a single smart person over for sherry. Or for Cuban tobacco. He smoked English cigarettes that stained his teeth.

Even years later, in fact, he held no tremendous hopes

for the advertising business until one day he was in New York—one day!—with all Mid-Atlantic Men it seems to start one day in New York.

Practically always they have started flying to New York more and more on business. He started flying over on the Fabrilex account. Fabrilex was going to run a big campaign in England. So he began flying to New York and getting gradually into the New York advertising life, which turned out to be a strangely . . . *stimulating*—all Mid-Atlantic Men come back with that word for New York, stimulating . . . strangely stimulating aura of sheer money, drive, conniving, hard work, self-indulgence, glamour, childishness, cynicism.

Beginning with the reception room of the —— Agency. It was decorated with the most incredible black leather sofas, quilted and stuffed to the gullet, with the leather gushing and heaving over the edge of the arms, the back and everywhere. There was wall-to-wall carpet, not like a Wilton but so thick one could break one's ankle in it, and quite vermilion, to go with the vermilion walls and all sorts of inexplicable polished brass objects set in niches, candelabra, busts, pastille-burners, vases, etc., and a receptionist who seemed to be made of polished Fabrilex topped with spun brass back-combed hair. She didn't sit at a desk but at a delicate *secretaire* faced with exotic wood veneers, tulipwood, satinwood, harewood. She also operated a switchboard, which was made to look, however, like the keyboard of a harpsichord. There was one large painting, apparently by the last painter in Elizabeth, New Jersey, to copy Franz Kline. Three different members of the firm, Americans, told him the reception room looked like "a San Francisco whorehouse." Three of them used that same simile, a San Francisco whorehouse. This was not said in derision, however. They thought it was crazy but they were proud of it. New York!

One of them told him the reception room looked like a San Francisco whorehouse while having his shoes shined at his desk in his office. They were both sitting there talking, the usual, except that a Negro, about 50, was squatted down over a portable shoeshine stand shining the American's shoes. But he kept right on talking about the San Francisco whorehouse and Fabrilex as if all he had done was turn on an air-conditioner. He also had an "executive telephone." This was some sort of amplified microphone and speaker connected to the telephone, so that he didn't have to actually pick up a telephone, none of that smalltime stuff. All he had to do was talk in the general direction of the desk. But of course! The delicious . . . *baldness* of it! Who gives a damn about subtlety? Just win, like, that's the name of the game, and the —— Agency had £70 million in accounts last year.

They always took him to lunch at places like the Four Seasons, and if it came to £16 for four people, for lunch, that was nothing. There are expensive places where businessmen eat lunch in London, but they always have some kind of coy atmosphere, trattorias, chez this or that, or old places with swiney, pebbly English surnames, Craw's, Grouse's, Scob's, Clot's. But the Four Seasons! The place practically exudes an air-conditioned sweat of pure huge expensive-account . . . *money*. Everybody sits there in this huge bald smooth-slab Mies-van-der-Rohe-style black-onyx executive suite atmosphere taking massive infusions of exotic American cocktails, Margaritas, Gibsons, Bloody Marys, Rob Roys, Screwdrivers, Pisco Sours, and French wines and French brandies, while the blood vessels dilate and the ego dilates and Leonard Lyons, the columnist, comes in to look around and see who is there, and everyone watches these ingenious copper-chain curtains rippling over the plate glass, rippling up, up, it is an optical illusion but it looks like they are rippling, rippling, rippling, rippling up this cliff of plate glass like a waterfall gone into reverse.

And some guy at the table is letting everybody in on this deliciously child-cynical American secret, namely, that a lot of the cigarette advertising currently is based on motivational research into people's reactions to the cancer scare. For example, the ones that always show blue grass and blue streams and blond, blue-eyed young people with picnic baskets, and gallons of prime-of-life hormones gushing through their Diet-Rite loins, are actually aimed at hypochondriacs who need constant reassurance that they aren't dying of cancer. On the other hand, the ones that say "I'd rather fight than switch" really mean "I'd rather get cancer than give up smoking"—New York!—the copper curtains ripple up. . . .

One interesting, rather nice thing he notices, however, is that they are tremendously anxious to please him. They are apparently impressed by him, even though he comes there very much as the beggar. They are the parent firm. Whatever they say about the Fabrilex campaign in England goes, in the long run. If they want to aim it at hypochondriac masochists who fear cancer of the skin, then that's it. Yet they treat him as a partner, no, as slightly superior. Then he gets it. It is because he is English. They keep staring at his suit, which is from Huntsman and has 12-inch side vents. They watch his table manners and then . . . glorious! *imi*tate him. Old George! He used to say to waiters, "*Would* you please bring some water" or whatever it was, whereas he always said, "*Could* you bring the cheese now, please?" or whatever it was—the thing is, the Americans say *would*, which implies that the waiter is doing one a favor by granting this wish, whereas the Englishman—class!—says *could*, which assumes that since the waiter is a servant, he will if he can.

And old George got that distinction right off! That's it with these Americans. They're incurable children, they're incurable nouveaux, they spell *finesse* with a *ph* to give it more *tone*—but they sense the status distinctions. And so by the second time old George is saying "Could you bring me some water, do you think?" and running do-you-think together into an upper-class blur over top of his sopping glottis just . . . like a real Englishman.

So all of a sudden *he* began to sense that he had it both ways. He had the American thing and the English thing. He could have his cake and eat it, too. They emerge from the Four Seasons, out on to 52nd Street—kheew!—the sun blasts them in the eyes and there it is, wild, childish, bald, overpowering Park Avenue in the Fifties, huge cliffs of plate glass and steel frames, like a mountain of telephone booths. Hundreds of, jaysus, millions of dollars' worth of shimmering junk, with so many sheets of plate glass the buildings all reflect each other in marine greens and blues, like a 25-cent postcard from Sarasota, Florida—not a good building in the lot, but, jaysus, the sheer incredible yah!—we've-got-it money and power it represents. The Rome of the twentieth century—and because wealth and power are here, everything else follows, and it is useless for old England to continue to harp on form, because it is all based on the wealth and power England had 150 years ago. The platter of the world's goodie sweets tilts . . . to New York, girls, for one thing, all these young lithe girls with flamingo legs come pouring into New York and come popping up out of the armpit-steaming sewer tunnels of the New York subways, out of those screeching sewers, dressed to the eyeballs, lathed, polished, linked, lacquered, coiffed with spun brass.

Ah, and *they* loved Englishmen, too. He found a brass-topped beauty and he will never forget following her up the stairs to her flat that first night. The front door was worn and rickety but heavy and had an air hinge on it that made it close and lock immediately, automatically—against those ravenous, adrenal New York animals *out there;* even New York's criminals are more animal, basic savage, Roman, *criminal*—he never remembered a block of flats in London with an air hinge on the front door—and he followed her up the stairs, a few steps behind her, and watched the muscles in her calves contract and the hamstring ligaments spring out at the backs of her knees, oh young taut healthy New York girl flamingo legs, and it was all so . . . tender and brave.

Precisely! Her walk-up flat was so essentially dreary, way over in the East Eighties, an upper floor of somebody's old townhouse that had been cut up and jerry-built into flats just slightly better than a bed-sitter, with the bedroom about the size of a good healthy wardrobe closet and a so-called Pullman kitchen in the living room, some fiercely, meanly efficient uni-unit, a little sink, refrigerator and stove all welded together behind shutters at one end, and a bathroom with no window, just some sort of air duct in there with the slits grimed and hanging, booga, with some sort of gray compost of lint, sludge, carbon particles and noxious gases. And the toilet barely worked, just a lazy spiral current of water down the hole after one pulled down that stubby little handle they have. The floor tilted slightly, but —brave and tender!

Somehow she had managed to make it all look beautiful, Japanese globe lamps made of balsa strips and paper, greenery, great lush fronds of some kind of plant, several prints on the wall, one an insanely erotic water-color nude by Egon Schiele, various hangings, coverings, drapings of primitive textiles, monk's cloth, homespuns, a little vase full of violet paper flowers, a bookcase, painted white, full of heavyweight, or middleweight, paperback books, *The Lonely Crowd, The Confessions of Felix Krull, African Genesis*—brave and tender!—all of these lithe young girls living in dreadful walk-up flats, alone, with a cat, and the faint odor of cat feces in the Kitty Litter, and an oily wooden salad bowl on the table, and a cockroach silhouetted on the rim of the salad bowl—and yet there was something touching about it, *haunting*, he wanted to say, the desperate fight to stay in New York amid the excitement of money and power, the Big Apple, and for days, if he is to be honest about it, he had the most inexplicably tender memory of—all right!—the poor sad way the water had lazed down in the toilet bowl. That poor, marvelous, erotic girl. At one point she had told him she had learned to put a diaphragm on in 15 seconds. She just said it, out of thin air. So bald.

Early the next morning he took a cab back to his hotel to change for the day and the driver tried to project the thing in manic bursts through the rush-hour traffic, lurches of acceleration, sudden braking, skids, screeches, all the while shouting out the window, cursing and then demanding support from him—"Dja see that! Guy got his head up his ass. Am I right?"—and strangely, he found himself having a thoroughly American reaction, actually answering these stupid questions because he wanted to be approved of by this poor bastard trying to hurtle through the money-and-power traffic, answering a cab driver who said, "Guy got his head up his ass, am I right"—because suddenly he found himself close to the source, he understood this thing—the hell with scarves, Pitt Clubs and pale silk ties, and watch out England, you got your head up your ass, and here comes a Mid-Atlantic Man.

His career back with the —— Agency in London picked up brilliantly for Mid-Atlantic Man. His momentum was tremendous when he came back. London was a torpid little town on a river. He began to cultivate the American members of the firm. Certain things about the advertising business that he had never been able to stomach, really, but

nevertheless swallowed silently—suddenly he began to realize that what it was, these things were American, bald and
cynical, only now he . . . *understood.* Yea-saying!

There was one American woman in the firm, and in the
most unconcerned way she would talk about the opening
of a big new American hotel that had gone up in London
and how the invitation list was divided into (1) Celebrities,
(2) VIPs, (3) CIPs and (4) just Guests. Things like that
used to make his flesh crawl, but now—now—the beautiful
part was the CIPs—Commercially Important People,
people important to the hotel for business reasons but
whose names meant nothing in terms of publicity, however. Marvelous!

He got to be a good friend of hers. One day they went
out to lunch, and there were a lot of people on the foot-
paths, and suddenly she spotted a woman about 20 feet
away and said, "Look at her! The perfect C-1." One of the
innovations, for the purpose of surveys and aiming cam-
paigns accurately, had been to break down consumers into
four categories: A, B, C-1 and C-2. A was upper class, B
was middle class, C-1 was upper working class or lower
middle class, in that range, and C-2 was plain working class.

"The perfect C-1!" she said.

"The perfect C-1?"

"Yes! Look. She's done her hair herself. She's wearing a
Marks & Spencer knitted dress. She bought her shoes at
Lotus. She's carrying a shopping basket"—with this she
moved right up next to the woman and looked in the
shopping basket—"she's bought pre-cut wrapped bread"—
she only barely turns back to him to announce all this out
loud —"she's bought a box of Wiz detergent with five free
plastic daffodils inside"—and the poor woman wheels her
head around resentfully—but he wants to shout for joy:
Bald! Delicious! A running commentary on a London
street about a perfect C-1!

That night he took her to the —— Trattoria, underneath those inevitable white plaster arches and black metal cylinder lamps. He came on breezy, first-naming the waiters as he walked in, like . . . a pal. Over the avocado vinaigrette he told her, conspiratorially, that the Agency was still hopelessly backward because it was run, in England, by the kind of Englishmen who think a successful business is one where you can get educated men to work for you for £2,000 a year and come to work dressed as if they make £10,000. After the wine he told her: "I've got the neuroses of New York and the decadence of London."

She thought that was—god!—great. So he sprung it, spontaneously as he could manage it, on many occasions thereafter. He also took to wearing black knit ties. Somehow they have become the insignia of Mid-Atlantic Man. He got the idea from David Frost, who always wears one. It is not that David Frost is a Mid-Atlantic Man, it is just that he seems so . . . classless, yet triumphant.

Instead of using Cockney or Liverpool slang for humorous effect, narked, knickers-job and all that, he began using American hip-lower-class slang, like, I mean, you know, baby, and a little late Madison Avenue. "Why, don't we throw it—" he would be speaking of somebody's idea— "and see if it skips across the pond." He always brought the latest American rock 'n' roll records back with him from New York, plus a lot of news of discothèques, underground movies, and people like Andy, Jane, Borden, Olivier. He always made a big point of telling everyone that he was expecting a call from New York, from *David* —and everyone knew this was a big New York advertising man—David!—David!—New York! New York!—hot line to the source!—land of flamingo legs and glass cliffs!—mine! mine!—

But then there were a few disquieting developments. The waiters at the —— Trattoria began *treating* him like an American. He would come on all pally—and they would do things like this: He would order some esoteric wine, Château whateveritwas, and they would bring him a bottle and pour out a little in his glass and he would taste it and pronounce it good and then one of his . . . *pals,* a waiter, would say, right out loud, in front of the girl he was with: We didn't have any more Château whateveritwas, sir, so I brought you Château thing, I hope it's all right, sir. All he can do is sit there and nod like a fool, because he has already tasted it and pronounced it good Château whateveritwas—oh christ.

And then, at the Agency, the Americans began to treat him as one of them. There was this stupid moment when A—, an American who ranked just above him, was going off on holiday, and he said to him, very solemnly, in front of several Englishmen:

"Think about Pube-Glo for me while I'm gone."

Not "think about the Pube-Glo account" or "work on the Pube-Glo campaign," but think about Pube-Glo, with that pure, simple American double-think loyalty to the product itself. He had to stand there, in front of other Englishmen, and solemnly agree to think about Pube-Glo. What was worse, he would have to show some evidence of having thought about Pube-Glo when A— came back, which meant he would actually have to spend time out of his life thinking about this vile fake-erotic concoction named Pube-Glo.

The hell of it was, he gradually found himself thinking English, not necessarily wisely, but rather fundamentally. Two New York Italians came over to take over—"hype up" was the term transmitted from New York—the art department, and he looked at them. They were dressed in flash clothes, sort of Sy Devore of Hollywood style, wearing tight pants like a chubby hairdresser, and right away they began changing this and that, like some sort of colonial inspector generals. They were creeps even by New

York standards. Even? Where was his love of that delicious, cynical . . . baldness . . .

Part of it was back in New York trampled to death.
Jaysus, he didn't want to say anything, but the more he went
to New York . . . sometimes the whole . . . attitude in
New York was hard to take. He was in New York, staying
at George's big apartment on East 57th Street, and he had
to get out to the airport. He had two huge heavy bags
because it was just before Christmas and he was bringing
back all sorts of things. So he half trundled them out to the
elevator, and at length it arrived and he said to the elevator
man: "Could you give me a hand with these, please?"

"I'm sorry, Mac," the elevator man said, "I can't leave
this elevator. My job is running this elevator. It's against
the law, I can't leave a running elevator," and so forth and
so on, even after he had dragged the bags on himself, a
lecture all the way down.

At the ground floor the doorman opened the door for
him but looked at the bags as if they were covered with
flies. Outside it was slushy and rainy, and there was a pond
of slush out from the curb. So he said to the doorman—this
time summoning up the ancient accent of British com-
mand:

"Could you get me a cab, please."

"No, I couldn't," the man says, with just a hint of
mockery. "I would, Buddy, but I can't. I can't get no cab
on a night like this. You'll have to take your best shot."

Finally he flags down a cab, and both the doorman and
the driver watch, with great logistic interest, as he navi-
gates the bags through the pond of slush, getting his shoes
and socks wet. In the cab he tells the man he wants to go to
the airport, and he answers, in a hideous impersonation of a
Cockney accent:

"Ow-kay, guv."

Then he turns up the car radio very loud to WQXR, the

classical music station, apparently to impress him. The piece is something horribly morose by that old fraud Stravinsky.

Back in London he learns that a few changes have taken place. The Hon.——, a melon-jawed ball of fire who is 31 and once had a job doing whatever it was, somewhere, has been brought in at a high level as a "consultant," and so has young Lady ——. Meantime, Peter ——, an Etonian, an Oxonian, first cousin of Lord ——, has suddenly been elevated to his level after ten months with the firm. And gradually it becomes obvious. Advertising may be a new industry, it may be an American art, it may be a triumph of the New World, but in the competition for new accounts, the clients—English new money as well as foreign clients—they want to be dealing with an upper-class Englishman, want to feel they are buying upper-class treatment for their £20,000 or whatever, want to let their blood vessels dilate and their egos dilate over lunch at the Connaught with upper-class Englishmen—

—but wait a minute, it can't *all* go back to that, he will hang in there, try to get that inviolable feeling again, the best of both worlds, and here amid the lyre-splat chairs, the bullion-fringe curtains, the old blacky Raeburn-style portraits, Roger! Have you met George? Cyril! Have you met George? Keith! Have you—

—and Peter. Pe-t-e-r . . . he watches Peter's lip curdle. It is as if it is taking forever, as in a Cocteau film, old George's eyes are frozen in the panic-grinning bobble, and—oh God of Fabrilex!—none of these smart bastards are coming over for sherry after all, are they, ever, ever.

THIRTY-NINE years old! A recluse! Bonafide! Doesn't go out, doesn't see the light of day, doesn't put his hide out in God's own unconditioned Chicago air for months on end; *years*. Right this minute, one supposes, he is somewhere there in the innards of those forty-eight rooms, under layers and layers of white wall-to-wall, crimson wall-to-wall, Count Basie-lounge leather, muffled, baffled, swaddled, shrouded, closed in, blacked out, shielded by curtains, drapes, wall-to-wall, blond wood, screens, cords, doors, buzzers, dials, Nubians—he's down in there, the living Hugh Hefner, 150 pounds, like the tender-tympany green heart of an artichoke.

He is revolving counterclockwise on his bed. The bed is round and has a motor in it like a turntable. His head is . . . floating to the left. His own TV camera is in there, in the bedroom, right nearby, not a TV set, a *camera*, putting . . . God knows what on videotape.

Look, Hef, while I've got you—*While I've got you?* This dapper little fellow, Lee Gottlieb, of Playboy, Inc., and some other fellow with a very wide nutty-looking Big Lunch tie on have made their way into the innards of

Hefner's mansion, to the edge of Hefner's bed, in fact, but they haven't *got* Hugh Hefner. Nobody's *got* Hugh Hefner. Hefner is at the center of the world. He is deep down inside his house—at the center of his bed. The center of the world!

Gottlieb and the man in the Big Lunch tie are right there, holding attaché cases, folders, notebooks, very much the businessmen here at eleven o'clock at night, standing up in the white wall-to-wall by the bed. Boy, that is a bed and a half. It is round, a circle, 7½ feet across, the biggest roundest bed in the history of the world, fitting into a bank of curving cabinets, and Hefner is at the controls. Dials in the headboard!

His knees are in the middle of the bed, dug down into the salmon percales. His hands are on the dials in the headboard and his back is bent over like a wire with a silk saffron bathrobe over it. Hefner is dressed for the day in his pajamas, bathrobe and slippers. Well, now—he is the creator of the $48-million-a-year *Playboy* magazine and club empire. Considering all that, he looks—well, kind of thin and pale; etiolate. But so what? Never mind the old idea of the *Playboy* world as a lot of girls from Akron with their gouda goodies lying all over a polar bear rug in front of the hearth. The whole thing is . . . the dials!

Hefner is thin and pale, but he has energy—his hands go after the dials. God, will he stop for just one second? Look, Hef—

Hefner pulls open a black leather headrest in the headboard, it opens on a hinge, revealing a panel of dials, and his hands are on the controls. Just—

 . . . a . . .

 . . . little . . .

 . . . twist . . .

 . . . here . . .

—a motor starts. The whole bed, the whole 7½-foot bed, starts going around like a phonograph. An efficient little turntable down under there somewhere is going

. . . rrr . . .   . . . rrr . . .   . . . rrr . . .

The whole thing starts revolving with Hefner in the middle on all fours. Suddenly he snaps upright. Heeee! He grins, his mouth pulls up into his head about three inches, his cheeks fold in, his high cheekbones slide out, his eyes turn on like a pair of pencil flashlights. He says,

"It goes 33⅓, 45 and 78!"

Unquenchable enthusiasm!

Gottlieb and Big Lunch stand there. Hefner's head is floating over this way.

"This changes the whole room!" Hefner says, on the way around. "It makes it three different rooms! It changes your entire field of vision, so that you— This is the hi-fi area!"

Hefner's head, his wiry back, his saffron bathrobe, float past the hi-fi area. His eyes burn like two gas-range pilot lights on top of his cheekbones. Hefner turns on with the most unselfconscious, hot-nerves enthusiasm, smiling, laughing, running over the top of his own words, batting around nervously—*This is the hi-fi area.* Damned right it is; such nice smooth, thick low cabinets, one can stand there and just look and almost *feel* how smooth, how thick, what a gleaming galaxy of speakers, tubes, rheenters, wheepers, flottoes and . . . dials must be behind the panel doors.

Hefner's thin jaws open, heading counterclockwise at two miles an hour: "This is the—living area—" he gestures toward the hearth and the fireplace, nicely sculptured and garlanded and so forth—"this can be great some afternoons, you know, the fireplace—there are some *damned romantic* afternoons in here, I'll tell you!"

. . . rrr . . .

. . . rrr . . .

. . . rrr . . .

"This is the conversation area—"

Conversation area. Over here, not 10 feet away from the bed, is a TV camera, not a set but a camera, a big gleaming Ampex television camera, for instantaneous transmission into a TV screen set into the wall there, or for videotapes of . . . God knows what.

Big Lunch says, "What's that for?"

"I have a whole $40,000 Ampex videotaping console," says Hefner, "so I figured I might as well have the camera, too. It would be like having a tape recorder and no microphone."

"But why is it in the bedroom?"

"Well—" Hefner smiles, his cheekbones come out, his eyes turn on— "Who knows when something *very beautiful* might happen in this bedroom!"

Gawdam, it's going to crash, the bed, it's going to crash into a Nasal Mist Helmet. The Nasal Mist Helmet is like a clear fiberglass space helmet. One puts it on over the head to combat head colds. A part of the helmet, the straps or something, is hanging over the edge of the cabinets that inclose the bed, and the headboard is about to hit that and the hi-fi muffler earphones and, damn, all this other apparatus up there. But Hefner is a quick fellow, like a hot wire, a lot of energy! His body snaps back, he is on all fours again, he catches the helmet in one hand, the earphones in the other. The bed comes to a stop with Hefner on all fours, like a scrambling going on.

Big Lunch Tie is saying to Gottlieb, "Listen, I'm sorry you have to stay out here this late on my account."

"No," says Gottlieb, "I wanted to come out here anyway. I've got some things I want to ask Hef about. Since he never comes to the office anymore—you know, you have to get in here to see him when you can."

Hefner has his arms full of apparatus, wires, fiberglass, tubes, and looks over his shoulder at Gottlieb. Gottlieb brightens.

"I was just telling him, Hef," he says, "I have to catch you in here when I can!"

"You don't go to the office at all?" says Big Lunch.

"I don't go out of the *house* at all!" Hefner says. A very enthusiastic fellow! His eyes go up to about 150 watts and he watches to see if all this is registering. "I'm a contemporary recluse! When was the last time I left this house, Lee? Three and a half months ago?"

"Um, there was Tony Bennett."

"That's right," says Hefner, "I went to Soldier Field to see Tony Bennett. I went to see Frank Sinatra, too. They're friends of mine, and that was the only way I was going to be able to see them. But generally—before that I must not have been out of here for three and a half months; I don't know, the last time was—I flew somewhere. Where was it I flew, Lee?"

"Los Angeles, Hef. About the only time Hef sees Chicago is when he's riding to the airport to go somewhere else!"

Hefner sits on the edge of the bed. Nice platinum-hazy light shines down from recessed rheostat dim-dim lovelies in the ceiling. His bathrobe collapses in nice highlife folds.

"How many times have I been out of this house in the last two years?" he says. He leans over and puts his head down practically between his knees. A wiry guy! "About nine times," he says, answering himself.

Then—

——*heeewack*——

—he snaps upright, he pulls that great angular smile into his face, his high cheekbones move out.

"But I don't need to leave here. Why should I? I've got more right here now inside this house than most people ever find in a lifetime!"

—his eyes turn on—old shining Ampex moon—"I've got everything I want right here. This place is run like a hotel. I mean, I'll take you down and show— No, it isn't! Hotels shut off about two o'clock in the morning, you want to get something— This place is run like a hotel ought to be run. It goes 24 hours a day. There's a full kitchen staff 24 hours a day, a chef, anytime I wake up, I can get anything I want. I've got a staff of 25 people here on a 24-hour schedule. I've got an Ampex engineer on the staff! That's right! There's so much equipment in here, I had to have a—this must be the only house in the country with an Ampex engineer on the staff! I sent him to the Ampex school in San Francisco. He's on 24-hour call."

He stares at the "hi-fi area" and glances at the TV camera. Then he stands up and stretches. Big Lunch's mouth opens, he's cranking up a question. Hefner leans forward and puts his head down, to concentrate.

"When did this all start?" says Big Lunch.

——*heewack*——

——lights——

—Hefner snaps upright and starts explaining, "Well, it got to the point where I was practically working around the clock over there at the office. I was doing nothing but working over there, eating, sleeping, getting up again, and working some more, so I decided, why not, I'd move the whole operation to the house and enjoy life.

"This operation is so personalized," says Hefner, "people are always trying to reach me, for everything. This way I can cope with that. I don't take calls anymore, I just return them. I don't have any In boxes and Out boxes. I don't have to arrange my life by other people's *hours*. I don't always have to be in some boring conference. I don't have to go through business lunches and a lot of formalities. I don't even shave if I don't feel like it. I don't have to get dressed. I don't have to put on a shirt and a tie and a suit every day. I just put on a *bathrobe!*"

Hefner smiles. Then he dims down his eyes.

"You know," he says, "people get the idea I'm a Barnum or something, putting on a show. People come by here, and you can tell—they want to find a flaw in it all. They want to think I can't be happy. They want to think it's got to be a lousy, unprofitable life I'm leading. Well, I can tell you something. It's a *damned full life!*"

"Do you get any new clothes, suits and things?"

"No, it's a funny thing"—Hefner's mouth pulls back up into his lit-up smile—"I don't seem to wear out many suits this way. You know! But it is rough on bathrobes. This must be about the third one since—"

One can imagine Hefner's tailor in there with the old measuring tape running down Hefner's wiry spine with his old stubby left thumb on the nape of Hefner's neck with the curly sprouts of Hefner's hair, where it's long in back, curling over the knuckle—making another bathrobe, a bathrobe, not a suit. Lollygag Heaven!

But who in New York will get all this? The idea of the high life in New York, when one owns a $48-million-a-year business, the idea is the old idea of *being seen.* There is always something like Monday night, the social night, at the Metropolitan Opera. Some five-foot-four chauffeur from Queens opens up the Cadillac door, and out comes Mr. Wonderful's patent-leather right pump with the grosgrain bow on it and his knuckly atrophied little right ankle. Then *she* emerges, all gold-thread slipper and alabaster and Chanel, careful, don't let that little weighted canvas Chanel hem ride up and show all that bad stuff just above the back of the knee where the colloidal tissue has dried up like old mutton, and then the swaddled little bellies and the hunker-

ing little shoulders, and everybody at the entrance looks to
see whose heads will be stuck on top of these grand stalks.
It's the . . . Trailer Truck King! the Jake Seat King! the
publisher's skull-faced son! it's Lennie the B! it's Jason the
Mason! it's Rudy! Wendy! Jackie! Kitty! Kiki!—*seen*
again, on *top* still, still winning the competition.

New York keeps trying to hang onto this, the old feudal,
patrimonial idea of status hierarchies, the being seen, meeting the right people and all of that. Practically nobody here
realizes what is going on out there—God, they know the
term, *out there*, the English say the same thing here, *out
here* they say when they get to New York—what is going
on out there in Chicago, in Columbus, Ohio; in Houston,
Los Angeles, San Francisco. They're all out there, with
Hugh Hefner at the very forefront, living the new life
style: contemporary recluse.

The New York style, this whole business, of asserting
superiority, observing esoteric status lines, making sym-
bolic gestures of rank, of living with snobbery, if one will
—all this has rather acutely embarrassed large masses of
Americans who have become well-to-do since World
War II.

Either they are middling people making a good living in
bureaucracies, usually private bureaucracies, Massachusetts
Mutual, Monsanto, Union Carbide, Metropolitan Life, any
of tens of thousands of firms. Or else they are the new
working class, men who have "working class" jobs so far as
status goes but middle-class incomes, boilermakers making
$15,000 or better a year, people like that.

In either case, these people have the money to make it in
the old status competition. They have all the objects it used
to take to make it socially, grand-looking homes, cars, big
lawns, well-dressed children, rugs in every room. They can
afford parties, evenings out, big weekends, status striving in

all its forms—but they don't have the talent and the in-clination for it. They're not up to the effort of competing socially in the old terms. They feel uncomfortable with the old status system, inherited from Europe. It makes one feel not snobbish, but curiously insecure, to try to assert one's status, even in petty matters like tipping in restaurants. Some crewcut Million Dollar Club life insurance salesman is in a coffee shop with the wife, the bill comes and—damn! he knew it! he doesn't have the right change to leave a tip and he'll have to go up to the cash register and pay the bill and get change and come back and leave the tip. But if they leave the table, the waiter, such a dour unforgiving-look dark little man with no teeth on top—he'll think they're going off without leaving any tip. So he starts up toward the cash register, and his wife gets up to follow, and he wheels around and starts jabbing toward her with his finger: Get back there! Get back there to the table! and so she heads back there and sits down, my poor fumbling hubby, he has left her there as a tip hostage for the Waiter King—

They are the new middle class with few of the old Babbitt status drives; a *lumpen* middle class. All these people might have had no choice. They have been stuck with the old European status system, the way their forebears always had been. But then—beautiful, bounteous, glorious war!— World War II started off a chain of good times and advances in electronic technology that is now enabling millions to live the full life as status dropouts: dropping out of conventional status competition in order to start their own league—in the privacy of the home, as it were.

The new lumpen middle class is gloriously bored with the old idea of *going out* and enriching one's life vicari-ously with spectacles, with concerts, plays, stage shows, speeches, lodge meetings, hustings, debates, prize fights, balls, luncheons and so on. And they have found a way to avoid *going out* and going through a lot of the old status tests involving face-to-face meetings with Mr. So-and-so on the street, admission to this or that club, sitting here or there in whatever restaurant it is, patronizing this or that shop.

The new status dropouts can pull it off precisely because twentieth-century technologies have made it possible for them to lead a full life—a *damned full life* here!—without *going out* amongst the community. Notably, the automobile, the telephone, the radio, television and all the electronic wonders of the new home.

They can turn their own households into the *stage*, only a stage this time with themselves at the center of it, isolated, insulated within discreet and rather marvelous electronic worlds. When it *does* come to going out, the lumpen middle class finds it intensely more pleasurable, more of a treat, to go to an auto show or a hi-fi show or to simply browse about in department store furniture sections or discount bazaars. These are spectacles—but spectacles in which you get in there and vicariously put all these great objects around yourself at your own homestead, and the hell with those tired old pretentious spectacles that Beckett, Arthur Miller or even Otto Preminger still put on. What the hell are they all about? As the movie industry itself knows quite well, only children, people 25 and under, *go out* to the movies anymore.

Only one man, at least, in exemplary fashion, has lived out the new style for all to see, the king of the status dropouts, exactly! Hugh Hefner.

Hefner has had the publicity and financial success to compete for status at the highest level. And yet the whole thing has been somehow *infra dig* by orthodox, European-style, Eastern status standards. First of all, Hefner is completely Midwestern. He was born in a God-fearing but socially only fair-to-middling family in

Chicago. He went to the University of Illinois. His first and only marriage—he was separated in 1954, divorced in 1959—was not "social." But, mainly, the source of his money has always carried a taint in traditional status terms: *Playboy*, a "skin magazine," as they say at Yale, and the Playboy Clubs, "those Bunny houses."

Worse still, he accomplished it all in Chicago, if one can imagine that. And even Chicago has been a little frosty about it. The Chicago *Daily News* recently published a list called "The 62 Best People in Chicago." This amounted to a status roster based not only on ancestry and corporate rank but on recent accomplishment. Almost anyone of any prominence in Chicago made it, but Hugh Hefner did not, despite the fact that he is perhaps the most successful entrepreneur Chicago has had since 1945 and certainly the best known.

Hefner has been the most successful new magazine publisher since World War II. He started out with $600 of his own money and $2,000 he borrowed and now has a business that grosses $48 million a year. *Playboy* magazine's circulation keeps on going up, from 742,000 in 1956 to 1,117,000 in 1960 to 1,877,000 in 1963 to almost 4,500,000 currently. Three-fourths of it is newsstand sales, which is the most profitable kind of circulation to have. Convincing people to subscribe and then mailing the magazines out to subscribers is expensive. *Playboy* sells for 75 cents a copy and does something no other slick magazine can manage; namely, it turns a profit on newsstand income all by itself. Hefner claims that all the advertising revenue is gravy, pure profit, and it is prodigious, up from $8 million in 1964 to an estimated $17 million for 1966.

Hefner opened the first Playboy Club in Chicago in 1960. Today, when Playboy people go abroad, they speak of it as World Headquarters. By 1963 Hefner had founded seven clubs and the membership was about 250,000. Today he has 17 clubs with more than 600,000 members. There are two full-scale foreign Playboy clubs, one in Jamaica and one, with gambling, on Park Lane in London. He has also taken over one of Chicago's most famous skyscrapers, the Palmolive Building—without even leaving The House to look at it—with a 63-year, $2.7 million leasehold and converted it into The Playboy Building. There, every night, the old Palmolive beacon, previously the Lindbergh beacon, revolves on top with a searchlight jet pilots can see 500 miles away.

Hugh Hefner is not "best people," however. By the old status standards he still doesn't rank, and he seems to sense it.

Hefner has had little taste for New York-style status competition or even the rabbity reflection of New York-style that goes on in Hollywood. For one thing, Hefner's *clothes* have never fit really well. His dinner jackets have been a little horse-collary and everything. Hefner has an apartment in New York—and has been in it twice. He also has an apartment in the making, in Los Angeles, with walls that revolve, converting rooms from libraries into bars into swimming pools into sauna baths, or something of the sort —but already that is . . . more like it.

Hefner's genius has been to drop out of the orthodox status competition and to use money and technology and to convert his habitat into a stage and to get on the stage, not in the spectator seats, and to be the undisputed hero himself. Through the more and more sophisticated use of machines, Hefner, and to a lesser degree millions of . . . *homemakers* outside of New York, have turned their homes into wonderlands, almost complete status spheres all their own. Certain basic technologies, the car, the telephone, television, radio, have enabled them to keep in touch with the basic realities of the . . . *outside world*, such as making a living, keeping in touch and so forth.

In or out of Chicago, of course, people can hardly think of Hefner without a picture of all those buttery-cheeked girls with their goudas protruding, the Playmates of the Month, folding out like hometown odalisques, and, more recently, movie stars, Carol Baker, Carol Lynley, Ursula Andress, Elke Sommer, with their real Movie Star mary poppins, their natural born aureolae, their *nature*, right there in rougey color in *Playboy*. Or, in the Playboy Clubs, the Bunnies, in satin Victorian corsets with *their* mammiforms floating in iron cups, melting vanilla custard, and their gouda buttocks décolletage squeezed out behind.

To account for Hefner's astonishing success—well, the *Playboy* aura of sex, by itself, is not enough. One must add another picture that has been shown often enough in *Playboy*—a large, *secure* bed, settled in a windowless corner, with smooth mellow walls, in a heavy wooden frame, low, smooth, modern—surrounded by smooth mellow-wood cabinets, with sliding panels that slide back to reveal *dials*. No girls anywhere in the picture! Just paradise; a bed, a fortress of smooth wood, windowless walls, and dials.

What Hefner has been offering is not merely a fantasy of some kind of potentate's serving of sex but also a fantasy of a potentate's control of the environment—all of a sudden made plausible by the new lumpen middle-class style of life. *Playboy* is running a series of picture features called "*Playboy* Pads." It shows the living quarters, apartments chiefly, of *Playboy* readers that measure up, in some degree, to the ideal environment *Playboy* is promoting. All of them are lesser versions of Hefner's own forty-eight-room dream-house—they have the same smooth, thick modernity, the wall-to-wall, the smooth thick cabinets, the rheostat lights, spiral staircases, and . . . the *dials*, the hi-fi, the projectors, the TV set into the wall. The décor, this ideal *Playboy* décor, is really a throwback to that vague concept known as 1930s or *Moderne* modern. It was an interim style whose smooth, thick surfaces finished off the old aristocratic style with its antique flutings, moldings and crested devices, redolent of feudal status competition. Yet it came before Modernity itself developed into a new kind of elite status competition with such delicate, esoteric stuff as Corbu chairs, Mies coffee tables, Paul Rudolph stairways, white walls, and wan waxy green interior-decorator plants.

Hefner moved into his mansion in 1960. The mansion or The House, as people in the Playboy organization usually call it, is at 1340 North State Parkway.

Inside, in the afternoon, *he* is asleep. Hefner's geographic position, whether he's horizontal, on his feet, sitting down, is a major piece of information, inside the House and at the *Playboy* office. He just got up, he just went to bed, he is in there working on The Philosophy—but Hefner does these things at unusual hours, which is to say, whenever he feels like it. He just went to bed; at 2:30 in the afternoon. He just got up; at 11 p.m. He is asleep; and one can sit underneath the fluorescent lights, over a gray metal desk, at the *Playboy* office over on East Ohio Street and imagine *him* with his head mashed down in the downy percale with his eyes closed and one arm writhed up under his cheek. He is working on the Playboy Philosophy while one is brushing one's teeth and watching the wispy red tide from the gums.

The official explanation of Hefner's long day-into-night night-into-day sessions in The House is that he is in there working incessantly on The Philosophy. And it is true that Hefner does devote enormous energy to this apparently endless project. The Philosophy is a solemn dissertation by Hefner on the absurdity of Victorian sex codes in the modern world. To the Eastern intellectuals, at any rate, the whole thing seems like a naïve and tedious set-to with a colossus that somebody or other must have killed off about

40 years ago. Nevertheless, Hefner has taken it through 23 installments in *Playboy* and figures he is only half through. It continues to draw a heavy mail response, much of it favorable comments—apostate thrill!—by ministers. The white wall-to-wall in the living room of Hefner's bedroom suite is covered with great hummocks of research material, marked "Sodomy," "Homosexuality," "Adultery" and so forth. He clodhops through it all and works away on a streamlined typewriter, sitting there in his pajamas and bathrobe. Actually, The Philosophy seems to be a rather conventional status performance by Hefner. The Philosophy imputes deep moral purpose to his enterprises, legitimizes them, in Weberian terms, just as the libraries helped Andrew Carnegie feel better about the whole thing. But so what? Just inches away, at all times, are the dials and the wonders of The House.

There is always a guide in The House, such as Michele, the dark-haired *dame d'honneur*, and the Nubians. Hefner has a staff of Negro servants in black-and-white livery, all tall, powerful-looking, wide in the shoulders, narrow in the waist, with close-cropped hair, all standing by straight, silent, all these silent Nubian powerhouses standing around there.

The guide, whoever, goes on about the sweet, modern, up-to-date *venery* of the establishment. There are rooms and dormitories high up in The House on the top two floors where about 30 Bunnies from the Chicago Playboy Club live. Alex and Sandra or Carl and Deborah—a significant look here—they are unmarried—some such couple is currently staying up there somewhere. And the parties here —well, if a boy and girl hit it off and what they want to do is go off hand-in-hand and climb the great stairs, well, nobody *says* anything, or they might say something, but nobody cares. Or when couples are in swimming—and here Michele has but to beckon, and a great silent Nubian comes over, bends at the waist, out from his white cuff comes a big black thongy hand and wrist and he pulls up a trap door in the floor of the main party room, the great hall, and one looks down into the Woo Grotto, a section of the swimming pool on the level below, a secluded pool in which *concupiscent* young bubbas can swim in the warm honey chlorine.

And yet none of the sweet warm honey venery of The House can quite compare with the true motif of The House—namely, the apparatus, the *dials*, the glorious controlled environment. Somehow just having silent Nubians reaching down with a belt of thongy wrist and starched cuff to open trap doors looking down into pools—that is the motif of The House.

Look, Hef, while I've got you—

Gottlieb has a few things he would like to go over with Hef. Big Lunch keeps cutting his eyes over at the TV camera Hefner has here in the corner near the big-boy round bed. Hefner is on his feet with his velvet slippers nestled in the wall-to-wall. He is lively, full of juice. His body snaps around a little.

Hefner suddenly propels himself toward the doorway, looking back for a moment and grinning. He comes back in a moment with a bottle of Pepsi-Cola in his hand. He tilts it up and down the gullet. Hefner always has a couple of Pepsi-Colas when he gets up. He drinks about twelve a day.

Hef—in a James Bond world. The contemporary recluse —the Consumer King! Hef—at the center of the world, amid the dials. And one can almost see the ultimate— appealing!—the Consumer King, his smile pulled on, his eyes lit up, his head back, sinking back into the middle of the biggest, roundest bed in the history of the world, reaching his hands back . . . just a bit, to the dials, and then—

. . . rrr . . . . . . rrr . . . . rrr . . .

—that great bed starts turning, into an orbit of its own, with the Ampex videotape on right there, coming over the screen, a videotape of a *very beautiful* thing that happened right there in that room, at the center of the world, the perfect moment, renewed with every revolution of the bed, every revolution of a . . . *controlled* universe, with one's own self as king, dropped, not *out,* but *in,* to the perfect rotation, around and around, in ever-decreasing concentric circles, toward . . . nirvana, *ambrosia,* while, following one's own perfect orbit, out there, for all to see, is the . . . *Playboy beacon!*—up on top of the yes! Playboy Building, sweeping the heavens of America with the two-billion-candlepower beam of American Hefnerism and the perfect . . . bliss . . . rrr . . . rrr . . . rrr . . .

4 *The Put-Together Girl*

In San Francisco, Broadway is "the strip," a combination of Macdougal Street in Greenwich Village and strip row on "East Bal'more" in Baltimore. It is about four blocks long, an agreeably goofy row of skin-show nightclubs, boho caves, saturated in black paint, with names like "Mother's," featuring light-projection shows, mono-loguists, *intime* jazz shows with brooding Negroes on the bass, and "colorful" bars with names like Burp Hollow. There is one tree on Broadway. It is about three inches in diameter, about 12 feet tall, and has 342 minute leaves on it and a tin anti-urine sleeve around the bottom. Carol Doda was standing under this tree as if it could hide her. A colored fellow from the parking lot up the street was standing out in the street trying to get her a cab. It is hard for Carol Doda herself to stand out in the street on Broadway and start waving for cabs. There is no telling what would happen or how many flaming nutballs would stop or—who the hell knows what?—because of "them," *them* being her breasts.

Old Italian women walk by her on the street and say to each other, "*Strega! Strega!*"—not knowing that Carol is a nice Italian girl herself from Napa Valley, and understands that they are saying, "Witch! Witch!" because of *them*.

Middle-aged women, the kind of Hard Lips who wear bib-chains on their eyeglasses and work behind hotel cigar counters, walk by at lunchtime and say, "Aw, go back to jail"—because of *them*.

About 3:30 p.m. grown men wearing rep ties and just emerging from long—tuh-*unh!*—liquid lunches walk by her and grin and aim their fingers at her like needles or guns or something and say, "Pop! Pop!"—because of *them*.

Even Carol Doda has started thinking of them as *them*. There they are secured to her pectoralis major like *acquisitions*.

"When a man asks me out, I never know if he is interested in me or *them*." That is the way she thinks about it.

Them! Carol Doda has had injections of a silicone emulsion put into her breasts in regular installments over the past three years. They have grown, grown, grown, enlarging like . . . dirigibles, almost as if right in front of the eyes of the crowds—they line up out there—who come every night of the week to see Carol Doda's "topless" act. Every night, seven nights a week, Carol Doda descends through a hole in the ceiling of the Condor Club. She comes down doing a dance called the Swim by herself on top of a piano that has been pulled up to the ceiling on pulley wires. The Condor modestly advertises her on the marquee outside as "Miss Carol Doda, the Girl on the Piano." But the crowds line up out there every night, where the sidewalk curves down the hill on Grant Street, it comes right into Broadway right there, and all those people are out there practically panting, Topless, topless, the girl who blew up her breasts, Wonder Breasts, Wonder Breasts, Gimme a mih . . .

Then all the spotlights shine up to the ceiling, and Sam the Man and everybody go into a rock 'n' roll song called

"Memphis, Tennessee." The lights shine on a nutty-looking thing, the bottom of a cocktail-grand piano, the top of which is flat up against the ceiling. Carol Doda! The piano starts coming down slowly on its pulley wires, and the first thing everyone sees is a hole in the ceiling with a heavy red ruffling inside of it, sort of like a gigantic Louis XIV version of a heart valve. Two legs are sticking out of it and down on the piano. Carol Doda! Carol Doda is descending, dancing the Swim. First, her legs, perfectly white legs, churning about, then her thighs, her hips—she is wearing a rather remarkable bikini cache-sex of some sort that starts up around her waist but has no side at all, just stretched down through her loins. She is also . . . *bottom-less*, as they say in the trade, but this room full of craning heads, tilted back in a silent glom, barely even notice that. They are all waiting . . . for *them*.

The piano settles down, Carol Doda is on top of it dancing the Swim, the Jerk, the Frug, the Jump, the Spasm, the—her face is up above there like a pure white mask, an Easter Egg yellow explosion of hair on top, a pair of eyes with lashes like two sets of military shoe brushes, ice-white lips, two arms writhing around, her whole ilial complex writhing around, but all just a sort of pinwheel rosette for *them*. Carol Doda's breasts are up there the way one imagines Electra's should have been, two incredible mammiform protrusions, no mere pliable mass of feminine tissues and fats there but living arterial sculpture—viscera spigot—great blown-up aureate morning-glories.

The whole performance is—it is not a strip tease, it is no kind of *tease*, it is an animated cartoon, like the old Tom & Jerry cartoons where Tom, the cat, sees the bulldog coming and about forty-four sets of round white eyes—*boing* —go springing out of his eye sockets. Carol Doda is not teasing anybody. Her prize is up there as if on a platter. She never smiles; she just draws her big ice-white lips into an O from time to time. She doesn't even have the old pig-bladder choreography of the burlesque houses; she just jerks, spasms, and writhes in the standard American twist-frug genre dances like any little high school bud from the garden apartment next door at the Saturday-night dance bumping away doing the Monkey under a strawberry Feather Duster coiffure while her mother looks on from the side with a pleasant smile on her face as if to say, Well, yes, Carmen is very social.

Sam the Man goes into an elaborate parody of ecstasy. He swings the saxophone down between his legs and then over his shoulders, he rolls his eyes, *Pretty woman walking down the street,* he flaps his brown jowls, he breaks into a sweat, he lolls his tongue out. Carol Doda does the Puppet. Oldie but goldie! "O" go her lips. They all break into *I Left My Heart in San Francisco*—Sam the Man starts moaning in front of the microphone as if in utter ecstatic depletion. "Oh-h-h-h-h-h, I can't s-t-a-n-d it! It's too mu-u-u-u-u-uch! Ah-h-h-h-h-h! O-o-o-o-o-o-o-o-o-o! Eee! Eee! U-u-u-u-u-u-um! Wheeeeedeeeeeeeeeee! Eeeeh! Yuh! Yuh! Oink! Blooogeeee! Snerk! Wiffle! Pooooom—poom-poom! Gush! Mips! Eeeeeeeh-yah! Eeeeeeeerrrrr-rrgggggh! Make her stah-ah-ah-ah-ah-ahp it! Lock me up! I'm going crazy! I'm flipping! I'm wigged out! I'm zonked! I'm erk-erk-erk blooooooooooooooogeeeeeeeeeeeeeeeeeeee! It's unbelieva-bobba-beeva-bova-bavvy-bipblap-blupbloop-poobog-mih-mih-scoony-scaggy-mimsy-poppy! Too mu-u-u-u-u-uch! Bad ma-a-a-a-a-a-a-a-an! Th ol' wild bird is gra-a-a-a-a-abbin' me! I caint tuh-*unh* tuh-*unh!*"—and so on and so forth. But all the Hard Worsted set just sits there refusing to take the comic cues—I'll be damned, so that's what they look like, yes, I'll be damned, look at that, you get that, there it is right up there in front of me. And even the women—they want to *study* this phenomenon. All right, it's *freakish*—see, they don't . . . *give*, they hold *forth*, they're substan—but what does it feel like? it must weigh—and then look at them all fastened on her, heads craned back, *goggling*—until the piano starts ascending toward the hole in the ceiling with Carol Doda still twisting and jerking about with the lights lighting *them* from below as she goes up. *I lost my heart, in San Fran-cis-co.* The silent anointed heads of all the worsted lovelies in here start craning back, back, back again while Tony Cassara and Sam the Man play the anthem of San Francisco, *I left my heart—*

The anthem indeed. The Topless, Carol Doda and *them* are suddenly one of San Francisco's great resources, along with the cable cars, the hills, the Bay, the View, and the Golden Gate. There are at least fifteen "topless clubs" in San Francisco. They are nightclubs, chiefly, like the Condor, offering bare-breasted girls in bikini versions of the G-string, like Carol Doda's, just standing up there and doing ordinary American dances, the Twist, the Frug, the Swim, and so forth. Yet there is no greater tourist and convention attraction in America, with the possible exception of Manhattan.

The most curious of all are two clubs, the Off Broadway and the Cellar, which have "topless waitresses," as they are called, serving lunch wearing nothing but flesh-colored bikini underpants and high-heeled shoes. The new business lunch for—

—the 6 a.m. specters of Russian Hill. At six o'clock in the morning one can look up Russian Hill, San Francisco's best apartment area, from the foot of Broadway, where it suddenly turns steep up the hill, above the tunnel, and down the hill, silhouetted against the first pink-ash light of dawn, come good straight cleaned-and-pressed figures in hard worsted, carrying attaché cases, the leather lunch pails of Wall Street, walking down the slope, one here, one there, the 6 a.m. specters of Russian Hill, well-to-do, anointed with after-shave and Stephan's hair oil which his regular barber lets him have—San Francisco brokers going to work on Montgomery Street, the financial district, at 6 a.m., since by then it is 9 a.m. in New York, and the Exchange is opening and won't wait, and down they come down the hill as if in some Fellini scene.

A group of "underground" moviemakers who live in quonset huts beside the Berkeley railroad tracks are still up with their hand-held camera filming some sequence in which three music students wrapped in Reynolds Wrap leap like Raji-Putra, the Indian dancer, against the first rays of the rising sun. They just stare stupidly at the anointed specters and miss the real movie. Leap, Raji-Putra! Anyway, by twelve noon, these same stock-broker specters of Russian Hill, along with more, sometimes hundreds of San Francisco businessmen, are filing up toward the Off Broadway, the Cellar, along with favored clients, for a "topless lunch." It's a *lark*, a novelty, I mean, one's clients really get a kick out of this screwy spectacle—but the same faces keep coming back, over and over.

The Off Broadway has a deep black-light Soho gloom in it. All the topless places in California set themselves in this gloom, presumably so the customers can feel that nobody can watch them watching the club's amateur galaxy of bare breasts.

The Style Show starts. Girls start parading up on the bandstand. Sandra has on a transparent lace bed jacket or whatever it is, just hanging down from the shoulders, and she parades about in her bikini underwear and high heels in the fashion-show manner. A girl at the microphone says in the boulevard manner of the fashion-show announcer, ". . . using heavy lace, of course, for *added support*."

The Off Broadway's *them*—the Off Broadway has a girl named "Yvonne D'Anger." She comes out from an illuminated theatrical gauze dressing room at one end of the bandstand—the star!—a round-faced girl, almost petite, but with great tumescent dirigible breasts sitting out.

She walks about the stage, then winds her way through the tables, then back to the stage, where she strikes a cheesecake pose, lying down with her legs curled up and her breasts pointing straight up, like vanilla sundaes, not mushing off to the side the way most girls' would, but sitting straight up, and then another topless girl comes out and takes a picture of her with a Polaroid camera—*flash!*— the flash catches all the craning Hard Worsted faces in an instant, the 6 a.m. Russian Hill specters sitting here, anointed, goggled.

They have missed the Off Broadway's most extraordinary show, however, which is in the kitchen. There is something unforgettable about half a dozen girls wearing nothing but high heels and cache-sexes straining at awkward angles over serving tables in the rising Veg Soup steam trying to balance salads on their arms while their breasts dangle hopelessly in the smeary Roquefort, French, Green Goddess and Thousand Island thickets and a battery of spade chefs yell at them like they were nothing but a bunch of unusually clumsy waitresses in the lunchtime rush . . .

Carol Doda's doctor on Ocean Avenue in San Francisco has an on-going waiting list of women of all sorts, not showgirls, who want the series of injections. Well, why should any woman *wait*—wait for what?—when the difference between dreariness and *appeal* is just a few centimeters of solid tissue here, a line stretched out there, a little body packing in the old thigh, under the wattles there—or perfect breasts? The philosophy of "You have only one life to live, why not live it as a blonde?"—that is merely the *given*. Even in old-fashioned New York there is hardly a single gray-haired woman left in town. And why stop short of the perfect bosom? Why do people talk about "the natural order"? Such an old European idea—one means, well, the *wheel* violated the natural order, for God's sake; hot and cold running water violated it; wall ovens, spice bars, Reddi-Tap keg beer and Diz-Poz-Alls fracture the natural order—what are a few cubic centimeters of silicone?

The silicone is injected in the form of an emulsion into the muscles and tissues all around the breasts where they join the chest. Exactly what happens to the emulsion after it is injected is not known. But some of it *moves around*. The shots bring the breasts up taut, at first, but then they begin to sag; continued booster shots are necessary. Sometimes a ring of shots seem to slip into a lake or puddle down in there somewhere. Sometimes the emulsion disappears; it goes off somewhere in the body. Whether or not it can cause cancer is simply not known.

But there are plenty of women in California who are willing to take the chances, whatever they are. There are about seventy-five doctors in Los Angeles giving the treatments, and one of them does twenty-five women a week. There are two hundred women taking the course in Las Vegas alone. More than half of all these patients are housewives, and some women bring their teenage daughters in there because they aren't developing fast enough to . . . compete; well, Carmen *is* social. And actually it's such a simple thing in a man's world where men have such simple ideas. After all, Carol Doda *developed*, from a bust measurement of about 35, up, up, month by month, to 44, through twelve months, eight sets of shots, $800. And why not? After all, one, anyone has fillings in the teeth, plates in the skull, a pin in the hip—what is the purpose of living, anyway? just to keep on living or to enjoy, be adored, favored, eyed—or—

Carol Doda turns around under the tree. A man in a white suit comes along. He just met her the other day. He

invites her into Enrico's, the café. The colored guy isn't
having any luck hailing a cab anyway. Enrico's is a kind of
Via Veneto café for San Francisco. It has an outdoor part,
under an awning by the sidewalk, and then a plate-glass
front and more café tables inside. All sorts hang out there,
actors, advertising men from the Jackson Square section
nearby, women from Pacific Heights down at North Beach
shopping. They head inside, but Carol Doda looks a little
apprehensive. Carol is wearing a thin white turtleneck
sweater, and *them* form a rather formidable shelf, but the
leather Eton jacket covers her up pretty well. Everybody
around Enrico's recognizes her; Burgess Meredith is in
there in a great sport jacket. Herb Caen the columnist is in
there. Larry Hankin and a lot of other people from "The
Committee" are in there. But there is always this possibility, this business of, well, frankly, getting thrown out.
Enrico's wife or somebody threw her out of there once,
and just the other day Mrs. Pacini over at Amilio's threw
her out. Carol is looking around a little in Enrico's.

"What do they say to you?"

"I don't know— She kept saying, 'We don't allow Topless here. Put your coat on, we don't allow Topless here.' I
wasn't *topless*. I mean I had a regular dress on, what I wear
all the time."

Carol Doda's mouth keeps changing from a smile to some
kind of bewilderment when she talks about all this. She has
a slightly husky voice but not a low voice. She has model-
goggle sunglasses up over her face like two huge shields,
and she keeps looking around.

"What did your friends think?"

"A lot of them . . . they don't have the same *air* about
them anymore. They used to treat you palsy-walsy. I mean
when I was a cocktail waitress. And then suddenly people
begin to change. They act like *I've* changed, like they think
I'm a snob or something now. It really used to bug me, I

couldn't figure it out; I mean, I hadn't changed, *they* had changed. It used to break my heart. Then I realized the public will not let you stay the same. I'm never snobbish. It's them, they refuse to accept you because you're well known. I don't know, maybe you have to change, because the public insists that you change."

She is sincere about all this; *changing*. She has a lot of the old North Beach I'm-searching, self-analysis syndrome. What is going on? She's a celebrity, and she likes that, but people have funny attitudes.

She *has* changed. Look at *them*; maybe that is what is on people's minds. But *she* hasn't changed, says Carol Doda. The silicone treatments were just a cosmetic; it wasn't all that drastic a thing. She was working as a cocktail waitress, and actually she had built up a big following in the Condor. Of course, people knew her. She used to wisecrack with them. She looked great. She had a great trim figure. Then she started dancing on the piano. It began almost like a gag. One night—this whole topless bathing suit thing had been going on, in the papers and everything, and the guys there said go ahead, go *topless*, Carol. So she did, right there, and Topless was born. There was Carol Doda, dancing in a topless bathing suit.

Carol Doda—Topless!—was great stuff from the start. Customers were piling in. But Carol—Carol had a nice figure, a trim figure, a real dancer's figure, but she wasn't . . . spectacular. It was one thing to have a nice overall figure, but if you were Topless, the thing was to be showing something spectacular; otherwise why take the top off? So guys around there started saying, Why didn't she get *the shots?*

"I was really scared when I went to the doctor," Carol is saying to her pal in the white suit. Then she brings her hands up. "The needle—well, it's about *this* long, it's like a horse needle or something. It really looks awful. Some of the shots he puts in all around here, near the surface. But some of them are really deep. When the needle goes in—it really scared me at first, these pains shoot all up through here and down your arms. You can feel it all the way down in your arms."

"Are you worried about the long-range effect, what the silicone might do to you?" says White Suit.

"No," Carol says, "the tissue grows around the silicone. It's just a short process."

"Does the whole thing make you—your breasts—feel any different?"

"Yes." She laughs but not very uproariously. "I'm conscious . . . of them . . . all the time. They weigh a lot more, a couple of pounds. I have to wear a special heavy brassière. I have to wear it to bed at night, and I can't sleep on my stomach, it's too uncomfortable. In fact, I can't sleep on my side, either, that's kind of uncomfortable, too. I have to sleep on my back.

"That's one reason I work out all the time. I work out with weights at a gymnasium to build up . . . my pectorals. It helps me support them better."

Self-improvement! But of course! She is a great self-improver. It goes along with the self-analysis. She doesn't smoke; she eats health foods; in fact, on her diet she builds up such tremendous energy, she has to find some outlet for it; the dancing isn't enough; that isn't even tiring; she goes to a gymnasium every day and works out; she lifts weights; she works seven days a week at the Condor, every night, coming down on that piano doing the Swim and the Watusi; it takes a lot of self-discipline, it really does; a side of it nobody knows about—

"Some days when I wake up, I just don't feel like getting up at all and going through the whole thing again," she says. The smile is kind of swimming off her face and then back on and then back off. "But I make myself get up, because if I don't, I'm not really hurting anybody else, I'm letting myself down."

"What are you aiming for, eventually?"

"Well, I'd like to have a big show. I want to be first-class, in New York or Chicago or Miami, some place like that. I've had a chance to go to Nevada, to Las Vegas, but I'm waiting for something big."

"You probably make a lot of money here now."

"Well, not really. Actually, I used to make more money as a cocktail waitress . . . the *tips* and everything . . ."

"You made more money *then?*"

"Yes—but, well. A lot of places here offer me more money and all that to move to their place, but I don't see any point in a lot of moving around like that. That doesn't really get you anything. I'm waiting for something first-class. How do you think the act would go in New York?"

A tall man with great rake features, long Barrymore hair, comes over all of a sudden, some guy she knows, and starts talking and says to Carol, "Hey, Carol, take off those glasses, I can't *see* you."

She looks up with her smile going on and off. "I can't," she says. "I don't have any eye makeup on, I'll feel undressed. I mean it!"

"Aw, come on, Carol—" This goes on for a while, and finally she pulls the glasses off, the great model-goggle shields, and—*strega*, honest *strega*—she is right. Her eyes blink there in the middle of her perfectly white face like something surprised in a nest.

"I always wear eyelashes, top and bottom."

But of course! A heroine of her times! Carol Doda wears false eyelashes, but only to go with her Easter Egg yellow hair, dyed from brown, which goes with her soapstone skin, so perfectly white from remaining forever, every night, within the hot meat spigot casbah of Broadway—

Electra of the Main Stem!—in order to show the new world a pair of—at last!—perfected twentieth-century American breasts. You have only one life to live. Why not live it as a put-together girl?

5 *The Noonday Underground*

JUST KEEP STRAIGHT. Keep your desk straight, keep your
Biros straight, keep your paper clips straight, keep your
Scotch tape straight keep your nose straight keep your
eyes straight keep your tie on straight keep your head
on straight keep your wife on straight keep your life on
straight and that is Leicester Square out there and that is a
straight square and this is a straight office, making straight
money—hey!—
  —Noses straight up there!
  —Line up those noses there!—there—is—an—office boy
here, Larry Lynch, a 15-year-old boy from the Brixton
section of London, staring up at the straight line of human
noses. Occasionally someone—what the hell is it with this
kid? Here he is, 15 years old, and he is dressed better than
any man in the office. He has on a checked suit with a
double-breasted waistcoat with a stepcollar on it and the
jacket coming in at the waist about like so, and lapels like
this and vents like this and flaps about so and trousers that
come down close here and then flare out here, and a custom-
made shirt that comes up like . . . *so* at the neckband,
little things very few people would even know about, least

of all these poor straight noses up here who make four times his pay and they never had a suit in their lives that wasn't off the peg. He is a working-class boy, and like most working-class boys he left school at 15, before the "O" level examinations. But he has been having his suits custom-made since he was 12 at a place called Jackson's. He has his hair regularly cut in a College Boy by a hairdresser named Andy. All—those—straight—

—noses up there have better jobs than he does, better addresses, they are nice old dads with manicured gardens out back and Austin 1100's, they have better accents, but he has . . . *The Life* . . . and a secret place he goes at lunchtime—

—a noonday underground.

Braaang—it is lunchtime. Why try to explain it to the straight noses? Larry Lynch puts this very straight look on his face, like a zombie mask, as if he were going to do the usual, go out and eat a good straight London lunch. All the straight human mummy-hubbies file on out for the stand-ard London office-worker lunch. Boy! Off to the pubs to slop down the jowls with bitter and sandwiches with watercress stems in them. Or to Somebody's Chop House or Trattoria for the Big Time lunch, basting the big noon-day belly and the big noonday ego with Scotch salmon, French wine and coq au vin. Or a Small Time lunch in some place that looks like a Le Corbusier cathedral with white grotto plaster and jazz-organ stained glass, serving nice steaming hot sliced garden hose on buns. But—Larry —Lynch—

—with—his—straight mask on walks over to Shaftes-bury Avenue and then almost to Tottenham Court Road, in the heart of the Oxford Street shopping district. The sun—the sun is out today—the sun shines off the glistening flaws on thousands of bursting lonely beetled faces on the sidewalk at noon, but Larry Lynch cuts in the doorway at 79 Oxford Street, a place called Tiles.

It is like suddenly turning off the light. The entryway is black, the stairs going down are black, black walls, black ceilings, winding around and around, like a maze, down into the blackness, until there is no daytime and no direction and suddenly—

—underground at noon—

—a vast black room heaving with music and human bodies. Up at one end is a small lighted bandstand. There is somebody up there at a big record turntable and rock music fills up the room like heavy water—

Bay-beh-eh

—and in the gloaming there are about 250 boys and girls, in sexy kaks, you know, boys in codpiece pants, the age of codpiece pants, mini-skirts, mesh stockings, half-bras, tailored mons veneris, Cardin coats, navel-deep button-downs, Victoria shoes, inverted pleats, major hair, major eyes—eyes!—eyes painted up to here and down to there, with silver and gold beads just set in there like Christmas balls, set in the false eyelashes—all of them bucking about, doing the Spasm, the Hump, the Marcel, the Two-backed Beast in the blackness while a stray light from somewhere explodes on somebody's beaded eyelashes—

—down in the cellar at noon. Two hundred and fifty office boys, office girls, department store clerks, messengers, members of London's vast child work-force of teen-agers who leave school at 15, pour down into this cellar, Tiles, in the middle of the day for a break . . . back into *The Life*. The man on the stage playing the records is Clem Dalton, a disc jockey. Off to one side in the dimness is a soft-drink stand, a beauty parlor called Face Place and an arcade of boutiques, a Ravel shoe store, a record shop, a couple of other places, all known as Tiles Street. There is a sign out there in the arcade that says Tiles Street, W1. The place is set up as an underground city for The Life.

Right away the music is all over you like a Vibro-Massage—and—Larry Lynch just starts waffling out onto the floor by himself—so what?—who needs a partner?—a lot of boys and girls come here at lunchtime and go into this kinetic trance, dancing by themselves, just letting the music grab them and mess up their minds. Berry Slee, a 19-year-old fellow from Brixton, is out there, in the darkness at noon, heh, going like a maniac, doing a dance called Rudy, by himself, with this maniacal suit on, with flaps on the pockets hanging down about eight inches, messes your mind right up, and Berry's friend, Ian Holton, who is also 19, is dancing by himself, too, and god, this *green* suit he has on, it *messes your mind up*, this waistcoat with the six buttons grouped in groups of two, great green groupy work by the great Jackson, like, one means, you know, the girls are all down here, too, but so what, the point is not making it with girls, there are plenty of girls out here dancing by themselves, too, the point is simply immersing yourself for one hour in The Life, every lunch hour.

Linda McCarthy from the Ravel store is out here, dancing with some guy, ratcheting her hips about in their sockets. Linda, with . . . The Eyes, is about to make it, as a model or something, it could happen, but just now she is 17 and she works in the Ravel shop and one moment she sells a pair of jesuschristyellow shoes and then the music gets her like a Vibro-Massage and she leaves the store and she goes out there and dances it out and then comes back, to the store, sell-a-shoe, and Jane Dejong is out there doing that, god, maniacal thigh-swivel dance she does. One knows? And Liz White and Jasmyn Hardwick, Chris Gray, John Atkinson, Jay Langford, a 15-year-old American kid, from Los Angeles, only he is really English now, from Willesden, and Steve Bashor, who lives down on the Strand, and is 17 but looks about 21, and he has already been to sea, in the Merchant Navy, and come back and now every day, in the dark, at noon, he comes down into

Tiles and stands on the edge of the bandstand and watches, he doesn't dance, he just watches and lets . . . the whole thing just take hold of him like the great god Vibro-Massage, and Sunshine Newman—oh god, Sunshine lost his job in the stationer's on Wardour Street but who gives a damn about that and Sunshine is going wild with some kind of yellow goggles on and his white turnover-neck jersey on, a checked jacket, sexy kaks. Who—cares—about—the —sack—in—

—the—Noonday—Underground. Tiles has the usual "beat club" sessions on at night, with name groups up on the bandstand, and it packs them in, like a lot of other places, the Marquee, the Flamingo, the Ramjam, the Locarno Ballroom and so forth. But it is the lunchtime scene at Tiles, the noonday underground, that is the perfect microcosm of The Life of working-class teenagers in England.

The thing is, The Life—the "mod" style of life that got going about 1960—has changed within the last year. It has become a life of total—well, these kids have found a way to drop out almost totally from the conventional class-job system into a world they control. Practically all of them leave school at 15, so why do that old-style thing? Why live at home until you are 20 or 21, putting up with it all, having your manic sprees only on the weekends, having Mod and Rocker set-tos in the springtime or just messing up your mind on Saturday night at some dance hall.

Over the past year thousands of these working-class mods have begun moving away from home at 16, 17, or 18, even girls, girls especially, in fact, and into flats in London. They go to work, in offices, shops, department stores, for £8 to £10 a week, but that is enough to get them into The Life. They share flats, three, four, five girls to a flat, in areas like Leicester Square—jaysus, *Leicester Square*— Charing Cross, Charlotte Street, or they live with their boyfriends, or everyone drifts from place to place. Anyway, it all goes on within a very set style of life, based largely on clothes, music, hairdos and a . . . super-cool outlook on the world.

It is the style of life that makes them unique, not money, power, position, talent, intelligence. So like most people who base their lives on style, they are rather gloriously unaffected cynics about everything else. They have far less nationalistic spirit, for example, than the orthodox English left-wing intellectual. They simply accept England as a country on the way down, and who gives a damn, and America as a country with the power, money, and if you can get some, fine, and the music is good, and you can get that, and they couldn't care less about Vietnam, war, the Bomb, and all that, except that English Army uniforms are indescribably creepy.

Their clothes have come to symbolize their independence from the old idea of a life based on a succession of jobs. The hell with that. There is hardly a kid in all of England who harbors any sincere hope of advancing himself in any very striking way by success at work. Englishmen at an early age begin to sense that the fix is in, and all that work does is keep you afloat at the place you were born into. So working-class teenagers, they are just dropping out of the goddam system, out of the job system, and into roles, as . . . Knights of the Codpiece Pants and Molls of the Mini Mons . . . The Life.

And nobody is even lapsing into the old pub system either, that business where you work your gourds off all day and then sink into the foamy quicksand of the freaking public house at night, loading up your jowls and the saggy tissues of your body with the foaming ooze of it all. Hell, one thing working-class teenagers know is that for five shillings, there is no way you can get drunk in the pub, but for five shillings you can buy enough pills—"purple hearts," "depth bombs" and other lovelies of the pharmacological arts—or "hash" or marijuana—Oh crazy Cannabis!—to stay high for hours. Not that anybody is turning on at Tiles in the noonday underground, but among working-class teenagers generally, in The Life, even the highs are different. The hell with bitter, watercress and old Lardbelly telling you it's time.

All that money, sodden with oozing foam, can better go into clothes. Practically all working-class teenagers in The Life devote half their pay, four to five pounds, to clothes. Some just automatically hand it over to their tailor each week because they always have him making something. There is no more contest between "mod" and "rocker" styles. The mod style and style of life have won completely. Working-class boys who do not dress in current mod styles—and they require a lot of money and, usually, a tailor—are out of it. Just like—shortly after Larry Lynch goes out there onto the dance floor, down into Tiles comes a 17-year-old kid wearing a non-mod outfit, a boho outfit, actually, a pair of faded Levi's and a jacket cut like a short denim jacket, only made of suède, and with his hair long all around after the mode of the Rolling Stones, and he talks to a couple of girls on the edge of the dance floor and he comes away laughing and talking to some American who is down there.

"Do you know what she said to me?" he says. "She said, 'Sod off, Scruffy 'erbert.' They all go for a guy in a purple mohair suit. That's what they call me, 'Scruffy 'erbert.' "

"What's your name?"

"Sebastian."

He turns out to be Sebastian Keep, who works in London as a photographer's assistant but comes from a wealthy family in Hastings. He comes down into Tiles from time to time during his lunch hour to see Pat Cockell, who is 19 and runs the Ravel store in Tiles. Both of them are from Hastings and at one time or another attended public schools and the hell with all that, but on the other hand they illustrate the class split that persists, even in the world of London teenagers.

All the articles about "Swinging London" seem to assume that the class system is breaking down and all these great vital young proles from the East End are taking over and if you can get into Dolly's, Sibylla's, or David Bailey's studio you can see it happening. Actually, the whole "with-it," "switched-on" set of young Londoners—or the "New Boy Network," as it is called, as distinct from the Eton-Harrow "Old Boy Network"—is almost totally removed from the working-class mods. It is made up chiefly of bourgeois, occasionally better, but mainly bourgeois young men and women in the commercial crafts, photography, fashion, show business, advertising, journalism. Aside from the four Beatles themselves and, possibly, two actors, Terence Stamp and Michael Caine, and two photographers, David Bailey and Terence Donovan, there are no working-class boys in the New Boy Network.

The New Boys, including a few upper-class adventurers and voyeurs, have borrowed heavily from the working-class mods in their style of life, but in a self-conscious way. Sebastian Keep's occupation, photographer's assistant, and his style of dress, 1964 Rolling Stones, are okay in the New Boy world. The suède jacket—cut and piped to look like a cotton denim pattern—cost 25 guineas, and this kind of reverse twist, like lining a raincoat with sable, is appreciated by the New Boys, but to the mods—well, 25 guineas is a hell of a mohair suit at Jackson's, with the lapels cut like so, like a military tunic, you know? and—yes.

Only the New Boys, the bourgeois, turn up to buy clothes in London's male fashion center, King's Road, in

Chelsea. Both, the New Boys and the Mods, turn up in Carnaby Street, but more often the mods browse Carnaby Street like some kind of show place, or ambience, and then go off and have clothes like that made somewhere else, where it is cheaper, even a big chain outfit like Burton's.

Browsing Carnaby Street! God, before there was Tiles, that was what Sunshine used to do every day at lunch. Sunshine, whose real name is Tony Newman, of Stamford Hill, Tottenham, and who used to be called Blossom—well, Sunshine tops Blossom anyway—Sunshine would cut out of the stationer's store with the straight lunch mask on and then head straight for Carnaby Street and then just walk up and down Carnaby Street's weird two blocks for an hour, past the Lord John, Male West One, the Tom Cat, men's boutiques with strange enormous blown-up photographs in the windows, of young men flying through the air with some kind of Batman jockstraps on and rock music pouring out the doors, and kids just like him, Sunshine, promenading up and down, and tourists, christ, hundreds of tourists coming in there to photograph each other in front of Male West One instead of Big Ben, and busloads of schoolgirls with their green blazers on and embroidered crests on the breast pocket, all come to see the incredible Carnaby Street, which turns out to be a very small street with shops and awnings and people standing around with cameras in their hands, and Sunshines, all the Sunshines of this world, trundling up and down for their whole lunch hour, not eating a goddamned thing, just immersing themselves in The Life.

That was before Tiles. On Saturday nights in Tiles there is an all-night session with kids stroked out from exhaustion on the steps at the far end of the arcade and then they revive and struggle upright again and jerk and buck a little in a comatose awakening and then they are awake and back out on the dance floor. It is like the Sisters in white dancing, by themselves, to the shout band at the funeral of Daddy Grace in Washington, D.C., going into that ecstatic kinetic trance, oh sweet Daddy, oh big bamboo, dancing until they dropped, and then they were dragged off to the side, prostrate, and they stayed that way until their heads started twitching and then they got up again, those mountains of devout fat got to writhing again.

On Whitsun weekend Tiles goes all day and all night and everybody gets a glimpse of the Total Life, the day when they can all really live completely, all day long, in a world of mod style, drenched in music, suited up, flipped out, whipped, flayed, afire, melded, living a role—Knights of the Codpiece Pants. Molls of the Mini Mons—rather than a job. The whole idea of working-class or this class or that class will be irrelevant, except that—

—oh god, if only you could somehow make money without leaving The Life at all, the way Clem Dalton does, being a DJ, playing the records at Tiles, coming on with some swift American-style talk, having these great *performers* hanging around all the time, like Lee Curtis who sings at these American clubs in Germany, and Lyn Wolseley, who used to be with the Beat Girls and is a great dancer and everything. A DJ! So all these boys want to be DJs and they will do anything for a break.

Like Sunshine—one of Sunshine's big fears is that he is going to get stuck on another job like the one at the stationer's where he has to wear a necktie, because the thing is, Sunshine has developed his own variation within the mod style, which depends on wearing turnover-neck jerseys with these great tailored jackets, well—you know— a *white* turnover-neck can look great, practically formal.

Anyway, Sunshine went to Kenny Everett, who used to run the noontime sessions at Tiles. Kenny is also a DJ, and Sunshine wanted to get a job as a DJ at Radio Caroline or Radio Luxembourg, one of the pirate stations. It would be

great, Sunshine heading out from shore for the first day, up
in the front of a small boat, with his head up and the wind
glancing off his yellow goggles, and his turnover-neck
jersey, a red one, perhaps, up high, and his hands in his
pockets. So Kenny Everett told him to make a tape and he
would see what he could do for him. He told him just to
come on with some patter like he was introducing a record,
just some light patter, movement, not regular gags or
anything.

So Sunshine got hold of a tape recorder and then the day
came when he got in his room and held up the microphone
of the tape recorder and then he concentrated on—what
the hell is it these DJs say?—where does all that stuff come
from?—and he could hear the voices of the DJs in his
mind, all that stuff they say, things like, "Now, baby, one
for the kidney machine, I mean one coming your way for
the kidney machine, all those guys and gals down at the
North College of Art, they're having their contest to raise
money for the kidney machine, and Elise Thredder, down
there at the college, you know what you wrote me about
Cilla Black, Elise, you said I said she said we said they said
oh my head, my head is—zowee!—now listen, Elise, I dig
her, I dig her, I dig that girl, I'm telling you that, I've told
you that, I dig her, I dig her, and I dig all those police
cadets, I mean it, and this one's for the kidney machine and
the police cadets, coming your way, and I'm sorry, if
anybody catches me with me hand in the shop window,
remember, I played this one for the police cadets, and the
kidney machine, and club members everywhere, bless their
little hearts, their lih-uhl 'earts, and their lih-uhl livers and
their lih-uhl kidneys, no, I'm serious, ladies and gentlemen,
and friends . . . I'm serious about this kidney machine,
these gals at North College of Art are undertaking a most
commendable endeavor, endeavoring to commendabobble
the undertaker, you might say, in behalf of all those won-

derful people with the—no—I mean that—and we're nothing until we're put to the test on the mountainside, and
here it is, Mr. Billy Walker, and . . . *A Little on the
Lonely Side*."

How do they do it! So Sunshine does it. But he plays it
back and it doesn't come out right somehow, he doesn't
know exactly why, so he hasn't given it to Kenny yet, but
someday, one day—
—one day Sunshine, and everybody, must find a way to
break through the way Linda has. Oh god, Clem Dalton is
the idol of the boys, they all want to be DJs, but Linda,
who works in the shoe store, is practically the idol of the
girls. Linda is on the verge of making it, of breaking
through, making a living totally within The Life, and she
is only 17.
Linda is a girl from Grays, in Essex. She left school at 15,
like most of her six brothers and sisters, but they stayed in
Grays, mostly, at home, until they grew up, but Linda, it is
not that she is a wild girl or anything, it is just that . . .
The Life, she was in it before she knew it. She could dance,
and the way she wore her clothes—Linda doesn't have a
skirt any lower than 7½ inches above the knees, that is the
truth, and these great bell-bottomed trousers, and her eyes,
well, she paints on these incredible eyes, a big band of
shadow, it looks an inch wide, between the upper lid and
the eyebrows, then a black rim underneath and then she
paints on eyelashes, paints them on, under her eyes, with
these stripes reaching in picket rows down to her cheekbones, and her black bangs in front come down and just
seem to be part of some incredible design ensemble with
her eyes, it is all a pattern, a mask—anyway, Linda moved
to London when she was 15, and she and three other girls
moved into a flat on the motherless Leicester Square and
pretty soon Linda was completely within The Life.

She took a job as a clerk, but it was, like—you know?—a total drag, and Linda started coming down to Tiles at noon, it was like a necessity, to get into The Life at midday before she flipped out in that flunky clerk world, and she was down there one day with her great face on, ratcheting her hips away, gone in the kinetic trance, and Pat Cockell saw her. He needed somebody, a girl, to come work in the Ravel shop in the arcade, somebody who would comprehend what all these working-class mod girls wanted when they came in. So he asked her.

Linda walked down the arcade and into the shop, and even in there, in through the door, she could hear the music from the bandstand. She could hear the music and the dance floor and all those kids would be about 50 feet away, that was all, and it would be like almost being in The Life all the time. So she took the job and pretty soon she would be selling a shoe and then nobody is in the shop for a moment, so Pat stays in there and she goes out to the dance floor and gets into the kinetic trance for one number and then comes back and sells some girl a jesuschristyellow pair of shoes.

Linda was making £9 10s a week. About 25 shillings went to taxes, £2 as her share of the flat, £3 or £4 a week to clothes, at places like Biba—and 30 shillings a week for food. That's all! Thirty shillings—but god, look, she looks great, and what are all these regular straight three-a-day *food injections* for, anyway. And then one day Linda was selling a pair of jesuschristyellow shoes or something and then ratcheting about on the Tiles dance floor and somebody told Marjorie Proops, the columnist, about her, and she ran her picture and then Desilu Productions, the TV company, was doing something about London and they put her in a scene, and now these photographers come by and take her picture—and Linda is *on the verge*, she could become a model or . . . a *figure*, a celebrity, however these things happen, with Pat Cockell as her manager, oh god, Linda could make it, living The Life totally . . . and yet Linda doesn't really give all that much of a damn about it.

People come in and talk to Linda, like this American who was in there, and she listens and she answers questions, but then Clem Dalton puts on something out there, like *Hideaway—*

Hideaway . . . Come on! . . . far from the light of day . . . Come on! . . . leaving the world behind.

—and Linda's eyes kind of glaze over and her legs, in the pinstripe bell-bottoms, start pumping and then she is out the door and out into the dark, at noon, in Tiles. *That's where we're gonna stay.* And so what if she doesn't make it. The Life is still there, it is still available for less than £10 a week, Clem Dalton will never forsake, Jackson will live forever, *I-love-you drops, I-miss-you drops,* and Ian Holton will be abroad in the streets of London with a green waistcoat on that messes your mind up, and Berry Slee and Jay, Liz, Jasmyn, Jane, all the Jays, Lizzes, Jasmyns, Janes of this world—and Larry Lynch—

*Hideaway—*Larry Lynch looks down at his wrist, beautiful the way that cuff just sort of wells out, white, out of the checked sleeve, a half inch of beautiful Brixton cuff, debouching, and christ, he is already twelve minutes over, and he heads back through the maze of Tiles, through the black, like unwinding himself, and up the black stairs—volt! —the sun hits him and nearly tears his eyes out, but the same bursting beetled faces are still bobbing and floating past on the sidewalks and the same shops, hacks, cops, the same Marks & Spencer . . . the same Leicester Square and—oh splendid!—he knew it would be this way, there, back in the office, even, even, straight, straight, the same rows of . . . straight noses, all pointing the same way, toward eternity, as if nothing had happened at all.

6 The Mild Ones

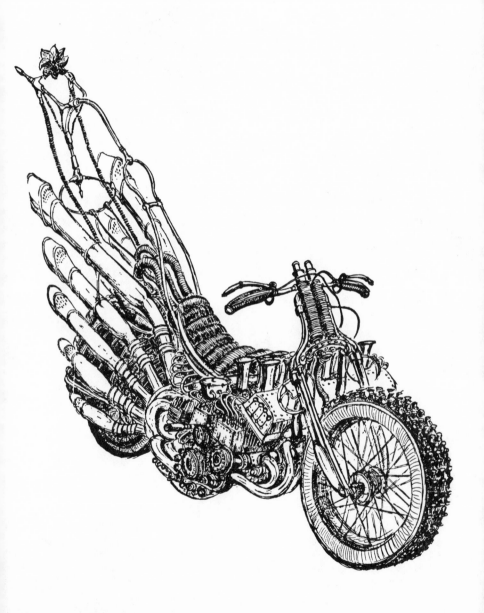

GOD knows how many thousands of work-a-daddy citizens of Columbus, Ohio, Tom's own city, drive past the Harley-Davidson agency at 491 West Broad Street every day without ever seeing *Tom's Bomb,* that weird monster in the show window. Yet there are many boys and men, religiosi of a sort, in Los Angeles, Oakland, Chicago, Cleveland, who know of it. They know of this *ecstatic* in Columbus, Tom Reiser—the stud who rides a motorcycle with an automobile engine in it—

Liberation!

Tom's Bomb is up on a platform in one corner of the window. It is a Harley-Davidson 74-XA motorcycle with a Chevrolet V-8 automobile engine in it. Reiser put a whole automobile engine in a motorcycle. He had to put it in crossways, so that half the block sticks out of one side of the bike and half out the other, right out of the frame there, right in front of the rider's legs and just in back of the front wheel. The proportions are like a boulder rammed through a sheet of plywood. The motorcycle frame weighs 300 pounds and the engine weighs 550 pounds, a Chevrolet V-8 with all the headers, the wires, the flywheel, everything showing.

Reiser got the idea from another one of the underground heroes of the motorcycle world, Ed Potter. Ed Potter, in motorcycling, is like what Chuck Berry, Muddy Waters, Hank Williams, or one of these people is in music, a *germinal* folk figure from back 'ere on Route 422 or something. Potter put a whole automobile engine in a motorcycle frame and called the machine the "Bloody Mary." But he didn't have any transmission in it, no gear shift. He couldn't start it off from a dead start and accelerate. He had to go out to the drag strip and get on and have his buddy Jimmy jack the rear wheel up off the ground. Then he would turn the throttle up until the rear wheel was turning at the equivalent of about 110 miles an hour. Then his buddy Jimmy would kick the jack out from under it and—holy jesus—the back wheel would hit the asphalt and shriek like a woman's scream and he would start careening down the strip, fishtailing every way you can think of, including straight into the crowd. There was a true ball buster.

Tom Reiser refined the whole thing. He invented a motorcycle transmission, the kind you operate on the handlebars of the motorcycle, for the Chevrolet V-8 engine. Reiser is a student of the motorcycle. That is one thing people do not generally understand about the motorcycle crowd. The kids who go in for racing, whether drag racing, like Reiser, or oval track racing or long-distance road racing, hill climbing or cross-country racing, are very studious. They develop a priestly passion for speed engineering. They are truly religious men, bound by their devotion to Liberation through the internal-combustion engine. They are sequestered from most secular concerns. They spend practically all their spare time working on the machines. They seldom drink much because it takes up too much time or even smoke much because it gets in the way when you're working on the machine.

Reiser looks a little like Slats in the comic strip, "Abbie and Slats." He is 29 years old, tall, blond, raw-boned, open, outgoing; *Western*-looking, one might say. He is married and has two children. His father, who is retired, was a florist and his mother was a seamstress; he went to South High School in Columbus and later was trained at the Harley-Davidson mechanics school in California. He was always a genius with motorcycles. And courage—raw nerve—it seemed like his priestly passion for the motor-cycle, for speed, made it so he would do practically any-thing to get speed out of a motorcycle. Reiser won the Canadian hill-climbing championship in 1965 and is after the speed record at the Utah salt flats. He put together "Tom's Bomb" in 1961, and thankgod they had just built the superhighway from Columbus west to Cincinnati, Route 71, because that was the chance to try it out.

The federal superhighway program has been a godsend for speed engineering in the state of Ohio. The beautiful time is right after a stretch of highway is built, but before it is opened to cars. Ohio's speed kids, the motorcyclists, the drag racers, both motorcycle and automobile, follow that beautiful superhighway system wherever the road con-tractors go with it. At night they sneak out onto the great smooth stretches of American superhighway and . . . *go.* Tom Reiser warmed up "Tom's Bomb" out on Route 71 under the moon and then he took it out to the drag strip near Newark, Ohio, for an exhibition. They all saw the machine rolling out toward the starting line, and a shriek went up—

"Well, when I started off," Reiser was saying, "the back wheel bit down so hard it threw me back and it felt like the whole motorcycle was going to go over backward. It was like the whole thing was just going to lift up and go over backward. It was like the whole thing was covered in smoke, me and everything. I couldn't see nothing. The guys thought the engine had exploded or something. It was the rubber burning, but they thought the whole thing was on fire and they were going to have to get me out of there with a fire hose. It was a weird feeling. It started off with a whole row of jerks. I don't know what that was, unless there was so much power, it was just running over the top of itself, and then all of a sudden it shot out of the cloud, and after that there wasn't anything to do but *hang on—*"

By the time he burst out of the cloud, Reiser was already going about 50 miles an hour. By the time he hit 60, he had his head practically down on the handlebars, to lower his body and cut down on the wind resistance. His body was stretched out over the Chevrolet V-8 engine, which was mounted in the frame between the seat and the front wheel. He was stretching more and more flat out with each split second of acceleration until his feet came up off the foot rests and his legs stretched out straight behind—

"When I hit about 90," said Reiser, "it was like the bike wasn't hardly touching the road any more—"

—and when he hit 130, he *knew* it wasn't—

"All of a sudden I was *sailing*—like I wasn't on the ground any more at all. I couldn't hardly see anything or hear anything. There was no gravity or nothing, I was just *sailing*—"

—and as he spoke, I could *see* it, the ultimate vision. I could see his body stretched out and pressing down tighter and tighter upon the V-8 engine until his thoracic cavity was practically bolted onto it. Its fiery combustions were his neural explosions and his neural explosions were its fiery combustions. His body and that roaring engine block were one and the same creature, sailing—at 140—160—180—200 miles an hour—*2,000* miles an hour—sailing!—at last, the winged American centaur, the American dream, at last: soaring over God's own good green Great Plains of America bareback aboard a 300-horsepower Chevrolet V-8 engine!

7 The Hair Boys

FRIDAY NIGHT, the night of the style cruise at Harvey's Drive-in, I was standing just inside the garage out back of Ed Roth the King of the Kustomizer's offices on Slauson Avenue in Maywood, a good . . . *rank* part of Los Angeles. Light from the cage lights mechanics use was lighting up my necktie, my seersucker jacket, white ducks, white shoes. Ed "Big Daddy" Roth was flat on his back underneath a yellow dragster he has, "Yellow Fang," and he twisted his head out from under the side of the thing and stuck his beard out and stared at me. George "The Bushmaster" Schreiber, who drives the dragster for Roth, was lowering a manifold plate onto the engine, and he looked up with his Fu Manchu beard hanging off his face and stared at me. Lou "Supermouth" Schorsch was just standing there meditating about some new . . . *rank* advertising copy for Roth's Ratfink doll—*made of 100% guaranteed lowest-grade Japanese plastic*—and suddenly Schorsch was staring at me.

"You can't go to Harvey's like that," Roth says. "They'll shoot us."

"They's *shoot* us, and they'll *kill* you," Lou Schorsch says.

"What do you mean? This is pretty casual, for me."

"Nah," Roth says, "nah. It doesn't make it." He starts to give a reason, but it is beyond even talking about. "Get him a T-shirt. Get him one of those surfing shirts. Maybe we can pass him off as a surfer."

The Oxford blue shirt, the necktie—that went first—the seersucker coat. All of a sudden I was in an area of High Style where I was out of style completely. Taking some fellow with a coat and tie on to Harvey's Drive-in would be like taking along the meter reader to Dior's in September, a meter reader in a khaki shirt and balloon-seat khaki pants with a leather pencil holster at his waist and a clipboard.

But of course! Harvey's Drive-in, on Firestone Boulevard, between Paramount Boulevard and Garfield Avenue, in Downey, a town just southeast of Los Angeles, is the world's major salon for the new High Style that is creating the most radical change in men's fashions since the disappearance of doublets, breeches and stockings in the early nineteenth century. Harvey's is the Dior, the Balenciaga, the Chanel of the new wave: men's clothes created not for jobs but for *life roles*, the role of High Liver, of Swinger, Artist, Hippie, Tiger Man, Hell's Angel.

Every Friday night at Harvey's, starting about 9:30 p.m., kids from all over the Los Angeles teenage netherworld, from West Los Angeles, Bell, Maywood, Hollywood, Gardena, San Pedro, white Watts, San Gabriel, even Santa Ana, Santa Monica, Covina—they all drive to Harvey's Drive-in in their cruising cars. Ostensibly they come in there to get something to eat, hamburgers, Dubble-Bubba-Burgers, French fries, Shrimp Splits, Mexicali Chili-Barbs, everything the glories of boiling lard and hot pepper have brought to America. The real reason they come, however, is simply to promenade, or, in the parlance of Harvey's Drive-in, to *cruise*. They cruise around in their cars in Harvey's huge parking lot, boys and girls, showing each other the latest in fashions in cars, hairdos (male and female) and clothes in the Los Angeles Teenage . . . and Second-Generation Teenage . . . modes. Rank moderne! Teenage Paris! Harvey's Drive-in!

I put on the black surfer's shirt. "That's better, Tom Coyote," the Bushmaster says. We get in Roth's 1955 Chevrolet and head over to Harvey's. Roth, Schorsch and Schreiber do not dress in the new High Style. Roth, for example, usually wears a T-shirt, revealing the huge tattoo on his upper left arm that just says, "Roth." But they all have a sense of the proprieties in the thing. We all went over in Roth's 1955 Chevrolet because the 1955 Chevrolet is one of the classic cars of hot rodding and customizing. The 1932 Ford is the other one. On the way over, we were tooling down the highway, past the shopping plaza signs, and three kids in a 1965 Mustang came up on the inside and started roaring past. Roth couldn't resist. He mashed the accelerator—*thraaagggh*—for a moment it was like the old days when Roth and Schorsch were growing up around Maywood and Bell, customizing cars, hot rodding, drag racing in the streets. Everybody was thrown back against the seats from the sudden thrust forward, and the three kids in the Mustang were blown out of the tub, as they say in stock-car racing. That just means they got left behind, nothing serious. Roth had a 427 cubic-inch engine in his Chevrolet.

That little exhibition match got everybody in the rank spirit of the thing. Supermouth tells about rank.

"Kids today like things that are rank," he says. "It's different from when I was a kid. It used to be it was a big deal if your old man got a Thunderbird or something. You'd run next door and say, 'Boy, my old man just got a Thunderbird. You ought to see it.' And the kid next door would say, 'Jesus, that's great. I wish my old man would do something great like that.'

"Today a kid doesn't give a damn if his old man gets a Thunderbird. The only thing his old man can do that's going to impress him is something *rank*. It's like if your old man calls your mother an——. Now that's rank. You know. The old man comes home, and right away she starts bugging him to get washed up for dinner. All he wants to do is go into the bathroom and sit down and do some light reading, like the competition's used-car ads. So he's in there sitting down reading the competition's used-car ads and she's yelling at him to come to dinner, and finally he says, 'Aw, shut up, you——.' " This word he uses is an ancient proctological word. "That's rank! Today a kid goes running next door and he says, 'Hey, listen! Guess what my old man just called my mother!' And the other kid says, 'No kidding! That's great. I wish my old man would do something great like that.' It's *rank*."

"Yeah," says Roth, "you ought to see some of the rank shirts the kids are buying now. I mean, there are some really rotten shirts now."

They bear legends such as: "Are you man enough to eat Granny Goose?" Roth himself produces T-shirts and sweat shirts for kids, but his have only relatively rank legends on them, such as "Mother Is Wrong."

Rank! Rank is just the natural outgrowth of Rotten. Roth and Schorsch grew up in the Rotten Era of Los Angeles teenagers. The idea was to have a completely rotten attitude toward the adult world, meaning, in the long run, the whole established status structure, the whole system of people organizing their lives around *a job*, fitting into a social structure embracing the whole community. The idea in Rotten was to drop out of conventional status competition into the smaller netherworld of Rotten Teenage and start one's own league.

Harvey's! Thousands of kids in their cruising cars were edging onto the asphalt of Harvey's Drive-in. They were lined up all the way out to Firestone Boulevard, just waiting to get in there and get on the cruising lanes. Harvey's is a huge drive-in, with a streamlined modern shed building. There are many streamlined modern shed buildings around Los Angeles, for drive-ins and car washes chiefly, also gasoline stations, with slanting roofs and a lot of upward hard-driving diagonal lines. Anyway, there are a lot of bright lights under the shed roof, and around it there are parking places for about a hundred cars. But a couple of thousand cars are edging onto the parking lot. Nobody really cares particularly about parking anyway. Everybody wants to . . . *cruise* in the cars and see everything. They just keep going around and around the cruising lanes, tooling around.

Strangely, there is a whole line of parking places up next to the curb by the shed, under the lights, where tough little buns with bare legs and black boots, the carhops, are up there hustling the Dubble-Bubbas, and there are only one or two cars parked there. "That's the Mickey Mouse area," Supermouth says. I never did figure out why. Roth doesn't care; he doesn't have to prove anything. He parks in the Mickey Mouse area and the kids still cruise by and yell, "Hey, Roth!" The kids roll by the shed, between lines of parked cars, and you can see that much of the old custom-car art has died out in California. They all have new cars, Lincolns even, Stingrays, Mustangs, with maybe a custom paint job, flake paint, and racing tires, Michelin Triple-X, so big they bulge out from under the fenders. Every now and then somebody comes by in one of the old classics, something like a 1960 Pontiac, chopped and channeled, lowered to about two inches off the ground with a hydraulic system to raise the big thing up if the cops come close, because those low cars are illegal now. But mostly here are screaming new cars. They keep going 'round and 'round. Sometimes you see one first with two boys in the front seat, and then the next time around one boy is in the back seat and each boy has a girl beside him, little yellow dandelion babies with black houri eyes. They aren't saying anything; they're just, you know, cruising. They must have had to say something at first, so the boys could pick them up and everything, but the main thing is just to ride around. Gradually, as they keep coming around, I begin to notice . . . the style.

The boys have the new Los Angeles car kids' look. They don't have the ducktail haircuts any more. The ducktail was combed back on the sides and forward on top, curling down over the forehead. The new look is to comb all the hair straight back, but up and high in the front, so that it gets a slight bouffant effect there, but all combed back into one massive, sculpted head of hair, practically completely smooth, all in place, piled high, impeccable. Other kids call them the Hair Boys. The Hair Boys have on the same kind of sweater, a cardigan, open down the front, a very fluffy sweater, in high pastels, magentas, peach, cerulean blue, a fluffy sweater with the arms cut very big, puffed out almost, but coming down tight at the wrists, and cut very full in the body, fluffing out—but with tight, thin-cut trousers, usually dark, coming down to various pointed shoes, gusseted boots and so forth, buckled winkle-pickers, Rip Van Winkle boots. Sometimes a plain T-shirt or a turtle-neck jersey, or else a soft shirt with a high collar, like a tab or a "Dino," but—one means, like, *given*—no tie.

There is something almost feminine about these boys. I refer to the high-piled, perfect coiffure, the attention to a fashion silhouette—the way the sweaters create big, soft, full lines, with the pants and shoes giving dramatic contrast, being narrow and thin. Of course, it is feminine only in comparison to the conventional adult standards for men. In another age—it is curiously close to what the men in power, the real movers and shakers, all wore. I am talking about the court fashions of seventeenth-century England.

At that point the suits of the most powerful men consisted of doublets, breeches and stockings. The doublets, like the Hair Boys' sweaters, had no lapels. They were full in the arms, and they were by the standards of today feminine, made from various weaves of silk—satins, damasks, velvets and so forth—or cloths with gold and silver threads, and laces and braids, ribbons. The perukes, or periwigs, those ornate curled wigs men wore, were very much like the bouffant coiffures of the Hair Boys today, something very *set* and stylized and high fashion. The breeches, stockings and buckled shoes gave the same dramatic contrast the Hair Boys try to achieve.

All these court styles of the seventeenth century, and, in fact, most of the styles recorded from the eighteenth century on back, symbolized some charismatic *role*. The ornate court fashions did not symbolize the *job* of ruling the country, but the majesty of the role, the godly rights, and so forth. A few styles from before 1800 still hang on in this country, and they all symbolize some charismatic— that is to say, god-inspired—role in life, Justice, Mercy, Wisdom. The gowns judges wear today date from the fifteenth century. The dresses nuns still wear are what widows wore in mourning in the sixteenth century. The mortarboards students graduate in are stiff versions of sixteenth-century scholars' caps.

The biggest revolution in men's fashions came in the nineteenth century with the industrial revolution. It happened in stages, but gradually men began to dress not for a role—Ruler, Man of God, Warrior, Savant, Carrier of Justice—but for a job. The rising business class simplified dress, partly as reaction against court life, partly for practical reasons, expense, for one. The coat, shorter and with a collar and a lot of pockets, replaced the doublet. Trousers replaced the breeches and stockings. Plain fabrics came in.

The fit of the clothes, not the cut, became the most important thing, fitting it to the measurements of the body. In court fashions, using heavy silks, it was not the measurements of, say, a doublet that counted, but the cut—the big flare of the sleeves, the flare of the skirt, flare, they like flare. The same—cut over fit—is true of women's fashions today.

But in men's clothes—one can see the drastic change the nineteenth-century business styles brought by looking in any office today. A woman in the office, an $80-a-week stenographer even, is not in there dressed to look like a stenographer. She, no less than a movie star, dresses to look like a woman—her *role* in life, as she sees it. But the men dress for jobs. They dress first of all to look like lawyers, bankers, sales managers, or messengers or janitors or window washers. Only secondarily, sort of by the way, does what they wear stress whatever role they have . . . as men.

After World War II, a number of sets of young men in California began to drop out of the rationalized job system and create their own statusspheres. In every case they made a point of devising new fashions, *role* clothes, to symbolize their new life styles. These were the beats, the motorcycle gangs, the car kids, and, more recently, the rock 'n' roll kids, the surfers, and, of course, the hippies. The hell with the jobs they had or might ever get. They wanted roles, as Rebels, Swingers, Artists, Poets, Mystics, Tigers of the Internal Combustion Engine, Monks of the Sea, anything that would be dramatic, exciting, not powerful or useful or efficient but . . . yes! a little bit *divine*, right out of the old godhead of the hero.

They have all been able to pull it off, set up their own styles of life and keep them going and make them highly

visible, because of the extraordinary amount of money
floating around. It is not that any of these groups is ever
rich. It is just that there is so much money floating around
that they can get their hands on enough of it to express
themselves, and devote time to expressing themselves, to a
degree nobody in their netherworld position could ever do
before. The beats, motorcyclists, rock 'n' roll kids, surfers,
hippies, all stress cut—flare—over fit in order to symbolize
the role they want to play, but they all stay fairly *low
style*. They want to look scruffy, by conventional standards, to express the Rebel role, for one thing. The surfers,
for example, wear wide-cut shorts and big nylon windbreakers that look like sails, and they grow their hair long
with a rabbinical devotion, but they don't shape it. They're
Rebels, they're Monks of the Sea. But the car kids—the
Hair Boys—even though they're known as Greasers to the
surfers, they keep moving into *high style*. It may be because they have always been dedicated to such an ornate,
glistening, high-style sculptural object, the American automobile, in the first place.

The idea of *role* clothes is beginning to take hold among
many older and wealthier men today. I see a style schizophrenia developing. These men have jobs and they go to
work dressed more or less like men in England and America have dressed to go to work at the office for the past 130
years. But after work and on the weekends—*role* clothes.
The role, in simplest terms, is . . . being a man; virile, a
free fellow with his Mennen-swabbed face in the wind.
They are buying all sorts of *heavy*, textured fabrics, navy-
style pea jackets, leathers, English lambskin coats with
fleece linings, heavy-ribbed turtle-neck sweaters, with all
that rough texture lying right next to one's own hide,
Danish bulky-knit sweaters, wide-wale corduroy pants, all
sorts of heavy *bootings*, Desert Boots, brogues that would
stagger a Highlander, gusseted boots, motorcycle boots,

tweed coats that practically have shepherd's barbed wire and tree bark woven right in there. None of this is at *casual* prices, either, with the lambskin coats weighing in at about $175, Danish sweaters at $45 to $55, and so on.

And the cuts—they're the cut of the hunter, the woodsman, the fighter, the motorcylist, the free stud's . . . *role.*

Great stuff! For years new men's styles have been created almost solely by the nobility. In 1666 Samuel Pepys tells how the King decided that he had discovered *the* finest style for all times, he would never change it and it would never change, a kind of vest he had dreamed up, only a vest as long and high-styled as a cassock, so he decreed this the style, and it became the style. As late as 1870, Albert Edward, Prince of Wales, Queen Victoria's eldest son, later Edward VII, created the style of wearing creases in pants. He was wearing white flannels on the way to a cricket match and got caught in the rain in a town. The flannels were ruined, so he stopped in a ready-to-wear shop, picked up a pair of flannel trousers out of a drawer and bought them and put them on and hurried to the matches. The pants were creased from lying in a pile in the drawer, but everybody saw Albert Edward wearing creases in his pants, and that was it, that was enough.

But today, in America—at Harvey's Drive-in—what is happening—one means—*blaaaaaaaaaaaaaaght—*

"What the hell is that?"

"That's somebody winging it back there," Roth says.

"They'll get him for that," says Supermouth. "They'll give him a ticket. There's a cop right back there waiting. That's real *rank*, the way they see it. Some kid just wants to wing it once, but that's real *rank* to them."

Some Hair Boy is back there in the cruising line in his Stingray with the huge Michelin Triple-X racing tires bulging out from under the fenders, and he has all this power under there, and all he wants to do is gun it once in neutral, *wing it,* blat all that power out through the headers once for everybody to hear at the style cruise. But the cops get it, too. It is like the rallying cry for—what?—nobody is quite sure. So the cop is giving the kid a ticket, Roth, Bushmaster, Supermouth and I look back, the cruise keeps going——

—*blaaaaaaaaaaaaaaaaaght*——

—the men's fashion trumpet of the Sixties is sounded and out of the dewy air of Harvey's Drive-in, there amid the Dubble-Bubba-Burgers, the French fries, Shrimp Splits, Mexicali Chili-Barbs and tough little bun carhops, comes, arising, the fashion vision, the *silhouette,* the Downey, Calif., doublets, fluffy, puffy, the breeches and stockings, stove pipe, blat pipe, the new *role* for Everyman, dropped out, blatted out . . . rank! blown out of the tub. Happy mass fop.

8 *What If He Is Right?*

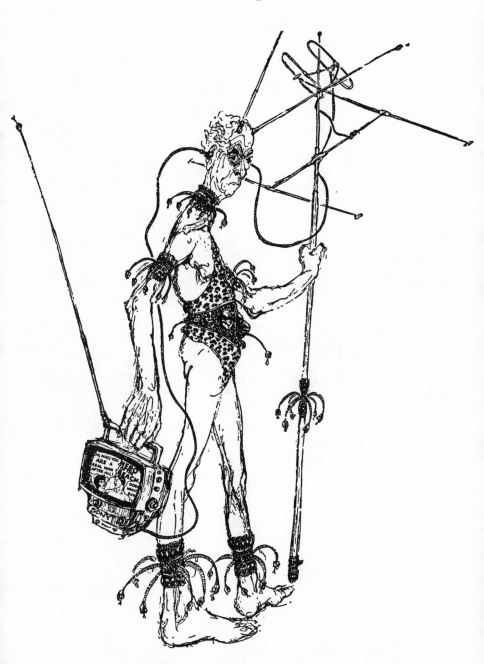

I FIRST met Marshall McLuhan in the spring of 1965, in New York. The first thing I noticed about him was that he wore some kind of a trick snap-on necktie with hidden plastic cheaters on it. He was a tall man, 53 years old, handsome, with a long, strong face, but terribly pallid. He had gray hair, which he combed straight back. It was a little thin on top, but he could comb it into nice sloops over the ears. Distinguished-looking, you might say. On the other hand, there were the plastic cheaters. A little of the plastic was showing between his collar and the knot of the tie. I couldn't keep my eye off it. It's the kind of tie you buy off a revolving rack in the Rexall for about 89¢. You just slip the plastic cheaters—they're a couple of little stays sticking out of the knot like wings—you slip them under your collar and there the tie is, hanging down and ready to go, Pree-Tide.

We were having lunch, five of us, out back in the garden of a French restaurant called Lutèce, at 249 East 50th Street. Lutèce is a small place but one of the four or five most fashionable restaurants in New York, I suppose. Certainly it is one of the most expensive. It is so expensive, only your host's menu has the prices listed. Yours just has a list of the dishes. That way you won't feel guilty about it. They put decanters of distilled water on the tables at Lutèce and they have a real wine steward. It is one of those places in the East Fifties in Manhattan where the Main Biggies and the Fashionable Matrons convene for the main event of the weekday, the Status Lunch. Executives, culturati, rich women who are written up in *Women's Wear Daily*, illuminati of all sorts meet there in a marvelous chorale of King Sano and Eastern Honk voices. The women walk in looking an ice-therapy 45, force-starved, peruked and lacquered at the hairdresser's, wearing peacock-colored Pucci dresses signed "Emilio" up near the throat, taking in "the crowd," sucking their cheeks in for the entrance, and calling Lutèce's owner by his first name, which is André, in a contralto that has been smoke-cured by fifteen to twenty years of inhaling King Sanos, the cigarette of New York Society women. The men come in wearing lozenge-shaped cuff links with real links and precious metal showing on the inside as well as the outside of the cuffs, not those Swank-brand gizmos that stick through and click, and they start honking over André and each other, speaking in a voice known as the Eastern boarding-school honk, a nasal drawl mastered by Nelson Rockefeller, Huntington Hartford, and Robert Dowling, among other eminent Americans. It was grand here, as I say. All honks and smoke-cured droning.

Our table was not the most illustrious, but it was in there trying: a movie actress; the daughter of one of the richest women in America; one of New York's top editors; and, of course, McLuhan. McLuhan, however, was not a celebrity at that time. I doubt that anybody else in the restaurant had ever heard of him.

And vice versa. McLuhan could not have been more oblivious of the special New York grandeur he had landed in. I don't think he noticed the people at all. He was interested in the little garden, or rather its thermodynamics, the way it was set out here in the heat of the noonday sun.

"The warmth steps up the tactile sense and diminishes the visual," he told us presently—as nearly as I can remember his words—I was following the plastic cheater. "It is more involving. It obliterates the distance between people. It is literally more 'intimate.' That's why these so-called 'garden restaurants' work."

Just before he made this sort of statement—and he was always analyzing his environment out loud—he would hook his chin down over his collarbone. It was like an unconscious signal—*now!* I would watch the tie knot swivel over the little telltale strip of plastic. It was a perfect Rexall milky white, this plastic.

At the time I didn't realize that McLuhan had been brought here, to New York, to Lutèce also, to be introduced to *haute New York*. He was about to make his debut, after a fashion. He was about to change from Herbert Marshall McLuhan, 53-year-old Canadian English professor, to *McLuhan*. He certainly didn't act like it, however. It had all been planned, but not by him. To him there was no *haute New York*. It was all past tense in this town. Toward the end of the meal his chin came down, the knot swiveled over the plastic—voices droned and honked richly all around us—and he turned his eyeballs up toward the great office buildings that towered above our little thermodynamic enclave.

"Of course, a city like New York is obsolete," he said. "People will no longer concentrate in great urban centers for the purpose of work. New York will become a Disneyland, a pleasure dome . . ."

Somehow, plastic cheaters and all, he had the charisma of a haruspex, the irresistible certitude of the monomaniac. I

could see New York turning into a huge Astrodome with
raggy little puberteens in white Courrèges boots giggling
and shrieking and tumbling through the atmosphere like
the snow in one of those Christmas paperweights you turn
upside down—

WHAT if he's right   What . . . if . . . he . . . is
. . . right   W-h-a-t i-f h-e i-s r-i-g-h-t

		R	
W		I	
H	IF	G	?
A	HE	H	
T	IS	T	

Quite a few American businessmen, it turned out, were
already wondering the same thing. There were many studs
of the business world, breakfast-food-package designers,
television-network creative-department vice presidents, advertising "media reps," lighting-fixture fortune heirs,
patent lawyers, industrial spies, we-need-vision board
chairmen—all sorts of business studs, as I say, wondering if
McLuhan was . . . right. At the time McLuhan was a
teacher working out of a little office off on the edge of the
University of Toronto that looked like the receiving bin of
a second-hand bookstore, grading papers, *grading papers*,
for days on end, getting up in the morning, slapping the old
Pree-Tide tie on, teaching English, grading more papers—
But what if—large corporations were already trying to
put McLuhan in a box. Valuable! Ours! Suppose he *is* what
he sounds like, the most important thinker since Newton,
Darwin, Freud, Einstein, and Pavlov, studs of the intelli-
gentsia game—suppose he *is* the oracle of the modern
times—*what if he is right?*—he'll be in there, in our box.
     IBM, General Electric, Bell Telephone, and others had
been flying McLuhan from Toronto to New York, Pitts-

burgh, all over the place, to give private talks to their hierarchs about . . . this unseen world of electronic environment that *only he sees fully*. One corporation offered him $5,000 to present a closed-circuit—*ours*—television lecture on the ways the products in its industry would be used in the future. Another contributed a heavy subsidy to McLuhan's Centre for Culture and Technology at the University of Toronto, which, despite the massive name, was at that time largely McLuhan's genius and some letterhead stationery. One day in New York, McLuhan was staying at Howard Gossage's suite at the Lombardy Hotel. Gossage is a San Francisco advertising man. McLuhan was staying there and representatives of two national weekly magazines called up. Both offered him permanent offices in their buildings, plus fees, to do occasional consulting work. Just to have him in the box, I guess—

"What should I do, Howard?" says McLuhan.

"Take 'em both!" says Gossage. "You need offices on both sides of town. Suppose you get caught in traffic?"

McLuhan looks puzzled, but Gossage is already off into his laugh. This Gossage has a certain wild cosmic laugh. His eyes light up like Stars of Bethlehem. The laugh comes in waves, from far back in the throat, like echoes from Lane 27 of a bowling alley, rolling, booming far beyond the immediate situation, on to . . .

. . . in any case, McLuhan never failed to provoke this laugh. Perhaps because there were really two contradictory, incongruous McLuhans at this point. Even his appearance could change markedly from situation to situation. One moment he would look like merely the English teacher with the Pree-Tide tie on, naïve, given to bad puns derived from his studies of *Finnegans Wake* and worse jokes from God knows where, a somewhat disheveled man, kindly, disorganized—the very picture of the absentminded professor. The next moment he would look like what he has, in fact, become: the super-savant, the Freud of our times, the omniscient *philosophe*, the unshakable dialectician. That was whenever the subject was The Theory, which it usually was. On those occasions the monologue began, and McLuhan was, simply, the master. He preferred Socratic dialogues, with six to ten people in attendance. A Socratic dialogue, like a Pentecostal sermon, is a monologue punctuated by worshipful interruptions. "Marshall is actually very polite," said one of his friends, meaning to be kind. "He always waits for your lips to stop moving."

Among his business clients, McLuhan was always that, monomaniac and master. The business studs would sit in their conference rooms under fluorescent lights, with the right air-conditioned air streaming out from behind the management-style draperies. Upward-busting hierarch executives, the real studs, the kind who have already changed over from lie-down crewcuts to brushback Eric Johnston-style Big Boy haircuts and from Oxford button-downs to Tripler broadcloth straight points and have hung it all on the line, an $80,000 mortage in New Canaan and a couple of kids at Deerfield and Hotchkiss—hung it all on the line on knowing exactly what this corporation is all about—they sit there with the day's first bloody mary squirting through their capillaries—and this man with a plastic cheater showing at the edge of the collar, who just got through *grading papers*, for godsake, tells them in an *of-course* voice, and with *I'm-being-patient* eyes, that, in effect, politely, they all know just about exactly . . . nothing . . . about the real business they're in—

—Gentlemen, the General Electric Company makes a considerable portion of its profits from electric light bulbs, but it has not yet discovered that it is not in the light bulb business but in the business of moving information. Quite as much as A.T.&T. Yes. *Of-course I-am-willing-to-be-patient.*

He pulls his chin down into his neck and looks up out of his long Scotch-lairdly face. Yes. The electric light is pure information. It is a medium without a message, as it were. Yes. Light is a self-contained communications system in which the medium is the message. *Just think that over for a moment—I-am-willing-to-be—*When IBM discovered that it was not in the business of making office equipment or business machines—

————but that it was in the business
of processing
information,
then it began
to navigate
with
clear
vision.
Yes.

Swell! But where did *this* guy come from? What is this—cryptic, Delphic saying: *The electric light is pure information.*

Delphic! *The medium is the message. We are moving out of the age of the visual into the age of the aural and tactile.* . . .

It was beautiful. McLuhan excelled at telling important and apparently knowledgeable people they didn't have the foggiest comprehension of their own bailiwick. He never did it with any overtone of now-I'm-going-to-shock-you, however. He seemed far, far beyond that game, out on a threshold where all the cosmic circuits were programmed. I can see him now, sitting in the conference room on the upper deck of an incredible ferryboat that Walter Landor, one of the country's top package designers, has redone at a cost of about $400,000 as an office and design center. This great package design flagship nestles there in the water at Pier 5 in San Francisco. The sun floods in from the Bay onto the basketwoven wall-to-wall and shines off the dials of Landor's motion-picture projection console. Down below on the main deck is a whole simulated supermarket for bringing people in and testing package impact—and McLuhan says, almost by the way:

"Of course, packages will be obsolete in a few years. People will want tactile experiences, they'll want to feel the product they're getting—"

But!—

McLuhan's chin goes down, his mouth turns down, his eyes roll up in his *of-course* expression: "Goods will be sold in *bins*. People will go right to bins and pick things up and *feel* them rather than just accepting a package."

Landor, the package designer, doesn't lose his cool; he just looks—*what if he is right?*

. . . *The human family now exists under conditions of a global village. We live in a single constricted space resonant with tribal drums* . . . That even, even, even voice goes on—

—McLuhan is sitting in the Laurent Restaurant in New York with Gibson McCabe, president of *Newsweek*, and several other high-ranking communications people, and McCabe tells of the millions *Newsweek* has put into reader surveys, market research, advertising, the editorial staff, everything, and how it paid off with a huge rise in circulation over the past five years. McLuhan listens, then down comes the chin: "Well . . . of course, your circulation would have risen about the same anyway, the new sensory balance of the people being what it is . . ."

Print gave tribal man an eye for an ear.

McLuhan is at the conference table in the upper room in Gossage's advertising firm in San Francisco, up in what used to be a firehouse. A couple of newspaper people are up there talking about how they are sure their readers want this and that to read—McLuhan pulls his chin down into his neck:

"Well . . . of course, people don't actually *read* news-papers. They get into them every morning like a hot bath."

Perfect! Delphic! Cryptic! Aphoristic! Epigrammatic! With this even, even, even voice, this utter scholarly aplomb—with *pronouncements*—

The phone rings in Gossage's suite and it's for McLuhan. It is a man from one of America's largest packing corporations. They want to fly McLuhan to their home office to deliver a series of three talks, one a day, to their top management group. How much would he charge? McLuhan puts his hand over the receiver and explains the situation to Gossage.

"How much should I charge?"

"What do you usually get for a lecture?" says Gossage.

"Five hundred dollars."

"Tell him a hundred thousand."

McLuhan looks appalled.

"Oh, all right," says Gossage. "Tell him fifty thousand."

McLuhan hesitates, then turns back to the telephone: "Fifty thousand."

Now the man on the phone is appalled. That is somewhat outside the fee structure we generally project, Professor McLuhan. They all call him Professor or Doctor. We don't expect you to prepare any new material especially for us, you understand, and it will only be three talks—

"Oh—well, then," says McLuhan, "twenty-five thousand."

Great sigh of relief. Well! That is more within our potential structure projection, Professor McLuhan, and we look forward to seeing you!

McLuhan hangs up and stares at Gossage, nonplussed. But Gossage is already off into the cosmic laugh, bounding, galloping, soaring, eyes ablaze—¡*más allá!*—¡*más allá!* just over the next skyline!—El Dorado, Marshall! Don't you understand!—

Looking back, I can see that Gossage, but not McLuhan, knew what was going to happen to McLuhan over the next six months. Namely, that this 53-year-old Canadian English teacher, gray as a park pigeon, would suddenly become an international celebrity and the most famous man his country ever produced.

McLuhan rose up from out of a world more obscure, more invisible, more unknown to the great majority of mankind than a Bantu village or the Southeast Bronx. Namely, the EngLit academic life. Tongaland and the Puerto Rican slums may at least reek, in the imagination, of bloodlust and loins oozing after sundown. EngLit academia, so far as the outside world is concerned, neither reeks nor blooms; an occasional whiff of rotting tweeds, perhaps; otherwise, a redolence of nothing. It is a world of liberal-arts scholars, graduate schools, *carrels*, and monstrous baby-sitting drills known as freshman English. It is a far more detached life than any garret life of the artists. Garret life? Artists today spend their time calling up Bloomingdale's to see if the yellow velvet Milo Laducci chairs they ordered are in yet.

English-literature scholars start out in little cubicles known as carrels, in the stacks of the university libraries, with nothing but a couple of metal Klampiton shelves of books to sustain them, sitting there making scholarly analogies—detecting signs of Rabelais in Sterne, signs of Ovid in Pound, signs of Dickens in Dostoevsky, signs of nineteenth-century flower symbolism in Melville, signs of Schlegelianism in Coleridge, signs of the oral-narrative use of the conjunctive in Hemingway, signs, analogies, insights—always *insights!*—golden *desideratum!*—hunched over in silence with only the far-off sound of Maggie, a Girl of the Stacks, a townie who puts books back on the shelves—now she is all right, a little lower-class-puffy in the nose, you understand, but . . . —only the sound of her to inject some stray, *sport* thought into this intensely isolated regimen. In effect, the graduate-school scholar settles down at an early age, when the sap is still rising, to a life of little cubicles, little money, little journals in which his insights, if he is extremely diligent, may someday be recorded. A Volkswagen, a too-small apartment, Department Store Danish furniture with dowel legs—before he is 30 his wife will have begun to despise him as a particularly sad sort of failure, once the cultural charisma of *literature* has lost its charm. How much better to have failed at oil prospecting or the diaper-service game than at . . . practically nothing!

McLuhan graduated from the University of Manitoba in 1933, then went to England and took another B.A. at Cambridge (in 1936; and, eventually, a doctorate, in 1942). At Cambridge in the thirties the literati were keen on PopCult. Movies, advertising, radio, display art were something to be analyzed as a "language," a kind of technological Creole that was understood instinctively (*ProleSlob!*) among the masses. It was up to the literati to discern its grammar and syntax (*O GaucheKick!*). Wyndham Lewis had written extensively on popular culture. F. R. Leavis had written *Culture and Environment.* Joyce's *Finnegans Wake,* Eliot's *The Waste Land* and Pound's *Cantos* seemed, in the fellows rooms of Cambridge, to be veritable nigger nightclubs of PopCult. Lewis, particularly, influenced McLuhan.

In 1936 McLuhan took his first teaching job, at the University of Wisconsin. He immediately found himself in one of the most exquisitely squalid hells known to middle-class man: freshman English at a Midwestern university. The teacher's evidently serious interest in the likes of Donne, Shakespeare, or Milton marks him at once, of course, as a pedantic and therefore all the more hopeless fool. One thing the poor nit can do in this situation is assign *The Old Man and the Sea, Of Mice and Men,* or some other storybook in words of one syllable and hope that will hold the little bastards for ten or twelve weeks.

McLuhan, however, had pride and ambition. He resorted to the GaucheKick PopCult of Cambridge. He showed the little bastards advertisements, the same advertisements their gummy little brains soaked up every day outside the classroom. What do these ads *really* convey? he would ask.

It works. It is a nice stratagem. Others have used it effectively, too, notably Orwell in essays like "The Art of Donald McGill." One presents a Gotham Gold Stripe nylon-stockings ad showing a pair of slick and shimmering female legs on a pedestal. Or a Lysol vaginal-wash ad showing a gorgeous woman in an evening dress sinking into a pool whose ripples are inscribed Doubt, Inhibitions, Ignorance, Misgivings. Or a Bayer aspirin ad showing a drum majorette wearing a military helmet and jackboots and carrying a mace-like baton captioned: "In 13.9 seconds a drum majorette can twirl a baton twenty-five times . . . but in only TWO SECONDS Bayer Aspirin is ready to go to work!" What is the true language of these ads? What do they *really* convey? Why, the wedding of sex and technology (The Mechanical Bride), the breakdown of the sexual object, Woman, into component machine parts: the Bakelite legs on a pedestal; the antiseptic, B.O.-free plastic vagina; the "goose-stepping combination of military mechanism and jackbooted eroticism."

Yes! *It is written—but I say unto you* . . . From Wisconsin McLuhan went to the University of St. Louis, Assumption University (Windsor, Ontario), and St. Michael's College of the University of Ontario. Along the way he became something of a charismatic figure in the phlegmy grim dim world of EngLit academia. He attracted circles of students and spoke to student groups, *extra cur-*

ricula, both in lectures and in Socratic gatherings. He showed slides of ads, comic strips, and newspapers, exploring the hidden language of "the folklore of industrial man," as he called it.

After Wisconsin, every institution McLuhan taught in was Roman Catholic. In the mid-1930's he had become a convert to Catholicism. His parents were Scotch-Irish Protestants from western Canada. McLuhan was apparently influenced by Catholic intellectuals in England, notably Chesterton and Hopkins. Twenty years later he was to discover a piece of PopCult that was to him a strangely Catholic and catholic force in the world: TV.

In 1951 McLuhan published his "industrial folklore" material in a book, *The Mechanical Bride.* The book went virtually unnoticed, then out of print, and he was left with stacks of copies himself. In 1966, before the book was republished as a $2.95 paperback, copies brought $40 and $50 apiece.

Compared to his two major books, *The Gutenberg Galaxy* (1962) and *Understanding Media* (1964), *The Mechanical Bride* is embarrassingly moralistic. It is written with the conventional nineteenth-century, anti-industrial bias of *the literary man,* a term McLuhan would later associate with the worst sort of intellectual obtuseness and rear-guardism. *The Mechanical Bride* is explicitly presented as a book designed to help Western man protect himself from the hidden persuasions of Madison Avenue, the press, and Showbiz. "Why not use the new commercial education as a means to enlightening its intended prey? Why not assist the public to observe consciously the drama which is intended to operate upon it unconsciously?"

The Mechanical Bride, however, as a book about folklore and the "collective public mind," led McLuhan more and more toward the work of anthropologists and historians. Certainly one of the great influences on his thinking was his friend and colleague at the University of Toronto, Edmund Carpenter, an anthropologist with whom he edited a book called *Explorations in Communication.*

Two books were published by university presses in 1950 and 1951 that changed McLuhan's life, I suppose you could say. They were *Empire and Communications* and *The Bias of Communication,* by Harold Innis. Innis was at the University of Toronto at the time. Innis gave McLuhan the basic insight of his career, which he was to compress into the aphorism: *The medium is the message.* You seldom hear anything about Innis in the many critiques of McLuhan. This is not McLuhan's fault, however. He gave Innis full credit in the *Gutenberg Galaxy* (p. 50): "Innis also explained why print causes nationalism and not tribalism; and why print causes price systems and markets such as cannot exist without print. In short, Harold Innis was the first person to hit upon the *process* of change as implicit in the *forms* of media technology. The present book is a footnote of explanation to his work."

McLuhan was also influenced by Henri Bergson. He adapted some of Bergson's theories about the central nervous system. They impressed Aldous Huxley as well. Bergson had the idea that the brain is a "reducing valve." The senses, he said, send an overwhelming flood of information to the brain, which the brain then filters down to an orderly trickle it can manage for the purpose of survival in a highly competitive world. Modern man, he believed, has become so rational, so utilitarian, so devoted to the classification of information for practical purposes, that the trickle becomes very thin and distilled, indeed, though efficient. Meantime, said Bergson, modern man has screened out the richest and most wondrous part of his experience without even knowing it. Implicit in this theory is the idea that sometime in the past primitive man experienced the entire rich and sparkling flood of the senses fully. It ties in with one of the most ancient metaphysical beliefs: the belief that out there somewhere, beyond the veil that blinds our egocentric modern minds, is our forgotten birthright, a world of wholeness, unity, and beauty. As a Roman Catholic, incidentally, McLuhan found the idea very congenial: "The Christian concept of the mystical body— all men as members of the body of Christ—this becomes technologically a fact under electronic conditions." *The All-in-One.*

McLuhan's great stroke was to bring Innis's and Bergson's ideas forward, beyond print, beyond the confines of the scholarly past, and into the present, like an anthropologist. In short, he turned their ideas on to PopCult, to television, motion pictures, radio, the telephone, the computer, photography, xerography: *the media.*

McLuhan had plenty of PopCult to look at in the 1950's. He had a house full of children. In 1939 he had married Corinne Lewis, an American actress. They had two sons and four daughters. They took over the place. Inside— TV, record players, radios, telephones, and children— while McLuhan wrote of tribal man and the Gutenberg revolution; of space and time and the collision of civilizations; of the seamless web and the electronic unification of mankind; on a ping-pong table in the back yard.

McLuhan is fond of quoting Daniel Boorstin's dictum, "The celebrity is a person who is known for his well-knownness." That pretty much describes McLuhan himself. McLuhan is one of those intellectual celebrities, like Toynbee or Einstein, who is intensely well known as a name, and as a *savant*, while his theory remains a grand blur. Part of the difficulty is that McLuhan is presented to the world as "the communications theorist." His first book, *The Mechanical Bride*, was a book about communication. Since then McLuhan has barely dealt with communication at all, at least if you define communication as "interchange of thought or opinions." He is almost wholly concerned with the effect of the means of communication (the medium) on the central nervous system. His theory falls squarely in a field known as cognitive psychology, even though his interests cut across many fields. Modern cognitive psychology is highly scientific, devoted to complex physiological experiments. McLuhan isn't. In fact, he is a theoretical cognitive psychologist.

This is made quite clear in *The Gutenberg Galaxy*. *Understanding Media* is really a chapbook for *The Gutenberg Galaxy*'s theory.

The theory, as I say, concerns the central nervous system. McLuhan makes a set of assumptions, à la Bergson, about how the central nervous system processes information. He believes that humans have a "sensory balance"—a balance between the five senses: sight, hearing, touch, smell, and taste. This balance, he says, changes according to the environment. For example, if the visual sense is dimmed, the auditory sense intensifies (as in the blind); if the auditory sense is increased, the sense of touch diminishes (as when a dentist puts earphones on a patient, turns up the sound, and thereby reduces his sensitivity to pain). Great technological changes, he goes on to say, can alter these "sensory ratios" for an entire people. McLuhan is concerned chiefly with two of these great technological changes: (1) the introduction of print in the fifteenth century (reputedly by Johann Gutenberg) and the spread of literacy in the next four hundred years: (2) the introduction of television in the twentieth.

Print, says McLuhan, stepped up the visual sense of Western man at the expense of his other senses. It led, he says, to "the separation of the senses, of functions, of operations, of states emotional and political, as well as of tasks." This, he says, had overwhelming historical consequences: nationalism and nationalist wars (cultural fragmentation);

the modern army, industrialism and bureaucracy (fragmentation of tasks); the market and price structure (economic fragmentation); individualism and the habit of privacy (fragmentation of the individual from the community)—and schizophrenia and peptic ulcers (caused by the fragmentation of both intellect and action from emotion); pornography (fragmentation of sex from love); the cult of childhood (fragmentation by age); and a general impoverishment of man's intuitive and artistic life (because of the fragmentation of the senses). And those are but a few of the results he mentions.

Enter TV. Television and the electric media generally, says McLuhan, are reversing the process; they are returning man's sensory ratios to the pre-print, pre-literate, "tribal" balance. The auditory and tactile senses come back into play, and man begins to use all his senses at once again in a unified, "seamless web" of experience. (Television, in McLuhan's psychology, is not primarily a visual medium but "audio-tactile.") The world is becoming a "global village," to use one of his happy phrases.

The immediate effects of TV on the central nervous system, says McLuhan, may be seen among today's young, the first TV generation. The so-called "generation gap," as he diagnoses it, is not a state of mind but a neurological fact. It is a disparity between a visual, print-oriented generation and its audio-tactile, neo-tribal offspring. School dropouts, he says, are but the more obvious casualties among a great mass of "psychic dropouts." These are children educated by the electric media to have unified, all-involving sensory experiences. They sit baffled and bored in classrooms run by teachers who fragment knowledge into "subjects," disciplines, specialties, and insist on the classification of data (rather than "pattern recognition," which is the principle of computers). This means, he says, that the educational system must be totally changed. In the long run, he says, the new neural balance will cause total change in everything anyway: "Total Change, ending psychic, social, economic, and political parochialism. The old civic, state, and national groupings have become unworkable. Nothing can be further from the spirit of the new technology than 'a place for everything and everything in its place.' You can't *go* home again." Many of the implications of the theory are very cheery, indeed: no more bitter nationalism—instead, the global village; no more shutout, ghetto-pent minority groups (racial fragmentation)—instead, all "irrevocably involved with, and responsible for," one another; no more tedious *jobs* (mechanistic fragmentation)—instead, all-involving *roles;* no more impoverished intuition (fragmented senses)—instead, expanded, all-embracing sensory awareness; and so on. Man made whole again!

MAN MADE WHOLE AGAIN

I gazed upon the printed page.
It tore me limb from limb.
I found my ears in Mason jars,
My feet in brougham motorcars,
My khaki claws in woggy wars—
But in this cockeyed eyeball age
I could not find my soul again.
Vile me.
And then—
       I touched a TV dial
And—pop!—
         it made me whole again.

To a clinical neurologist or psychologist, McLuhan's neurology is so much air. McLuhan's subject matter, as I say, is not communication but the central nervous system. The central nervous system is today perhaps the greatest dark continent of the physical sciences. Precious little is known about even the crudest neural functions. It was not until the 1950's that experimenters discovered, piecemeal, through experiments in several countries, the actual processes by which even so primitive an impulse as hunger is transmitted through the brain (Neal Miller in America, W. R. Hess in Switzerland, Konorski in Poland, Anand in India, *et alii*). It has taken half a century, since the development of the technique of stereotaxic needle implants, to reach even such tiny thresholds as this. It was not until 1962 that physiologists, using microelectrodes, discovered how the eye transmits shapes to the brain. To move from this level to the postulate that TV is altering the neural functions of entire peoples or even one person— this could only strike a clinician as romanticism.

McLuhan, however, was ready for the criticism. He insisted he was not presenting a self-contained theory but making "probes." He sees himself as trying to open up the dark continent for systematic exploration by others. He says he is not drawing conclusions but using what facts are available as "means of getting into new territories." He even says that if he could persuade enough investigators to study the effects of the new technologies systematically, he would gladly return whence he came, viz., to "literary studies." At the same time, he has sought to give his theory some scientific underpinning by setting up psychological studies of sample groups in Canada and Greece, studying their "sensory balance" before and after the coming of TV to their locales. The Canadian study has been completed, and I understand that the results, unpublished as of this writing (January, 1968), were inconclusive.

What, then, has been the nature of McLuhan's extraordinary splash? It certainly has not been scientific, despite the fact that he now characterizes himself as a scientist, speaks of the "clinical spirit," and compares his methods to those of modern psychiatry, metallurgy, and structural analysis.

A clue, I think, may be found in the parallels between McLuhan's history and Freud's. In any historical perspective the two men are contemporaries (Freud died in 1939). Both have come forth with dazzling insights in a period (1850 to the present) of tremendous intellectual confusion and even convulsion following what Nietzsche called "the death of God"; and Max Weber, "the demystification of the world." Both men explain *all* in terms of—*Santa Barranza! something common as pig tracks! under our very noses all the time! so obvious we never stepped back to see it for what it was!* Freud: sex. McLuhan: TV. Both men electrified—outraged!—the intellectuals of their time by explaining the most vital, complex, cosmic phases of human experience in terms of such lowlife stuff: e.g., the anus; the damnable TV set. The biggest howl Freud ever caused was with a two-page paper that maintained that anal sensations in infancy were capable of imprinting a man's mature personality in a quite specific way. Freud was the subject of as much derision in his day as McLuhan in his; and, like McLuhan, benefited from it. Freud said to Jung: "Many enemies, much honor"; McLuhan might well say the same. After all, where there's smoke, there's . . . *what if he is right?* McLuhan said to his disciple and amanuensis, Gerald Stearn: "No one believes these factors have any effect whatever on our human reactions. It's like the old days when people played around with radium. They painted watch dials and licked the brushes. They didn't believe radium could affect people."

Freud, of course, was a doctor of medicine and a trained clinician and a more certifiably scientific thinker than McLuhan. But Freud, like McLuhan, strove after the cosmic insight. The more rigorous psychologists today, as

well as most research physicians, regard Freud as a roman-
ticist, almost a metaphysician. They cast the old boy as a
sort of Viennese Bishop Berkeley. There is a suspicion that
Freud poked around—*aha! very significant!*—amid the
plump velvet and florid warps and woofs of a few upper-
bourgeois Viennese households, including his own—*Dad,
that bugger, seduced my sis*—and then rerouted his insights
through the front door of the clinic as findings explaining
the behavior of all mankind. One cannot help but wonder
something of the sort about McLuhan. Here sits the master
out back at the ping-pong table. And there, inside the
house, sit the kids, gazing at their homework—amid a
raging, encapsulating sensory typhoon of TV sets, transistor radios, phonographs, and telephones—and yet they
make it through school all the same—*Very significant!*
Amazing, even. A neo-tribal unity of the senses. "The
family circle has widened. The worldpool of information
fathered by electric media—movies, Telstar, flight—far
surpasses any possible influence Mom and Dad can now
bring to bear."

PING-PONG

I walked into the living room.
They rocked me with a stereo boom.
No haven here downstairs at all.
Nymphets frug on my wall-to-wall
And boogaloo in my private den
And won't let poor work-a-daddy in.

How glorious!
Übermenschen! golden gulls!
With transistor radios plugged in their skulls.
Radiant! with an Elysian hue
From the tubercular blue of the television.
Such a pure Zulu euphoria
Suffuses their hi-fi sensoria!

How glorious.
I shall stand it long as I can,
This neo-tribal festival.
Their multi-media cut-up,
The audio-pervasion of their voices,
Leaves me with two choices:
Shall I simply make them shut up—
Or . . . extrapolate herefrom the destiny
Of Western Man?

Freud and McLuhan both became celebrities at the same period of life, their early fifties, and under similar circumstances. Both began with rather obscure cliques of academic followers. Freud had a little group of adherents who held discussions every Wednesday night in his waiting room and were known as the "Psychological Wednesday Society." McLuhan had his adherents in several Canadian universities, and they, plus Americans interested in his work, often met in his home. If one were to choose a precise date for Freud's emergence as a public figure, it would probably be April 26, 1908, when a *Zusammenkunft für Freud'sche Psychologie* (Meeting for Freudian Psychology) was held in the Hotel Bristol in Salzburg, with Jung, Adler, Stekel, and others in attendance. In McLuhan's case it would be January 30, 1964, when faculty members of the University of British Columbia staged what was known to his followers as a "McLuhan Festival" in the university armory. They suspended sheets of plastic from the ceiling, forming a maze. Operators aimed light projections at the plastic sheets and at the people walking through them. A movie projector showed a long, meaningless movie of the interior of the empty armory. Goofy noises poured out of the loudspeakers, a bell rang, somebody banged blocks of wood together up on a podium. Somebody else spewed perfume around. Dancers flipped around through the crowds, and behind a stretch fabric wall—a frame with a stretch fabric across it—there was a girl, pressed against the stretch fabric wall, like a whole wall made of stretch pants, and *undulating* and humping around back there. Everybody was supposed to come up and *feel it*—the girl up against the stretch fabric—to understand the "tactile communication" McLuhan was talking about.

Neither event, the Meeting for Freudian Psychology or the McLuhan Festival, received any very great publicity, but both were important if esoteric announcements that *this* is the new name to be reckoned with. As Freud says . . . As McLuhan says . . . McLuhan's friend, Carpenter, had already put it into words: "McLuhan is one of the epic innovators of the electronic age. His *Gutenberg Galaxy* is the most important book in the social sciences of this generation, overshadowing in scope and depth any other contribution."

Both Freud and McLuhan attracted another obscure but important source of support: young artists and young literary intellectuals who saw them as visionaries, as men "who divined the famed riddle" (Sophocles, *Oedipus Rex*), to quote from a medallion that Freud's Wednesday Society friends gave him on his fiftieth birthday in 1906. Both McLuhan and Freud present scientific theories, but in an ancient priestly-aristocratic idiom that literary and artistic souls find alluring. Both buttress their work with traditional literary erudition. Freud, of course, presents his most famous insight in the form of a literary conceit, i.e., "the Oedipus complex." To sense Freud's strong literary bias, one has only to read ten pages of Freud and then ten pages of Pavlov. The difference in mental atmospheres, the literary vs. the clinical, stands out at once. Freud had the typical literary respect for artistic genius. He depicted the artist as one who has the power to express openly and faithfully the world of fantasy—the link between the conscious and the unconscious—that ordinary mortals grasp only fitfully in daydreams. Freud became the patron saint of the Surrealists, who saw themselves as doing just that (Dali visited Freud shortly before Freud's death, sketched him, and told him that surrealistically his cranium was reminiscent of a snail).

McLuhan, of course, was trained as a literary scholar. He begins *The Gutenberg Galaxy* with three chapters carrying out a somewhat abstruse analysis of *King Lear*. A la Freud's Oedipus, he begins his discussion of "sensory ratios" with a Greek legend (the myth of Cadmus: the Phoenician who sowed dragon's teeth—and up sprang armed men; and introduced the alphabet to Greece—and up sprang specialism and fragmentation of the senses). It is all quite literary, this neurology. Joyce, Matthew Arnold, Dr. Johnson, Blake, Ruskin, Rimbaud, Pope, Cicero, Dean Swift, Montaigne, Pascal, Tocqueville, Cervantes, Nashe, Marlowe, Shakespeare, Ben Jonson, St. Augustine—they twitter and gleam like celebrities arriving by limousine.

Artists, meanwhile, have precisely the same role in McLuhan's galaxy as in Freud's. They are geniuses who detect the invisible truths intuitively and express them symbolically. They are divine *naturals*, gifted but largely unconscious of the meaning of their own powers. McLuhan sees artists as mankind's "early warning system." They possess greater unity and openness of the senses and therefore respond earlier to the alteration of the "sensory ratios" brought about by changes in technology. McLuhan today is the patron saint of most "mixed-media" artists and of many young "underground" moviemakers (for such dicta as "The day of the story line, the plot, is over"). He was very much the patron saint of the huge "Art and Technology" mixed-media show staged by Robert Rauschenberg and others at the 27th Street Armory in

New York in 1967. The artists, incidentally, are apparently willing to overlook McLuhan's theory of how they register their "early warning." It is a rather retrograde perform- ance, as McLuhan sees it. The "avant garde" of each period, he says, is actually always one technology behind. Painters did not discover The Landscape until the early nineteenth century, when the intrusion of machine-age industrialism caused them to see the technology of agricul- ture—i.e., The Land—as an art form for the first time. They did not discover machine forms (cubism) until the electric age had begun. They did not discover mass-pro- duced forms (Pop Art: Roy Lichtenstein's comic strips, Andy Warhol's Campbell Soup cans) until the age of the conveyor belt had given way to the age of electronic circuitry. McLuhan says that this is the early warning, nevertheless—and the idea has made artists happy.

Older literary intellectuals, however, have reacted to McLuhan with the sort of *ressentiment*, to use Nietzsche's word, that indicates he has hit a very bad nerve. The old guard's first salvo came as far back as July, 1964, with a long piece by Dwight Macdonald. It contained most of the objections that have become so familiar since then: the flat conclusion that McLuhan writes nonsense (a typical reac- tion to Freud), that his style is repetitious and "boring," that he is anti-book and for the new barbarism (TV, electronic brains), or, obversely, that he is amoral, has no values. Once again the example of Freud comes to mind. After Freud's Clark University lectures were published, the Dean of the University of Toronto said: "An ordinary reader would gather that Freud advocates free love, re- moval of all restraints, and a relapse into savagery." In fact, of course, Freud savaged and very nearly exterminated traditional Philosophy, the queen of the sciences through- out the nineteenth century. What was left of the lofty metaphysics of God, Freedom and Immortality, if they were products of the anus and the glans penis?

McLuhan, in turn, has been the savager of the literary intellectuals. He has made the most infuriating announcement of all: You are irrelevant.

He has hit a superannuated target. The literary-intellectual mode that still survives in the United States and England today was fashioned more than 150 years ago in Regency England with the founding of magazines such as the *Edinburgh Review*, the *Quarterly*, *Blackwood's*, the *London Magazine*, the *Examiner* and the *Westminster Review*. They became platforms for educated gentlemen-amateurs to pass judgment in a learned way on two subjects: books and politics. This seemed a natural combination at the time, because so many literati were excited by the French Revolution and its aftermath (e.g., Byron, Wordsworth, Shelley, Hazlitt, Francis Jeffrey). The *Edinburgh Review* had covers of blue and buff, the Whig colors. Remarkably, the literary-intellectual mode has remained locked for more than a century and a half in precisely that format: of books and moral protest, by gentlemen-amateurs, in the British polite-essay form.

McLuhan has come forth as a man with impeccable literary credentials of his own to tell them that the game is all over. He has accused them of "primitivism" and ignorance of the nature of the very medium they profess to value: the book; they "have never thought for one minute about the book as a medium or a structure and how it related itself to other media as a structure, politically, verbally, and so on. . . . They have never studied any medium." He has challenged them to come to grips, as he has, with the objective, empirical techniques of exploration developed in the physical and social sciences in the past fifty years; if the literary intellectual continues to retreat from all this into the realm of values, says McLuhan, "he's had it."

This has been the sorest point for the literary fraternities, as he calls them. During the past five years their response to the overwhelming sweep of scientific empiricism has been *the literary retrenchment*—an ever more determined retrenchment into the moralist stance of the Regency literati ("intellectual" protest against the tyrants and evils of the times). Literary intellectuals even sound the cry in so many words today, asserting that the task of the intellectual in a brutal age is the preservation of sacred values (e.g., Naom Chomsky's manifesto, "The Responsibility of the Intellectuals," in *The New York Review of Books*). Intellectuals thus become a kind of clergy without ordination. Macdonald, for example, has devoted the past two decades of his career to the *retrenchment*. He has been busily digging in against all forms of twentieth-century empiricism, from sociology to linguistics. He even sallied forth against so conservative and benign an intrusion of empiricism into the literary world as the third edition of Webster's Dictionary —on the quaint grounds that it had abdicated its moral responsibility to referee Good vs. Evil in grammar and diction. All the while, from inside the trench, he has been running up the flag of "values."

McLuhan's Nietzschean (*Beyond Good and Evil*) "aphorisms and entr'actes" on this subject have been particularly galling: "For many years I have observed that the moralist typically substitutes anger for perception. He hopes that many people will mistake his irritation for insight. . . . The mere moralistic expression of approval or disapproval, preference or detestation, is currently being used in our world as a substitute for observation and a substitute for study. People hope that if they scream loudly enough about 'values' then others will mistake them for serious, sensitive souls who have higher and nobler perceptions than ordinary people. Otherwise, why would they be screaming? . . . Moral bitterness is a basic technique for endowing the idiot with dignity."

Even more galling to the literati, I suspect, is that there is no medium they can turn to, books or otherwise, esoteric or popular, without hearing the McLuhan dicta thundering at them, amid the most amazing fanfare.
Ecce Celebrity.

McLuhan's ascension to the status of international celebrity has been faster than Freud's, due in no small part to the hyped-up tempo of *the media* today—and the fact that the phenomenon of Freud himself had already conditioned the press to exploit the esoteric guru as a star. Freud's ascension was more gradual but quite steady. His emergence, at the Meeting for Freudian Psychology, was in 1908. By 1910 his writings prompted barrages of heated reviews in both American and European intellectual journals, sometimes running to more than a hundred pages apiece. In 1915 his two essays, "Thoughts for the Times on War and Death," were a popular hit and were widely reprinted. By 1924 he was very definitely *Freud;* both the Chicago *Tribune* and the Hearst newspapers offered him huge sums, private ocean liners, etc., to come to the United States and make a psychoanalysis of the sensational thrill-killers, Leopold and Loeb (he declined).

Both Freud and McLuhan experienced their great publicity booms after trips to the United States, however. Freud's followed a series of lectures at Clark University in Worcester, Massachusetts, in 1909 on the twentieth anniversary of its founding. When his boat landed in New York on August 27, he was mentioned, and merely mentioned, in only one newspaper, and as "Professor Freund of Vienna," at that. By the time he sailed for Europe on September 21, he had his first honorary doctorate (from Clark) and was well on the way to becoming a proper sensation and outrage.

McLuhan's pivotal trip to the U.S. came in May, 1965.

As I say, American corporations had already begun to import him for private lectures. The publication of *Understanding Media* in 1964 had prompted that. There was first of all the sheer intriguing possibility—*what if he is right?* There was also the strange wrong-side-of-the-tracks sense of inferiority such firms seem to feel toward the academic and intellectual worlds. Any scholar with good credentials who will take a serious, vaguely optimistic, or even neutral interest in the matters of the business world, e.g., technology, will be warmly received. McLuhan's May, 1965, trip to New York, however, was at the behest of two rather extraordinary men from San Francisco, Howard Gossage and Dr. Gerald Feigen.

Gossage is a tall, pale advertising man with one of the great heads of gray hair in the U.S.A., flowing back like John Barrymore's. Feigen is a psychiatrist who became a surgeon; he is dark and has big eyes and a gong-kicker mustache like Jerry Colonna. He is also a ventriloquist and carries around a morbid-looking dummy named Becky. Gossage and Feigen started a firm called Generalists, Inc., acting as consultants to people who can't get what they need from specialists because what they need is the big picture. Their first client was a man who was stuck with an expensive ski lift in Squaw Valley that was idle half the year. They advised him to start a posh and rather formal restaurant-nightclub up the slope that could be reached only by ski lift. So he did. It was named High Camp and immediately became all the rage. One thing that drew Gossage and Feigen to McLuhan was his belief that the age of specialists (fragmentation of intellect) was over.

Gossage and Feigen invested about $6,000 into taking McLuhan around to talk to influential people outside the academic world, chiefly in the communications and advertising industries, on both coasts. Gossage says they had no specific goal (no fragmentation; open field). They just wanted to play it "fat, dumb and happy" and see what would happen.

So in May 1965 they had a series of meetings and lunches set up for McLuhan, at Laurent, Lutece, and other great expense-account feasteries of the East Fifties in Manhattan, with men of the caliber of Gibson McCabe. The first meetings and a cocktail party in Gossage's suite at the Lombardy were set for a Monday. McLuhan never showed up. Gossage finally got him on the telephone in Toronto that evening. Marshall, what the hell are you doing—

"I'm grading papers."

"Grading papers?"

"And waiting for the excursion rate."

"The excursion rate! What excursion rate?"

—the midweek excursion rate on the airlines. He could save about $12 round-trip if he didn't come to New York until Tuesday morning.

"But Marshall, you're not even *pay*ing for it!"

—but that was the English prof with the Pree-Tide tie. He had a wife and six children and thirty years behind him of shaving by on an English teacher's pay. So there he was in the bin, grading papers, scratching away—

"Listen," says Gossage, "there are so many people willing to invest money in your work now, you'll never have to grade papers again."

"You mean it's going to be fun from now on?" says McLuhan.

"Everything's coming up roses," says Gossage.

By January, 1966, the McLuhan boom was on, and with a force, as I say, that McLuhan himself never dreamed of. I remember seeing McLuhan in August, 1965, in Gossage's firehouse offices in San Francisco. Gossage and Feigen were putting on their own "McLuhan Festival," as they called it. They invited small groups of influential West Coast people in for Socratic dialogues with McLuhan every morning and every afternoon for a week. One afternoon McLuhan was sitting at the round table in Gossage's own big, handsome office with half a dozen people, Gossage, Feigen, Mike Robbins of Young & Rubicam, Herbert Gold the novelist, Edward Keating, then editor and publisher of *Ramparts* magazine, and myself. Someone asked McLuhan what he thought of a large-scale communications conference that happened to be going on in San Francisco at that moment, at the Hilton Hotel, with a thousand scholars in attendance, headed by the renowned semanticist, S. I. Hayakawa.

"Well . . ." said McLuhan, pulling his chin in and turning his eyes up, "they're working from very obsolete premises, of course. Almost by definition."

By definition?

"Certainly. By the time you can get a thousand people to agree on enough principles to hold such a meeting, conditions will already have changed. The principles will be useless."

The Hayakawa conference . . . evaporated.

I thought of this remark four months later. McLuhan had a long-standing invitation to speak before the regular monthly luncheon meeting of a New York advertising group. This group always met in a banquet room off the mezzanine of the Plaza Hotel. Attendance was seldom more than a hundred. Suddenly McLuhan's appearance took on the proportions of a theater opening by a blazing new star. The luncheon had to be transferred to the Plaza's grand ballroom—and was attended by . . . a thousand.

McLuhan, as I look back on it, was magnificent that day. Rather than gratify the sudden popular clamor, he stood up at the podium and became his most cryptic, Delphic, esoteric, Oriental self. He was like a serious-faced Lewis Carroll. Nobody knew what the hell he was saying. I was

seated at a table with a number of people from Time-Life,
Inc. Several of them were utterly outraged by the performance. They sighed, rolled their eyeballs, then actually
turned their chairs around and began conversing among
themselves as he spoke. It could not have been more reminiscent of the Freud phenomenon fifty years before. *Many
enemies, much honor!*

I have heard friends of McLuhan say that his publicity
boom has become so intense, he is in danger of overex-
posure and trivialization. Perhaps; certainly some of his
recent gestures, such as an article in *Look* on "The Future
of Sex" (co-authored by a *Look* editor), have sounded
trivial enough. But I think that all in all he has handled the whole thing like a champion. Like Freud, he
never stops to debate a point ("I want observations, not
agreement"). Mainly, he has just continued to pour it on,
in every medium he can get hold of, books, magazines, TV,
radio, lectures, seminars, symposia. He has even broken
through the meaning barrier. As late as the winter of
1965–66 people from the Canadian Broadcasting Company
told me they would like to put McLuhan on Canadian TV,
but they felt he would be unintelligible to their audience.
Today that objection would be a laugh, even at the CBC. It
would be like saying, We can't show Richard Burton—
he doesn't finish his sentences.

McLuhan's monomania for his theory—and his conse-
crated pursuit of it amid the whole spume of his celebrity—
has lent him a weird peace. It is the peace of the eye of the
hurricane or of what Professor Silenus, the architect, describes in Evelyn Waugh's *Decline and Fall*. Professor
Silenus describes life as being like one of those whirling
discs at the old amusement parks. They are like a gigantic
phonograph record, 50 feet across. You get on the disc and

it starts spinning, and the faster it goes, the more centrifugal force builds up to throw you off it. The speed on the
outer edge of the disc is so great you have to hold on for
dear life just to stay on. The closer you can get to the
center of the disc, the slower the speed is and the easier it is
to stand up. In fact, theoretically, at the very center there is
a point that is completely motionless. In life, most people
won't get on the disc at all. They shouldn't get on. They
don't have the nerve or the *élan*. They just sit in the stands
and watch. Some people like to get on the outer edge and
hang on and ride like hell—that would be people like
McLuhan's madman impresarios, Gossage and Feigen.
Others are standing up and falling down, staggering, lurch-
ing toward the center. And a few, a very few, reach the
middle, that perfect motionless point, and stand up in the
dead center of the roaring whirlygig as if nothing could be
clearer and less confused—that would be McLuhan.

Yes. I once took McLuhan to a Topless Lunch in San
Francisco. This was at a place on North Beach called the
Off Broadway, where the waitresses served lunch bare-
breasted. Gossage, Feigen, and Herb Caen, the famous San
Francisco columnist, joined us. All of us had heard about
the Topless Lunch, but none of us had ever seen it. I found
out that a curious thing happens when men walk for the
first time into a room full of nude girls. Namely, they are
speechless. I saw it happen many times that afternoon. The
whole vocabulary of masculine humor about female nudity
is actually based on the premise that they are partly
clothed, that much is being revealed, but by no means all.
When men walk into a restaurant and find a dozen girls
walking around in nothing but flesh-colored cache-sexes
and high heels, they just don't know what to say—not even
a sophisticated boulevardier like Caen. Everyone was
struck dumb; everyone, that is to say, except McLuhan.

Inside of thirty seconds McLuhan had simply absorbed

the whole scene into . . . the theory. He tucked his chin down.

"Well!" he said. "Very interesting!"

"What's interesting, Marshall?"

"They're wearing *us*." He said it with a slight shrug, as if nothing could be more obvious.

"I don't get it, Marshall."

"We are their clothes," he said. "We become their environment. We become extensions of their skin. They're wearing *us*."

We sat down. The place was packed with businessmen. It was kept in a black-light gloom, apparently to spare embarrassment, just like in the old burlesque houses. Except that huge heavy expense-account lunches were being served by bare-breasted waitresses. Their breasts dangled and jiggled and sweated over your plate as they stretched in the meat crush to hand out the soups, the salads, the bread, the cocktails. You could barely see the plate in front of you, only glistening breasts in a nighttown gloom. It was a pure nutball farce, that was all one could seem to get out of it. Unless you were McLuhan.

"When you dim the visual sense," he said, "you step up the sense of taste. That's why these so-called 'dim-lit restaurants' work. That's why they are literally 'intimate.' You are brought together sensually and sensorially, forced out of the isolation of the visual man."

Later on we fell to discussing the relative charms of our sweating seraglio houris, and Caen happened to single out one girl as "good-looking"—

"Do you know what you said?" said McLuhan. "Good-*looking*. That's a visual orientation. You're separating yourself from the girls. You are sitting back and *looking*. Actually, the light is dim in here. This is meant as a *tactile* experience, but visual man doesn't react that way."

Everyone looks to McLuhan to see if he is joking, but it is impossible to tell in the tactile night. All that is clear is that . . . yes, McLuhan has already absorbed the whole roaring whirlygig into the motionless center.

Just after the meal, the Off Broadway presented its Style Show. This consisted of several girls with enormous tits—"breasts" just doesn't say it—blown up by silicone injections and sticking clear out of the various gowns and lingerie they were "modeling." All the while a mistress of ceremonies was at a microphone giving a parody version of that feathery female commentary you hear at fashion shows. "And here is Denise," she would say, "in her lace chemise"—and a young thing comes forward with a pair of prodigious dugs swollen out in front of her, heavily rouged about the nipples, and a wispy little stretch of lace dripped over her shoulder and tied with a bow at her neck. "This latest creation," says the M.C., "is made of *heavy-duty* Belgian lace . . . for that so, so *ne*cessary *ex*tra support . . ."

After the show, McLuhan calls to the M.C., the woman at the microphone—she was clothed, by the way—he calls her over to our table and says to her, "I have something you can use in your *spiel*."

"What's that?" she says. Her face starts to take on that bullet-proof smile that waitresses and barmaids put on to cope with middle-aged wiseguys.

"Well, it's this," says McLuhan—and I have to mention that Topless performers had recently been brought into court in San Francisco in a test case and had won the trial—"It's this," says McLuhan. "You can say, you can tell them"—and here his voice slows down as if to emphasize the utmost significance—"*The topless waitress is the opening wedge of the trial balloon!*"

Then he looks at her with an unfathomable smile.

Her smile, however, freezes. The light goes out in her eyes. She suddenly looks like an aging pole-axed ewe. She stares at McLuhan without a word or an expression—

But of course!

—*what if he is right?*

Part Two

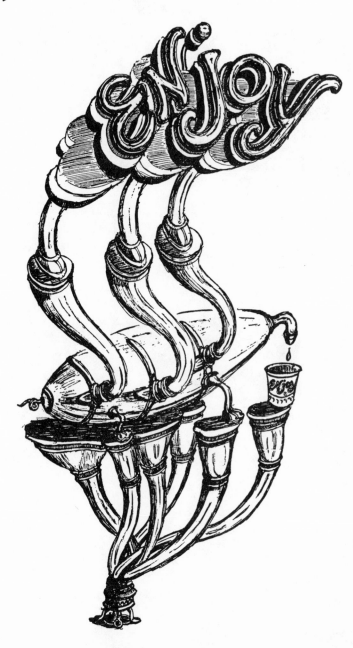

Look! She beckons! With those deep high-class black eyes! Here at a dinner party in Alfred Barr's apartment, in a room full of men who get their shirts hand-laundered at 90 cents a shirt by Forziati on East 74th Street and women who start getting ready for dinner with, first off, a little hair action at 4 p.m. by Kenneth on East 54th Street—here in this room she beckons. Liza, Liza Parkinson, Mrs. Bliss Parkinson, president of the Museum of Modern Art, daughter of Cornelius Bliss, niece of Lillie P. Bliss, who was one of the founders of the museum, sister of Anthony Bliss, the president of the Metropolitan Opera Association—Liza, the very embodiment of all that is most social, high class, Protestant tree-of-life and embossed-watermark-writing-paper in this whole art world social thing—Liza beckons to Spike. And Spike catches Bob's eye across the room. And Bob gives Spike the high sign. Go, girl, go. This is the moment—beckoning black eyes!—

Bob and Spike—*Spike*—when Bob, Robert Scull, America's most famous collector of pop and other avant-garde art, first met his wife, Ethel, Ethel Redner of West 86th Street, on a blind date back in 1943, he said to himself,

"Ethel, what a terrible name." So he called her Spike. Spike's family had some dough, but Bob and Spike were so broke that they were living in one room on West 56th Street with a Murphy bed. They got a $12 membership in the Museum of Modern Art, three blocks away, on West 53rd Street, and used the museum, the garden, the restaurant and everything, as their living room, to entertain guests in. Is that irony or isn't it? Bob got very interested in the art there and started a phantom art collection, writing down the names of pictures he wished he had, on a piece of shirt cardboard in his wallet. In 1947 or 1948 Bob started in the New York taxicab business, which was a very rough business at that time, full of—well, don't ask. Half the guys were rejects from the Mafia shape-up for hotel house dicks. But Bob started making money, and the rest is history. He started actually buying pictures himself. He had to put up with a lot of ridicule and everything, like the time in 1959 when he bought Jasper Johns' beer cans, two cans of Ballantine Ale, as a matter of fact, but everybody called them the beer cans, and the magazines and newspapers came around to take pictures, and he was very proud about buying Jap's beer cans. Would you believe they were only making fun of him? Yeah! Kids used to come to his kids in school and say, "Hey, is your old man the nut who bought the beer cans?" But he kept on collecting, and pretty soon Robert Scull became synonymous with pop art, and Bob and Spike are just getting in tight with the very social Museum of Modern Art crowd and finally here is the big dinner in Alfred's apartment—Alfred Barr is the curator of the Museum of Modern Art—

Here amid the crystal and the silver asparagus holders and the Forziati ironing jobs are people the magnitude of Liza and Philip—that's Philip Johnson, the architect, socialite and art savant—and Bob and Spike are looking great. Bob, who is 49, is just emerging, sartorially, from the 57th

Street Biggie phase. The 57th Street Biggie look is the look of the men in New York who are in their 40s or 50s and the money is starting to come in and their hair is thinning in the crown but they comb it straight back like the real studs of the American business world do, like Lyndon Johnson does, as a matter of fact. They are getting an opulent plumpness about them, not fat exactly, and they don't have double chins, just sort of a great smooth tan fullness in the jowls set off by some good Sulka shirt work and a little Countess Mara in the necktie and a suit from Frank Brothers and a wife with apricot-colored hair—they all have wives with apricot-colored hair for some reason—and they take the Christmas cruise on the *S.S. France*. Only Spike didn't go the apricot-hair route. She has already graduated to the big time in fashion. She is slender and quite pretty. Her hair, which is mostly kind of pineapple blond, is great, and Kenneth does it. Her dresses come from St. Laurent, Dior, Chanel, Courrèges, Mainbocher, Cardin, Ken Scott, you name it. And she didn't like the Christmas cruise on the *S.S. France*. All the women came to the breakfast table wearing furs and enough diamonds to sink the boat. Spike took to her stateroom and wouldn't come out.

Finally—the moment arrives. Bob and Spike are both eating with the Continental style they now use, holding the fork in the left hand and the knife in the right. Liza Parkinson beckons, motions to Spike to come aside so she can talk to her. Those deep dark aristocratic eyes—she is the *whole thing* in the whole social thing of the art world—and Bob gives Spike the high sign, and right away, without having to say a word to each other, Bob and Spike both figure the same thing. This is the moment. Liza is going to say to Spike something like, Could you serve on this board or whatever, or could we get yours and Bob's advice on this or that vital project, or, at the very least, would you come to such-and-such a dinner—you know, something that will symbolize the fact that Robert and Ethel Scull are now in the inner circle of the whole thing—and Liza draws Ethel aside and then Liza—regal eyes!—pops the question—

Afterwards, when Spike comes back, Bob can hardly wait.

"What did she say?"

"Are you all set?" says Spike.

"Yeah—"

"You sure your heart's O.K.?"

"Yeah—"

"She said, 'Ethel, would you mind telling me who does your hair?'"

Who does your hair?

"Well—what did you say to that?"

"I told her."

"Then what did she say?"

"She said would I ask him if he could do hers."

"That's all she said?"

"No. She wanted to know how much it was."

Well, there it is. It is just an incident, but it gives an idea of what Bob and Spike are up against in this whole art world thing. Bob does everything right, better than right, in fact. He rises out of the Lower East Side and its psychological affiliates, the Bronx and Long Island, to an eight-room apartment on Fifth Avenue overlooking the park and a summer place in East Hampton. He amasses a collection of pop art and op art and primary art, in fact, everything since abstract expressionism, that is actually better than the Museum of Modern Art's in that area. Like a lot of ambitious guys who had to take the night-school route, he studies his field very thoroughly, talks to the artists themselves for hours on end, until he probably knows more about pop art and post-pop art than anybody in the country except for Leo Castelli, Ivan Karp, Henry Geldzahler and a couple of others. He probably knows a lot more about it than Alfred Barr. Yet what do they want from Bob and Ethel Scull at the Museum of Modern Art? They want $1,000 a year so they can be on the International Council and they want Ethel to help organize a party—and where does she get her hair done?

Who needs that? This season Robert and Ethel Scull are transferring their backing from the Museum of Modern Art to the Whitney. All right, the whole art world is not going to flip over backward like Charlie Brown in the comic strip over this, but it's a sign of this whole social thing in the art world that nobody knows anything about. They can talk about *modern art and contemporary art* all they want. But it's the same old social thing that's been going on in art for a hundred years, the flutey bitones of the Protestant cultural establishment, and—

But then Spike looks at Bob, and Bob looks at Spike and he shrugs and wraps his clavicles up around his head and breaks into a smile, in a primordial gesture of the New York streets, the What Are You Gonna Do Shrug, and he says:

"Spike, you know what my philosophy is? My philosophy is, *Enjoy*."

Enjoy! So a few things aren't panning out here at the top of the ladder. The main thing is that you're up here. Right? That is one thing nobody ever seems to understand about people who go through something like the Lower East Side–West Bronx route and make it in New York. A few slights, a few disappointments, a little sniggering along the way—you're going to cut your throat over that? The main thing is that Robert and Ethel Scull are one of *the* great social success stories of New York since World War II.

In eighteen years they have *made it* all the way, or practically all the way, from point zero—up from the Lower

East Side, the West Bronx, up from that point just eighteen
years ago when Bob Scull was a nobody, a 31-year-old
businessman whose business had gone down the chute and
he and Spike woke up every morning in that Murphy bed,
to . . . Today. Today they have made it to the greatest
address in New York, Fifth Avenue across from Central
Park, and not just in terms of money, but right into that
whole world of opening nights and the parties they write
about in the papers, chauffeurs who are practically one of
the family, apartments where the lobby and the doorman
look so great you feel like you have to dress up to step on
the sidewalk or you're letting down the building, esoteric
New York day schools for the younger children and boarding schools for the older ones, lunches at La Grenouille
where expensive matrons in Chanel suits have two bloody
marys and smile—teeth!—at tailored young men with names
like Freddy, Ferdi and Tug, petite plaques on the exhibition
wall that say "from the collection of Mr. and Mrs. Robert
C. Scull," photographs in the women's magazines in court-
photographer Shah and Farah Diba poses, fashion stories in
which they say that this new madras wool gabardine coat is
on the backs of Mrs. William Paley, Mrs. Palmer Dixon,
Mrs. Samuel Pryor Reed and Mrs. Robert C. Scull, and a
social set in which Chester is Chester Beatty who owns the
diamond mines, and Nicole is Nicole Alphand the wife of
the former French ambassador, and Bob is Robert Kintner
the former chairman of NBC, Susan is Susan Stein the
heiress, Alex is Alex Liberman the editorial director of
Vogue, Marina is Marina Consort the wife of Prince
Michael of Greece, Jap is Jasper Johns the painter, Dean is
Dean Acheson, Sammy is Sammy Davis, Ave is Averell
Harriman, Andy is Andy Warhol, Lady Bird is Lady Bird
—All right! People are getting shot and blown up in Vietnam. China is a restless giant. The black ghettos are bran-
dishing the fist of liberation. God has gone and died. And

yet what Bob and Spike have done, made it, is still the only name of the game in New York. What is more, they have made it the way people dream of making it in New York; namely, right now. The hell with just making the money and setting things up for your children and waiting for the reflected glory of it when your daughter at Wellesley, the bird-song genius, gets invited up for a weekend in the country at the Detergent King's in North Egremont.

Make it—now!

That cry, that cry, burning like valvulitis in so many hearts in New York tonight . . .

Bob and Spike are the folk heroes of every social climber who ever hit New York. What Juarez was to the Mexican mestizo—what John L. Sullivan was to the Boston Irish—what Garibaldi was to the Sardinian farmers—what the Beatles are to the O-level-dropout £8-a-week office boys of England—what Antonino Rocca is to the Garment Center aviator Puerto Ricans of New York—what Moishe Dayan is to the kibbutzim shock workers of the Shephelah—all these things are Bob and Spike to the social climbers of New York.

In a blaze of publicity they illuminated the secret route: *collecting wacked-out art.* It was a tricky business. Art has been a point of entry into New York Society for seventy-five years or more. Duveen, of course, made millions selling *cultural immortality* to John D. Rockefeller and Henry Clay Frick in the form of Old Masters. After World War I the Protestant elite turned to Recent Masters as well. The Museum of Modern Art, after all, was not founded by intellectual revolutionaries. It was founded in John D. Rockefeller, Jr.'s living room, with Goodyears, Blisses, and Crowinshields in attendance. They founded the museum in order to import to New York the cultural cachet of the European upper classes, who were suddenly excited over the Impressionists and post-Impressionist masters such as

Cézanne, Picasso, and Braque. In either case, Old Masters or New, the route was through art that had been certified in Europe.

Bob Scull had started out collecting Renaissance bronzes, but he quickly found out two things: (1) after World War II the prices of certified art, even in an esoteric field like Renaissance bronzes, were rising at a rate that made serious collecting out of the question; (2) the social world of certified art, even modern art, was a closed shop controlled—despite a dazzling aura of cultural liberalism—by the same old Protestant elite.

Then, in the late 1950's, a great thing happened: Pop Art; and pop publicity for Pop Art. In the financial world they speak of the tens of millions a man would be worth today had he invested $10,000 in IBM in 1926. But who ever has the daring or the foresight to do these things at the time? Bob Scull. Socially, Scull achieved a stock coup of IBM magnitude by plunging on the work of a painter, Jasper Johns, in 1959 and 1960. Rather amateurish stuff it was, too, renderings of flags, targets, numbers—and two bronzed ale cans. *How they sniggered over that!* But Johns became the "axe man for abstract expressionism," as Scull likes to put it. The ten-year-rule of abstract expressionism, which had seemed like *the final style*, was over, and in came a new movement, with Johns and Robert Rauschenberg as the key figures. Two years later, in 1962, it picked up a name: Pop Art.

Abstract expressionism was so esoteric it had all but defied exploitation by the press. But all the media embraced Pop Art with an outraged, scandalized, priapic delight. Art generally became the focus of social excitement in New York. Art openings began to take over from theater openings as the place where the chic, the ambitious, and the beautiful congregated. Art museum committees replaced charity committees as the place where ambitious newcomers could start scoring socially.

By 1961 the Sculls were being invited everywhere. "It was a whole thing going on," Scull told me, "where we got invitations from important people we didn't even know. You feel a little strange—you know, you go to some famous person's to a party or a dinner and you don't even know them, but you figure some friend of yours asked them to invite you, and then you get there and you find out there's nobody you know there. They just invited you. And everybody is very friendly. It's great. They come up and embrace you like you're the oldest friends in the world.

"I'll never forget once in Washington, at a gallery, Dean Acheson was there and I heard that he wanted to meet me. He came all the way over and shook hands with me very warmly and congratulated me on my collection—the whole thing was just as if we had gone to school together or something. Acheson—he was always practically a *god* to me, you know? One of the great leaders. And I walked in and here he walks all the way across the room and says *he* had looked forward to meeting *me*. And all the time I had always thought there were two worlds, this world full of all these people who did these great things, all these great, faultless people, and then this other world the rest of us were in."

From *hoi polloi* to *haute monde*—just so!

The success of Bob's original plunge, investing in twenty of Johns's works at one clip like he did, might be called luck. But the way Bob and Spike traversed that difficult interval from *hoi* to *haute* proved they had something else: *Fifth Avenue guts*, east side of the Park.

Throughout the period of transition—*how they sniggered!*—Bob and Spike were blessed with that gyroscope a few lucky people get built into them growing up in New York. It is an attitude, a Sat'dy aftuh-noon *Weltanschauung*, that always keeps them steady somehow. It is the cynicism of the cab driver with his cap over one eye. It is the fatalism of those old guys who sit out in front of the stores in the Lower East Side on Saturday afternoon in old bentwood chairs of the 1930's drugstore variety and just survey the scene with half a smile on, as if to say, look around you, this town is a nuthouse to start with, right? So don't get your bowels in an uproar. Relax. Enjoy.

There was, for example, the ticklish business—*how they sniggered*—of Bob learning how to dress. As I said, Scull is emerging from the 57th Street Biggie phase. Somebody turned him on to the big time in men's fashion, the English tailor shops on Savile Row, which is in the sort of 57th Street and Fifth Avenue area of London. The Savile Row shops still like to maintain the impression that they are some kind of private clubs and that you have to be recommended by an old customer. O.K., said Bob Scull, enjoy, enjoy, and he had two wealthy English friends, Harry Lawton and Murray Leonard, recommend him. All the same he can't resist it; he has to swing from the heels. So he walks into this place, amid all the linenfold paneling and engraved glass with all the "by appointment" crests, HRH King George, The Prince of Wales, etc., and a man about 55 in a nailhead worsted suit with a step-collared vest comes up and Scull announces that Harry Lawton and Murray Leonard recommended him and he wants . . . a sport jacket made of the material they make riding pinks out of.

"I beg your pardon, sir?" says the man, turning his mouth down and putting a cataractic dimness into his eyes as if he hopes to God he didn't hear correctly.

"You know that material they make the riding pinks out of, those coats when they go hunting, riding to the hounds and everything, that material, they call it riding pink."

"I am familiar with that, yes, sir."

"Well, I want a sport jacket made out of that."

"I'm afraid that's impossible, sir."

"You don't have the material?"

"It's not that—"

"I know where I can get you the material," says Scull. "There's this place, Hunt & Winterbotham."

Now the man looks at Scull with his lips tight and tilts his head back and opens his nostrils wide as if his eyes are located somewhere up his nose. Telling a Savile Row tailor that there is this place, Hunt & Winterbotham, is like telling a Seventh Avenue coffee shop that there is this thing called a cheese Danish.

"We are aware of the availability of the material, sir," he says. "It's just that we don't do that sort of thing."

"You can make a sport jacket, can't you?"

"Oh, yes, sir."

"And you can get the riding pink."

"Yes, sir."

"Then why can't you get the riding pink and make a sport jacket out of it?"

"As I said, sir, I'm afraid we don't . . ."

". . . do that sort of thing," says Scull, finishing the sentence.

"Yes, sir."

"Well, all I know is, Harry Lawton and Murray Leonard said you could take care of me."

"Oh, you come very highly recommended, sir, it's just that we . . ."

". . . I know . . ."

It is at this point, if not before, that Savile Row tailors are used to seeing Americans, 1960's style, at any rate, bow out, shuffling backwards like they are leaving the throne room, thoroughly beaten, cowed, humiliated, hangdog over the terrible gaffe they have committed—*a sport jacket out of traditional riding pink*—but Bob Scull just starts in again, still exuberant, smiling, happy to be on Savile Row in Harry Lawton and Murray Leonard country, and he says, "All right, let's go over this thing again. You can make a sport jacket and you can get the material . . ." They are so amazed to see an American still standing there and talking that they go ahead and agree to do it, and they take his measurements.

A week or so later Scull comes back in for the first fitting, and they bring out the riding pink, with the body of the coat cut and basted up and one arm basted on, the usual first fitting, and they put it on him—and Scull notices a funny thing. Everything has stopped in the shop. There, in the dimness of the woodwork and the bolt racks, the other men are looking up toward him, and in the back, from behind curtains, around door edges, from behind tiers of cloth, are all these eyes, staring.

Scull motions back toward all the eyes and asks his man, Nostrils, "Hey, what are they doing?"

Nostrils leans forward and says, very softly and very sincerely, "They're rooting for you, sir."

Enjoy! Enjoy!

Scull is so pleased with this, he goes back and starts shaking hands with everybody in the place, right down to the Cypriot seamstresses who made buttonholes and can't speak any English.

"I got news for you," says Scull, by way of congratulating those who are happy and consoling those who are desolate over the riding pink sports jacket, "you're going to be very proud of this jacket when we get through."

Later on, as Scull tells it, he saw one of his friends and said, "Well, I went to your tailor, and I want to thank you, because they made me a very nice jacket."

"Oh, that's very nice. I'm very glad."

"You know, it was funny. They didn't want to make it at first. I walked in and I said, 'I want a sport jacket made out of riding pink' and . . ."

"You *what!* Bob—you didn't use my name, did you . . ."

Afterwards Bob Scull tells me, "It's funny. The English treat their tailors like they were clergymen. Yeah. And their clergymen like they were tailors."

Spike's parents had money, and, if the truth were known, helped set Bob up in the taxi business in 1948. But as for social cachet—well, Spike had to learn all the subtleties of *chic* the same way Bob did, namely, the hard way—*how they sniggered*—but she always showed *class*, in the New York street sense of that term; *moxie*. When the going got tough, Spike just bulled it through and made it work. In the midst of the social galas attendant upon the opening of the Venice Biennale in 1966, I saw Ethel Scull stroll at twilight through Venice, heading for Countess Anna Camerana's in a dress of silver gossamer, see-through by St. Laurent, and silver shoes. The citizens of Venice and the tourists of all nations, including a man whose monocle fell out of his skull, stared bug-eyed at this vision of scientific-Cinderella chic with her head held high and one perfect rose in her hair. She topped this off by standing on one foot and hoisting the other one up and rubbing it and delivering the last word on strolls through Venice at twilight: "I got news for you, this girl's got sore feet."

Bob hasn't lost the common touch, either. Today he has 130 cabs in his fleet, the Super Operating Corporation, which is $2,625,000 worth of medallions alone, and a big taxi insurance business involving a lot of fleets. He goes up there every day to his garage in the Bronx, at 144th Street and Gerard Avenue, in the Mott Haven section, about 10 blocks south of Yankee Stadium, and he deals directly with the drivers right there in the garage, guys like Jakey, The Owl, Cream Cheese, Moon and this guy who used to be there, Do-Nut or whatever they called him.

You know what would be funny? It would be funny to

pick up Liza or Philip or Nicole or Peggy—that's Mrs. Peggy Guggenheim of New York and Venice, who has one of the world's greatest private art collections—or Chester or Alex or Bob or Dean or any of the other wonderful people who make up the art world set Robert Scull now moves in—it would be funny to pick up some of these people and suddenly sit them down in the grease moss at the Scull garage in the Bronx and let them try to handle a New York taxi operation for about one hulking hour. Never mind the heavy problems. Just imagine Philip or Alex or Ave dealing with a minor problem, like Do-Nut.

Philip! Ave! Do-Nut was a driver, a huge guy, and every morning he started out from the garage with a big brown paper bag full of donuts and pastries on the seat beside him. He kept on eating the day away and getting bigger and bigger and Scull tried everything. He had them push the seat in Do-Nut's cab back so far, to make room for his belly, it got so the only fares he could pick up were infants and midgets. Then they took the padding off the seats so he was back up against the metal plates. And then one day it was all over. He managed to get into the seat, but he couldn't turn the wheel. It would turn about 15 degrees and then just lodge in his belly.

"Bob, I got news for you," says Do-Nut, there behind the wheel. "This don't make it."

"You want to know something?" says Scull. "This is the day I dreaded."

"Wait a minute," says Do-Nut, "look at this. If I hold my breath, I can turn it."

"Yeah," says Scull, "but what about when you let it out."

Do-Nut exhales and the wheel disappears like a strawberry under a gush of whipped cream. Do-Nut looks up at Scull. Scull shrugs, pulling his shoulders up over his ears like a turtle, in a primordial gesture of the New York streets, the Hopeless Shrug, which says, What can I do after I've said I'm sorry. The guy had eaten himself out of the profession.

Scull still has to shake his head over that. Those guys. But the great thing is, the men, Scull says, the men . . . "generally speaking they're very proud of my art kick. They're proud that their boss is something special. They want a boss they can look up to. That's class."

Bob's art kick, as I say, was tricky business. The economics of collecting *the latest thing* in art, as Bob has been doing, are irrational. A collector can count on *the latest work* by almost any of the current avant-garde artists to depreciate more drastically than a new car; it will lose one third to one half its value the moment it is bought. The explanation gets at the heart of the whole business of collecting the latest, the most avant-garde, the most wacked-out in painting. The price of, say, a new Lichtenstein or a new Johns or a new Stella is not determined by market demand in the usual sense (i.e., a mass of undifferentiated consumers). Aside from museums, the market is, in effect, some ten or twenty collectors, most of whom are striving to become Bobs and Spikes, although they would bridle if it were ever put to them just that way. The game, when one is collecting the *latest thing*—as opposed to certified Old or Recent Masters—is to get one's hands on just that: *the latest thing* by a promising avant-garde artist and, preferably, to be publicized for purchasing it. One has . . . *the new Lichtenstein! the new Poons! the new Rauschenberg! the new Dine! the new Oldenberg!* The competition to buy it hot from the studio is what drives the price up in the galleries. Once that little game is played out, the re-sale value may be but a fraction. The galleries dealing in the hottest avant-garde artists are driven to frantic juggling to make sure each of the handful of players wins a bout every now and then and remains interested. Collector X got the first shot at the last hot one—so Y gets first shot at the next one; and so on.

So Bob Scull got an idea. Why not get to the artists before their work reaches the gallery even? Why not do even better than that—why not *discover* them?

One evening a friend of Bob's, a psychiatrist, said to him: "Bob, did it ever occur to you that when you commission young artists to create works of art, you may be influencing the course of art history?"

Patron. Shaper of history. If the truth be known, it had already crossed Bob's mind that he had influenced art history by buying twenty works by Johns in 1959 and 1960. Before that, Johns was just some kind of odd man out in the art world, some guy from South Carolina trying to bug the establishment with his fey, representational rendition of banal objects. The fact that he was actually being *collected* —well, that's what started Pop Art. Yes, that thought had crossed Bob's mind. But why not go even one step further—*discover* the greats of tomorrow yourself and *commission* the future of art history. Stalk their very studios. That was how Bob ran into Walter De Maria.

It was a Saturday. Another Culture Sabbath. Bob Scull was walking down Madison Avenue, and you know, it's funny on Saturday in New York, especially on one of those Indian summer days—God, somehow Culture just seems to be in the air, like part of the weather, all of the antique shops on Madison Avenue, with a little blaze of golden ormolu here and a little oxblood-red leathery marquetry there, and the rugs hung up in the second-floor display windows—rich!—a Bakhtiari with a little pale yellow setting off the red—and the galleries, God, gallery after gallery, with the pristine white walls of Culture, the black wooden

191 : *Bob and Spike*

floors, and the Culture buds, a little Renoirish softness in the autumn faces.

Through the window of this particular gallery, Scull can see two girls who are tending the place, and one is sitting with her legs crossed, a short skirt on, great pre-Raphaelite hair, the perfect Culture bud, and it is not that he wants to make a pass or anything, it is just part of this beautiful atmosphere of Culture in New York, Indian summer, Culture Sabbath, all the rest—so he goes in. It is just a pleasure to go on in there and let the whole thing just sort of seep through you like hot coffee.

But what a freaking show. Here is some wooden sculpture of some sort, two very tall pillars of wood—and then there is a bunch of drawings. Except that there doesn't seem to be anything on the paper, just a lot of framed blank paper on the wall. What the hell is this? Scull goes up very close to a drawing and then he can see there is a hard little design on the paper done with a hard pencil, a No. 8 or something, so you can hardly see it. Then down at the bottom, also in this hard pencil, are these poverty-stricken little words: "Water, water, water."

So Scull turns to the girl and he says, "I've seen a lot of things, but how does this guy think he's going to sell these?"

"Well . . ."

"I mean, I don't know what this whole art thing is coming to. You can't even *see* what's on the paper."

He looks back at it again and it still says "Water, water, water." That's all that's up there. Well, the girl says, it's by a young artist, they never handled him before. She shrugs. Scull is really bugged by this whole thing.

"All right," he says, finally, "how much is this drawing?"

She gives him a look—what the hell, this girl never even thought about the price before. Nobody ever asked. Finally she says, "It's $110."

"All right," says Scull, "I tell you what. This whole thing bugs me. I'll buy this drawing for $110 if you'll give me the artist's name, address and telephone number. I want to see what he has to say about this."

So she says all right, and it's Walter De Maria. So the following week Scull calls up the number. The thing is, the whole thing *disturbs* him, and so this guy may have something he ought to know about. The telephone conversation disturbs him some more. This Walter De Maria comes to the phone and Scull says, "This is Robert Scull."

"Yes." That's all he says.

"Do you know who I am?"

There's this long pause. Then this hesitant voice: "Yes. You're the man who bought my drawing."

"That's right," Scull says. "I'd like to come to your studio and see some more of your work."

There's a big silence. Scull starts saying, Hello, hello. He thinks the guy must have hung up.

"I don't know," the guy says. "I won't be available."

"Look," says Scull, "I bought your drawing and I want to see some more of your work. Can't I even come and look at it?"

"I don't know. I'm glad you bought the drawing, but you bought the drawing from the gallery, not from me, and I'm not available."

Scull is really rocked by this, but he keeps arguing and finally De Maria gives in and says O.K., come on down to his studio. The studio is downtown up in a loft building, about five flights up, and Scull climbs up there. His heart is banging away from the freaking stairs. There's a small room and then a bigger room beyond, and in the small room here are these two pale, slender figures, Walter De Maria and his wife. Mrs. De Maria is kind of backed off into a corner. She doesn't say anything.

"Well," says Scull to De Maria, "I'd like to see some more of your drawings."

So he shows him one and this time Scull has to put on his *glasses* to see if there's anything on paper. He looks up, and by this time De Maria is pacing around the room and running his hands through his hair in a terrible state of agitation.

What the hell is this? Scull says to himself. You could get a heart attack walking up these freaking stairs, and after you get up here, what's going on? He's sorry he even came up. But as a last gesture, he asks De Maria to show him what he had been doing before he did the drawings. Here, says De Maria, that's what I've done. What's that? says Scull. That's a sculpture, says De Maria. Here is this Skee-Ball, like in the amusement arcades, on a wooden board, and it says on there, "Place ball in upper hole," and so Scull dutifully places it in the upper hole and pow! it falls down into a hole at the bottom. Scull stares at the ball. And De Maria, like, he's watching Scull this whole time, waiting for a reaction, but Scull can't come up with any, except that he's still bugged.

"How long have you been a sculptor?" he says.

"Six years."

"Well, can I see some of your earlier work?"

"It's in the other room."

The other room is bigger, a studio room, with all white walls and a white floor—and nothing else. It's empty. Yeah, well, where is it? Scull says. Over here, says De Maria. Over here? De Maria is pointing to a little filing cabinet. He's done a lot of successful sculptures, he says. The only thing is, he never made them. He never made them? No. He couldn't afford the materials. Well, yeah, says Scull, then he says, What's in the file? De Maria riffles through and here are more of these sheets of paper with something on there you can't even see, a few lines and more "Water, water, water" and so forth.

The whole thing now has Scull so bugged he says, "Look—if I commission you to do one for me and I get you the materials, will you make one?"

De Maria says O.K. A couple of months go by and finally De Maria says he has completed a design and he'll need a large plate of silver. Silver? says Scull. Why can't he use stainless steel. It's got to be silver, says De Maria. So Scull gets him the silver. Through all this Bob and Spike get to know De Maria a little better, but it's an unusual relationship. Sometimes one of them says something and there is no response, nothing at all. Other times, they're all out on the street and De Maria walks way ahead, as if he didn't know them. Who are these people following him? Bob says to himself: Ah, he's been through a lot of excitement because of all this. That's all it is.

Then three and a half or four more months go by, and— nothing. Bob is on the verge of going back there and getting his silver back. But then one day De Maria calls up and says the sculpture is ready. He brings it up in a truck, and they bring it up into the apartment; it's the big moment and everything, and here is this big object with a velvet drapery over it. Bob pulls a string and opens up the drapes—and there it is, the piece of silver, the original plate of silver, with nothing on it. Bob stares at the piece of silver. De Maria is watching him just like he did the first day with the Skee-Ball.

"What is it?" says Scull.

"Look on the back."

On the back is a little piece of chrome inscribed "Nov. 5, 1965, made for Mr. and Mrs. Robert C. Scull." There are also instructions to photograph the plate of silver every three months and keep the pictures in a photograph album. The sculpture is entitled *The Portrait of Dorian Gray*. The thing is, says De Maria, the silver will tarnish, and the plate will get blacker and more and more corroded and the film will record the whole process. Every three months until 1975, presumably, Bob or Spike will pull the velvet drapes and take a picture of this piece of corroded metal and then paste it in the scrapbook. *The Portrait of Dorian Gray!* But of course!

"I was overwhelmed by it," Scull told me later. "It's impossible to describe what happens to a collector when he commissions something and it turns out right."

Bob and Spike went out to New Jersey to the studio of George Segal. Segal is famous for his plaster-cast sculptures. Bob and Spike commissioned him to make one of them. So Segal started encasing them in the plaster. It was kind of a wild time. Sometimes the plaster starts sticking to the skin when it dries. Spike lost one of her Courrèges boots in the struggle to get out, and Bob—they had to pull his Levi's off him to keep him from being a permanent living cast. The shape of history, all right. Bob and Spike decided to unveil the sculpture at a party for a couple of hundred celebrities, artists, columnists, and editors. They didn't even know half of them—but they would come, they would come.

The afternoon before the party, Jasper Johns's latest show opened at the Leo Castelli gallery, 4 East 77th Street. There were four huge paintings in the show and Bob wasn't going to get any of them. For a variety of reasons. For one thing, three of them had been spoken for, by museums. Nevertheless, Bob was in a good mood. Spike didn't even show up, but Bob was in a good mood. Castelli's, especially at an opening like this, was where it was at. You could tell that at a glance. Not by the paintings, but by the Culture buds. They were all there, all these gorgeous little Culture buds, 20, 21, 22, 23, 24 years old, along in there, their little *montes Veneris* in the sweet honey grip

of Jax slax that finger into every fissure, their serious little
Culture pouts hooded in Sassoon thrusts and black Egypt
eyes—their lubricous presence, like that of the whalebird,
indicating where the biggest fish in the sea is.

Out in the middle of the bud coveys Bob is talking to
Leo Castelli. Castelli, New York's number-one dealer in
avant-garde art, is a small, trim man in his late fifties. Bob is
Leo's number-one customer. Leo is the eternal Continental
diplomat, with a Louis-salon accent that is no longer Italian; rather, Continental. Every word he utters slips through
a small velvet Mediterranean smile. His voice is soft, suave,
and slightly humid, like a cross between Peter Lorre and
the first secretary of a French embassy.

"Leo," says Bob, "you remember what you told me at
Jap's last show?"

"Noooooooo——"

"You told me—I was *vulgar!*"—only Bob says it with
his eyes turned up bright, as if Leo should agree and they
can have a marvelous laugh over it.

"Noooooo, Bob——"

"Listen, Leo! I got news——"

"Nooooooo, Bob, I didn't——"

"I got news for you, Leo——"

"Nooooooooooo, Bob, I merely said——" Nobody says
No like Leo Castelli. He utters it as if no word in the entire
language could be more pleasing to the listener. His lips
purse into a small lubricated O, and the Nooooooo comes
out like a strand of tiny, perfect satiny-white pearls . . .

"Leo, I got news for you——"

"Nooooooooooo, Bob, I merely said that at that stage of
Johns's career, it would be wrong—"

"*Vulgar* you said, Leo—"

"—would be wrong for one collector to buy up the
whole show—"

"You said it was *vulgar*, Leo, and you know what?"

"What, Bob?"

"I got news for you—*you were right!* It *was* vulgar!" Bob's eyes now shine like two megawatt beacons of truth; triumphant, for the truth now shines in the land. For one of the few times in his life, Castelli stares back blank; in velvet stupefaction.

That night, the big party—it was freezing. For a start, Spike was very icy on the subject of Jasper Johns; another of their personal tiffs, and Johns wasn't coming to the party. But enjoy! Who else is even in a position to *have* tiffs with the great of the avant garde? It was also cold as hell outside, about 17 degrees, and all these people in tuxedos and mini-evening dresses came up into the Sculls' apartment at 1010 Fifth Avenue with frozen heads and—*kheeew!*—right inside the door is a dark velvet settee with a slightly larger than life plaster cast of Ethel Scull sitting on it, legs crossed, and Bob standing behind it. Standing next to it, here in the foyer, are the real Bob and Spike, beaming, laughing, greeting everybody—*Gong*—the apartment has been turned into a gallery of Bob's most spectacular acquisitions.

Everywhere, on these great smooth white walls, are de Koonings, Newmans, Jasper Johns's targets and flags, John Chamberlain's sculpture of crushed automobile parts, Andy Warhol's portrait of Spike made of thirty-five blown-up photos from the Photo-Matic machine in the pinball arcade at 52nd Street and Broadway, op art by Larry Poons with color spots that vibrate so hard you can turn your head and still, literally, see spots in front of your eyes. That is on the dining room walls. There used to be a Rosenquist billboard-style painting in there with huge automobile tire treads showing. Tonight there is a painting by James Rosenquist on the ceiling, a painting of a floor plan, the original idea being that the Sculls could wake up in the morning and

look over their bed and see the floor plan and orient themselves for the day. Over the headboard of their king-size
bed is an "American nude" by Tom Wesselmann with two
erect nipples sitting up like hot cherries.

Many prominent people are moving about in the hub-
bub, talking, drinking, staring: George Segal the movie
actor, George Segal the sculptor, Leonard Lyons the columnist, Aileen Mehle, who is Suzy Knickerbocker the
columnist; Alex Liberman; Mrs. Jacob Javits; Robert Kintner. Larry Poons comes in with his great curly head hung
solemnly, wearing a terry cloth Hawaiian shirt with a
picture of a shark on it. *Poonsy!* Spike calls him Poonsy.
Her voice penetrates. It goes right through this boilup of
heads, throats, tuxedoes. She says this is a big concession for
Poonsy. She is talking about the Hawaiian shirt. This is
formal for Poonsy. To some parties he wears a T-shirt and
a pair of clodhoppers with Kelly green paint sloshed on
them. *Awash.* People are pouring through all the rooms.
Gong—the World's Fair. Everybody leaves the apartment
and goes downstairs to where they have three Campus
Coach Line buses out on Fifth Avenue to take everybody
out to the World's Fair, out in Flushing.

The World's Fair is over, but the Top o' the Fair restaurant is still going, up in the top of a big mushroom tower.
The wreckage of the fair, the half-demolished buildings,
are all hulking around it in silhouette, like some gigantic
magnified city dump. The restaurant itself, up there at the
top, turns out to be a great piece of 1930's *Modren* ele-
gance, great slabs of glass, curved wood, wall-to-wall, and,
everywhere, huge plate-glass views of the borough of
Queens at night.

Scull has taken over half the big complex at the top of
the tower, including a whole bandstand and dance floor
with tables around it, sort of like the old Tropicana night
club in Havana, Cuba.

After dinner a rock 'n' roll band starts playing and people start dancing. Mrs. Claes Oldenburg, a pretty, petite girl in a silver mini-dress, does a dance, the newest boogaloo, with Robert Rauschenberg, the artist. The band plays "Hang on, Sloopy." Rauschenberg has had an outrageous smile on all evening and he ululates to himself from time to time—Ooooooooooo—Gong—the dancing stops and everybody is shepherded into a convention hall.

There is a movie screen in here and rows of seats. The lights go out. The first movie is called *Camp*, by Andy Warhol. A group of men and women in evening clothes are sitting in a very formal pose in a loft. One of them is Jane Holzer. A fat boy in some kind of Wagnerian opera costume comes out in front of them and does some ballet leaps, sagging and flopping about. The men and women in the evening clothes watch very stiffly and respectfully. Another fat boy comes out with a yo-yo act. A man in drag, looking like a faded Argentinian torch singer, comes out and does a crazy dance. The basic idea is pretty funny, all these people in evening clothes watching stiffly and respectfully while the performers come out and go into insane acts. It is also exquisitely boring. People start drifting out of the convention hall in the darkness at the Top o' the Fair. So they stop that film, and the lights go on and a young man named Robert Whitman comes up and puts on his film, which has no title.

This one is more elaborate. It involves three screens and three projectors. The lights go out. On the left screen, in color, a slender, good-looking girl, kind of a nude Culture bud, with long pre-Raphaelite hair and good beach skin, is taking a shower, turning this way and that. At first water comes out of the nozzle, and then something black, like oil, and then something red, like wine. She keeps waffling around. On the righthand screen, also in color, some nice-looking buds are lying on the floor with their mouths open.

You're looking down at their faces. Food and liquid start falling, cascading down, into their mouths, onto their faces, onto their noses, their eyes, all this stuff, something soft and mushy like pancake mix, then a thin liquid like pineapple juice, then chopped meat, chopped liver or something, raw liver, red and runny, all hitting the old bud face there or going straight down the gullet. Only they keep smiling. Then the whole thing goes in reverse and all the stuff comes back up out of their mouths, like they're vomiting, only they're smiling out of these pretty faces the whole time.

On the center screen, all this time, in black and white—nobody can tell what the hell is going on at first. There are these sort of, well, *abstract* shapes, some fissures, folds, creases, apertures, some kind of rim, and some liquid that comes from somewhere. But it doesn't add up to anything. Of course, it could be some of the abstract forms that Stan Brakhage uses in his films, or—but then, after about fifteen minutes, while Black-haired Beauty on the left waffles in the shower and the Open-jawed Beauties on the right grin into eternal ingestion, it adds up—the girl who was sitting on the rim gets up, and then some large testicles lower into view, and then the organism begins to defecate. The film has somehow been made by slicing off the bottom of a toilet bowl and putting a glass shield in place and photographing straight up from inside the bowl. Black-haired Beauty pivots in the shower, luxuriating in oil, Strawberry Beauty smiles and luxuriates in chopped liver.

And here, descending head-on into the faces of the 200 celebrities, artists, columnists, editors . . . is an enormous human turd.

Marvelous! The lights go on. All these illuminati are sitting here in their tuxedos and mini-evening dresses at the Top o' the Fair above grand old Nighttime City Lights New York City, above the frozen city-dump silhouette of the New York World's Fair, like an assembly of poleaxed lambs.

Walter De Maria! Walter De Maria is on the drums, high up on the Tropicana bandstand, snares, brushes, blond wood, those sturdy five-story loft walkup arms going like hell—Walter De Maria is on the rise. Bob Scull patronized him, helped him out, and De Maria is now among the rising young sculptors. Blam! He beats the hell out of the drums. On the dance floor they've seized all the equipment at the Top o' the Fair, the artists. The band looks on from the side. Walter De Maria has the drums, Claes Oldenburg has a tambourine, his wife Pat, in the silver dress, has a microphone, and Rauschenberg has a microphone. Rauschenberg's friend Steve Paxton, the dancer, is dancing, waffling, by himself. Rauschenberg and Pat Oldenburg are both ululating into the microphones, wild loon wails—*Sloopy!* —filling up this whole mushroom-head glass building overlooking frozen Queens. Where are the poleaxed lambs? They have been drifting off. The Campus Coach Line buses have been leaving every half hour, like a bus route. The pop artists, the op artists, the primary artists, have the place: De Maria, Rauschenberg, Rosenquist, Segal, Poons, Oldenburg, they have the Top o' the Fair. Larry Poons pulls off his shark terry cloth Hawaiian shirt and strips down to his Ford Motor Company Cobra T-shirt, with the word COBRA stacked up the front about eight times. Poons waffles about on the edge of the dance floor, with his head down but grinning.

Bob Scull beams. Spike is delighted. Her voice penetrates —yes!

"Look at Poonsy! When I see that boy smile, I really enjoy it, I'm telling you!"

Bob Scull sits at a table on the edge of the dance floor, beaming. Rauschenberg and Pat Oldenburg go into ululation, mimicking rock 'n' roll singers, and then somebody there says, "Sing the dirty song!" Just as if she knows what he means, Pat Oldenburg starts singing the Dirty Song. She has the microphone in that Show Biz grip and her legs roil around in her silver mini-gown and she sings.

"You got a dirty ceiling, you got a dirty floor, you got a dirty window, you got a dirty door, oh dirty dirty, dirty dirty dirty, oh dirty dirty, dirty dirty dirty—"

Scull just beams and gets up from the table and takes his chair practically out onto the dance floor in front of her and sits down—

"—oh dirty dirty, dirty dirty dirty, dirty dirty, oh, you got dirty hair, you got dirty shoes, you got dirty ears, you got dirty booze, dirty dirty, dirty dirty dirty, oh you got a dirty face you got a dirty shirt, you got dirty hands—"

Rauschenberg ululates in the background, De Maria explodes all over the drums in some secret my-own-bag fury, Oldenburg beats the tambourine, Poons waffles and grins, everybody looks at Scull to see what he's going to do. Scull seems to sense this as some sort of test. Enjoy!

"I like it!" he says to Pat Oldenburg.

"—oh dirty dirty, dirty dirty dirty, dirty dirty—"

"That's very good ! I like it!"

He beams, Rauschenberg ululates, blam bong—*Gong*—*2:30 a.m.*, out, out of here, Poons, De Maria, Segal, Rauschenberg, Rosenquist, they're off, down the elevator, they disappear. Bob and Spike take the last elevator down, with Jonathan and Stephen. They get to the bottom, and it is cold as hell, 2:30 a.m., 17 degrees, in the middle of Flushing, Queens, frozen Flushing with the troglodyte ruins of the World's Fair, frozen-dump garbage, sticking up in the black—and suddenly the artists are gone—and so is the last bus. It's unbelievable—Bob and Spike—deserted—abandoned—in the middle of Queens. There must have been some stupid mistake! Either that or somebody told the last bus, and the last bus driver, "This is it, we're all here, take off," and he took off, all those Campus Coach Line buses. A station wagon pulls out. It has a few remaining magazine editors in it, the *Time* and *Life* crowd. It disappears. Suddenly it is all quiet as hell here, and cold. Bob Scull stares out into the galactal Tastee-Freeze darkness of Queens and watches his breath turn white in front of him.

THE ETIQUETTE BOOKS struggle to "update," to keep up with new customs among the upper orders of mankind. By last year they were including remarkable sections such as guidelines for petting by the younger set. The etiquette of petting; just so. Etiquette, after all, is only generally accepted rules of conduct; and there must be rules for braces of nubile adolescents secreting hot civet musk and exploring one another's nodules, mounds, fleshy processes, and tingly striations in the Naugahyde gloamings. Yes; and that is but one example. Already, in New York, the entire Book of Etiquette is being rewritten, because of two developments:

(1) *The rationalization of politesse;* i.e., the adapting of social etiquette to purely business ends.

(2) *Nostalgie de la boue;* i.e., the adoption by the upper orders, for special effect, of the customs of the lower orders.

The new Book of Etiquette will have many new headings:

The Monkey Dinner
Dying Institutions:

(1) The Cocktail Party
(2) The Hostess
Pariah Styles
Shit! Fuck! & Other Polite Interjections
The Social Kiss
The Etiquette of Pot

The rationalization of politesse. First, a very common example—the New York business lunch—by way of illustrating the principle. Historically, etiquette has been derived from the *paternal charisma* of the feudal system. The highest social honor (short of intermarriage of offspring) that one nobleman could pay another was to *fete* him. The New York business lunch is the feudal *fete* harnessed to rational economic ends. An entire belt of restaurants in the East Fifties of Manhattan derives its livelihood from the eternal business *fetes*. The feast may include two cocktails per person, *haute cuisine* in the French or Italian mode, wine, coffee, brandy, and cigars and may last three hours. If the host (i.e., corporation) has done his work well, the client or customer being feted will feel the euphoria of the ancient *status honor* implicit in the feast. This principle applies in many of the new social practices in New York. Such as—

The Monkey Dinner. The term comes from what until recently was thought of as a mere frivolous *sport* in the genealogy of New York manners; namely, Mrs. Stuyvesant Fish's original monkey dinner at 19 Gramercy Park in 1908. Mrs. Fish invited the *haute monde* of her day to a dinner in honor of the Prince del Drago. Nobody bothered to ask who the Prince del Drago was, but they all came. And there was the Prince, at Mrs. Fish's right at dinner, a full-grown Chambezi baboon in evening clothes. Mrs. Fish had fitted him out in a wing collar and tails. She put him at her right at the table so everybody could watch him gibber and nod over the various courses. He smeared aspic over a Victoria Cross on his magenta taffeta sash, and Lord Whatdyecallit felt obliged to leave the room. The first monkey dinner; this grand gesture was Mrs. Fish's way of showing how contemptible *Society* had become in her day, willing to go anywhere, for whatever purpose, if it seemed grand enough.

Today the monkey dinner is no cynical gesture; it is a convention. One receives an invitation from someone of the social magnitude of Bill and Babs Paley (I use these names merely to indicate the caliber) inviting one to a dinner party in honor of someone of even greater magnitude, such as Averell Harriman. One envisions a dinner for twelve or sixteen given by the Paleys—in short, an evening in the very bosom of the New York aristocracy. Dreamer! This being the 1960's, in the age of the monkey dinner, there are not twelve or sixteen for dinner, but two hundred. Everybody is there, all those wonderful five-foot-four blue-jowled floor-liquid and body-cream magnates with eyes like walnut shells. And one need get no further than the catered lobster *au cardinal*, with the thawed and warmed-up oleaginous sauce, to know what comes at the end. At the end the guest of honor is trotted out like Prince del Drago, the monkey king, and there is a speech for a worthy philanthropy: The Cancer Fund, Heart, Liver, Gizzard, thyroxine-eyed children, Mississippi Negroes, the Rehab of JD's—who remembers? Then a servant passes out the pledge cards and—well, what is there for one to do but get it up? It is too sublime for anger. One can only sit there amid catered stemware of five different shapes realizing that something beautiful and perfect has taken place; the rationalization of politesse.

So many charity monkey dinners have been perpetrated in the last two years, using real-life Prince del Dragos, that serious freelance hosts and hostesses in New York have started adding at the bottom of invitations, "No fund raising." In the new era of New York manners the charity monkey dinner is merely the super-rationalization of a subtler form of monkey dinner that has been common in New York ever since the war; namely—

The Angle Dinner (or private monkey dinner). Today the most sought-after species of monkey figure for angle dinners is an artist or museum director, someone on the order of Andy Warhol, Robert Rauschenberg, Roy Lichtenstein, Jasper Johns, Alfred Barr. He is, however, only the guest of honor, the window dressing. The party, all the while, is really being given for another, inconspicuous guest, someone like a vinyl-wallet-manufacturing baron, who wears neat white shirts with spring-metal stays in the collars. The whole point of the party—the angle—is to put this man next to another guest, one of the host's colleagues or clients who is a small wholesaler out for a soft distribution deal. The host could have given the party in honor of the vinyl-wallet baron, of course, but who would have come? None of those opulent biggies in Welsh broadcloth shirts and Revatti ties. None of those opulent lovelies with feathery eyes and white lips. None of those people one knows and loves, who can create New York's . . . status euphoria . . . for a vinyl-wallet baron.

After-dinner Guests. The monkey dinner itself is for a very specific and serious purpose, namely, a piece of business. Therefore, one cannot have too many sheerly decorative types at the dinner table, making sand piles in their own egos. Therefore, the hosts of the new era have instituted the curious custom of ringing in after-dinner guests. It has an antecedent in the old Society custom of calling in entertainers and paying them to perform after dinner.

Some singer or dancer would use the pantry or some such place as a dressing room, then come popping out of the wings to burst into a dance for a loll-glut of sated diners nodding over cognac, under the Rundell shields, on zebra-wood chairs. The night the dancer Irene Castle danced and then *mingled* with the guests at Mrs. Whowasit's house was considered sick-making by some and epoch-making by all. Today, hosts bring in guests after dinner for about the same reason—for color, atmosphere, style. On the face of it at least, the after-dinner guest is an equal, a bona fide guest, even a socialite, perhaps. At Allan's and Dorothy's salon— the heavyweights sit over dinner, pondering the big things in life, and then, as if on cue, the doors fly open and here, arms outstretched, lips outstretched, grinning *loudly*, it is *Uncle Miltie*—Milton Berle!—"Dottie! Al!"—now the delicious *fun* part of the evening begins.

Status Introductions. A man who wants to use a monkey dinner in a serious, businesslike manner has to be able to identify people very quickly, separate the potted plants from the heavyweights, and so forth. This has led to several odd new manners.

Even twenty years ago it would have been unthinkable to introduce people to one another at a party by status. But at the modern monkey dinner this is one of the host's duties. "This is Harry ——; Harry makes television commercials. This is Lionel ——; he writes. This is Arthur ——; with Sullivan & Cromwell." It goes on and on. It is like the college application that asks for "religion." Supposedly the question is to help out the college chaplain in his ministrations. Actually, it is for status detection—the detection of Jews, Irishmen and Italians. By the same token, introducing people with their occupations appended to their names is supposed to get conversation going easier. Actually, it is a form of quick status identification. There was a time when nobody would have dreamed of asking somebody he just met at a party, "What do you do?" The question, of course, really asks, What is your status? Today, it is not only common but considered polite. The very essence of conduct at a monkey dinner is ascertaining at once the status of any stranger one is talking to.

Dying Institutions: (1) The Cocktail Party. New York "society," and its new etiquette, centers almost completely on dinners. Only editorial writers, theologians, and college literature majors still speak of the cocktail party as where the *haute monde* in New York meets in sophisticated communion. They still compose such locations as "Meanwhile, cocktail party savants were spreading the word that . . ." In fact, the only people with money in New York today who seem to find any use for cocktail parties are institutions—firms, hotels, art galleries, museums, foundations, trade associations. One gives a cocktail party today when there are a large number of people whom one really doesn't think will be of much use but—well, it might be the wise thing to give them some kind of token attention. One gives cocktail parties for "the press." The manager of the Beatles gives a vast party in the Plaza Hotel for "the press," those bloody gibbering bahstads. Or outfits like the National Book Award Committee. They put on the award ceremony in some place like the Hilton Hotel or Philharmonic Hall at Lincoln Center and then give an enormous cocktail party afterwards for all the dear authors, subeditors, and publishing-house "editorial assistants," who pour into the place because, unfortunately, they are never invited *any*where else. The real literati and publishing nabobs sidle out early to private dinners at "21" and such places in the East and West Fifties. The idea behind cocktail parties today, in almost every instance, is, *There*, get in there and swill it up; that ought to hold you useful but dreary little bahstads.

In "society," however, there must be food, a meal, dinner—one has to be able to sit down with someone over food. That is one of the rules of the new etiquette. It is based on the ancient idea that one is paying a man a compliment by inviting him to sit down and eat. The schema, in England and here, has been that an aristocrat invites only his equals, other "top people" presumably, to dinner. He can invite equals or near equals to lunch with him and he can invite practically anybody to "tea."

The cocktail party, in the schema, is the modern equivalent of the "tea." Thus, who can honestly feel good over being invited to a cocktail party? There are abrasive details about New York cocktail parties today. A guest who doesn't know the host or hostess personally seldom feels obliged to look him up and meet him. And nobody, other than close friends, feels the slightest compulsion to thank him or say goodbye on leaving. It is, as they say, some place to go.

Dying Institutions: (2) *The Hostess.* New York's social life, like Boston's, used to be ruled by great hostesses such as Madame Fish. In New York today there remain a few great hostesses; Mrs. C. Z. Guest, Mrs. Gilbert Miller, Mrs. Elsie Woodward. They are anachronisms. With the rise of the monkey dinner, entertaining has become a man's domain. The wife may get the credit on the social pages, but she is really only some kind of social secretary. The man is using the dinner as an integral part of his career and, eventually, takes over the most minor details. He stays up nights studying books on English silverware, Lebanese lacework and French wine châteaux. He plans the seating arrangement. After all, the practical side of the monkey dinner is the fact that it gives men a chance to sit down and talk. It is almost an axiom. A stand-up party, such as a cocktail party, is at best a way of diluting one's social burden. One doesn't have to talk to anyone at length; one barely has to pay attention to them. A sit-down party, set up for talk, is by definition more serious, and therefore, today in New York, men insist on controlling it.

Even harmless enterprises, such as the philanthropies, have been taken away from women in New York. There is too much money and status involved. Today, women are not the leaders of New York's "social" charities but the slaveys; lady soldiers, who go out to *im*plement.

At the very point where New York's most prominent hostesses think they are recouping and creating a new, charismatic grouping for the "top people," there is not only a man behind it, but a man with a plan with ancient caste traditions built right into it; "pre-fab," as it were. One receives an invitation from a group of socially prominent women to join in the founding of the *Nine O'Clocks*, a social elite that will give four, let us say, *exclusive* dinner dances a year. In the Rainbow Room, which is trying to reestablish itself as a prominent nightspot. Such tradition about it! Such a confluence of traditions! The dinner dance—so like Washington society, when there *was* a Washington society, one understands; so like the best Mayfair atmosphere of the old grand hotels in New York, when there *were* grand hotels, as one will recall; so—so right out of the swallow-throat gravure pictures in *Vanity Fair*— and why should anyone feel spiteful, later on, when they all realized that the mastermind of the *Nine O'Clocks*, with all those caste moldings, was a public relations man, Earl Blackwell, founder of Celebrity Service? After all, here was a man for the new age; he gave them instant tradition, pre-fab, pre-tested; a most rational and efficient politesse.

Nostalgie de la boue. Socially, New York today is highly redolent of London during the Regency period (roughly, 1800 to 1830). The Regency was a period of unparalleled

affluence in England. The middle classes had so much new
money they threw traditional social lines into great confusion in London. In *Society*, manners took a rakehell turn.
Girls began dispensing with foundation garments and wearing filmy dresses that revealed a great deal of breast and
other flesh. They also started wearing knickers. Young
men gave up breeches for tight-fitting trousers and wore
clothes of bizarre cut and high color that were often
denounced as effeminate. Both homosexuality and fashionable whores were widespread. The courtly dances of the
late eighteenth century, such as the minuet, gave way to the
dervish spins of the waltz.

"This was thought to denote a general decline in moral
standards, if not the onset of national decadence," wrote
one historian. Both young men and women of the upper
classes were swept by *nostalgie de la boue*—a longing to
recapture the raw and elemental vitality of the lower
orders. They took on the manners and dress of the more
dashing lower-class types as a fashion. Young gentlemen
affected the dress of coachmen, wearing capes and conical
beaver hats and driving their own horses to various small
sports phaetons at wild speeds on the outroads of London.
Even more popular was the "bruiser" pose, after the manner of the prize fighters of the day: swaggering about in
skin-tight boots and pantaloons, and the hell with bourgeois respectability. A young chemist named Humphry
Davy discovered nitrous oxide (laughing gas), which,
when sniffed from a silken bag, seemed to open doors in the
mind to sublime mystical experiences. "The laughing gas
was a furore," wrote R. J. White. "Poets and painters,
potters and antiquaries, statesmen and popular novelists,
Maria Edgeworth and Isaac D'Israeli and Josiah Wedgwood, everyone who was anyone might insert his or her
nose in the silken bag and record his or her sensations."

The various modes of *nostalgie de la boue* were in large

part the young aristocrats' means of setting themselves apart from the middle classes. Wealth was no longer a buffer between the classes; but the old aristocratic manner of *confidence* was. The middle classes had money but lacked the confidence to be anything but ever more ornately respectable. The aristocrat had the confidence to be as shocking and outrageous as a navvy and get away with it. The bourgeois was hipped on gentility—genteel language, genteel conduct, the *gravitas* of the good burgher. The aristocrat shone by his own brilliance without regard to popular opinion, by which he usually meant the middle classes.

And in New York today—

Pariah Styles. But of course. In New York Society today one must understand, appreciate, know how to handle dozens of *outrageous* mannerisms and styles. Outrageous is such a quaint word. Words! Dinner-table expletives such as *Fuck!* and *Shit!;* also clinical commentary at dinner about various exotic feminine diseases and sexual hysterias; also homosexual movies, camp jesters, this and that—it is all part of the new *chic* of Society in New York. Such a marvelous book of etiquette one must now write!

New York Society today is the kind of elite that has no natural style of life of its own. "Society"—the minority that establishes manners—is today a publicity aristocracy. Fewer and fewer people are in Society today because of their ancestry or any other kind of inherited or immutable status. They are in Society today because of their success. They have triumphed in their careers and are publicized for it. Their careers are diverse, although more and more of them are in newer fields of information and communication—television, show business, publishing, the arts, advertising. They have had no common meeting ground or tradition out of which a style of life could grow.

Yet, like every status group, New York's new Society does need a style of life. Only through a style of life can a status group assert its position publicly and show that it is unique. But where are they to find styles? American life is getting more and more homogenized at its center of power. Unique styles, today, tend to be developed by various marginal, religiously possessed, netherworld, outcast— "pariah"—groups. Such as: teenagers, artists & bohemians (or "hippies"), Negroes, narcotics users, homosexuals & camp culturati. They have felt out of it, so they have banded into status groups and created their own styles of life, to fortify their own morale. And now—Santa Barranza!—here are "socialites" slithering and jerking among them, taking up their styles, doing the most *delicious slumming*.

Shit! Fuck! & Other Polite Interjections. In Society, currently, the words *shit* and *fuck* are used as routine expletives by both men and women. More elaborate but quite common expressions refer to quaint anatomical impossibilities. No one's eyebrows arch today when the most *chic* and charming young ladies in Society say such things as:

"Look, pussycat, I've taken just about enough shit from him, I mean, fuck! You know? Next time I'm just going to tell him, 'Go fuck yourself, pussycat.'"

The Etiquette of Pot. From Negroes, for example, Society has drawn its favorite form of insult, the "put on." From narcotics users Society has acquired a few "hip" expressions, but chiefly it has acquired, in a word, *pot*, which is marijuana. Most of New York Society's "hip" expressions are actually what is known as "square hip" among the narcotics avant garde, which is in California. In

California one refers to marijuana as "grass." New York's top people are stuck with pot.

The use of marijuana in New York today has almost the same status as the use of alcohol during Prohibition; which is to say, it is a minor vice that is largely winked at in the upper reaches of Society because of its very prevalence. It is more than winked at; its illegality lends it the luster of daring; it is the stuff of legends and reminiscences. There is no whisky bore alive who is so boring as a true pot bore.

In Society, hosts and hostesses should, preferably, have marijuana on hand, even if they do not use it themselves. In any case, they should never object to their guests' using it. The table manners of marijuana have changed markedly since the early days (1964). In the early days, the marijuana cigarette (joint) was passed from hand to hand between drags (tokes) in order not to waste the weed, since it was hard to get. Similarly, it was inhaled with a vigorous and esoteric display of air-sucking, lung-expansion, and eyeball-bugging. The butt (roach) was saved, to be added to more marijuana in the future or mixed with cigarette tobacco and smoked as a "cocktail." Pot heads made a big point of saying that they did not drink; alcohol users were considered bourgeois dullards with a dreary, mind-clotting vice. That was in the early days.

Today, in Society, the use of marijuana is in the "second convolution" phase. The joint is smoked like an ordinary cigarette and, preferably, there is one per person. Bug-eyed air-suckers are regarded as *square hip*, which is worse than merely being square, since it bears the connotation of failed pretensions. The butt is thrown away. Marijuana smokers today are also "second convolution" about alcohol. They now regard it as a low-grade but pleasant sort of drug, a convenient *downer*, and even sip it while smoking marijuana or hashish. Hashish, incidentally, is socially preferable to marijuana because of its more exotic aroma, dearer price, and cultural credentials (Coleridge, Baudelaire, *et alii*).

Social Negroes. Pariahs! Poets, bohos, photographers, music-hall Englishmen . . . Negroes . . . Social Negroes, part of the new style of life. One good Negro at dinner, even if he chooses to sit there and lacerate these poor white liberals—"What you people don't see—what you people don't *want* to see is—" yes, yes, nod, nod, and never mind, he is Our Negro tonight—Negroes! Yes. Lately, however, there has been a new social Negro of a rather engaging variety. Some white, chunky, raspberry-mottled lawyer puts down his $100 for two tickets to the Emphysema Ball at the St. Regis roof, and he and his wife are seated between a *very nice*, as they word it later, a very nice sharkskin and taffeta Negro couple—and he says, "Hello," and the colored woman says, without preamble, "I work for Mr. C—." Mr. C—'s maid. That's nice. Old C—, he got fed up to here with charity dinners, the whole monkey charity route, so he gets it up as usual, the $100, but gives his tickets to the maid, who brings her husband along, and they sit there along with everybody else amid the white and gold, sandwiched into the St. Regis roof room, while stertorous Italian waiters drift their larded bellies over the back of one's head, handing out the *saumon fumée*, to all, assembly-line style. Yes! Fashion! The *chic* thing, today, as they say, is to send one's Negro maid to the abominable charity dinners and then say, "I told them I'd gladly pay not to have to go myself."

The "pariah" styles generally have led to a condition curiously kin to French Society under Louis XIV at Versailles. Louis caused a separation of "power" and "grandeur." Power, under Louis, tended to be in the hands of rather plain men, often bourgeois. "Grandeur" was the preserve of his courtiers. They performed all the decorative displays and functions that made Louis' Court Society one of the most elaborate in history. It is the same in New York today with the men of power in government, finance, and industry. For example, they, almost to a man, refused invitations to Truman Capote's famous masked ball of 1966. But all of New York's "grandeur" was there; as always, it is far more fragile beings—artists, uptown bohos, and the like—who exhibit . . . most gloriously . . . the styles that make up Society's new style of life. The comparison, curiously, extends even further. Under Louis, the manners of Society varied sharply from those of respectable persons elsewhere in France. Only at Versailles did men ask to be let into a room by scraping on the door with an elongated little fingernail. Likewise, the manners of New York Society today are sharply divided from those in the rest of the country.

The Social Kiss. Only in New York, for example, is the social kiss such a favored form of greeting. The social kiss is an ancient form of exhibiting one's status. Herodotus wrote of the Persians' elaborate status kissing: equals kissed each other on the lips; near-equals, on the cheeks; inferiors prostrated themselves before superiors. Constantine Porphyrogenitus, in his manual on etiquette, goes on and on for pages, elaborating on who kisses whom, where—on the head, the hands, the breast, lips or cheek, or wherever. In New York Society, the social kiss follows the pattern of European royalty. Members of royal families—wet smack! —always embrace each other in public, even if they loathe each other to the point of odium or have never laid eyes on each other before. In New York Society even men have taken to giving each other the social kiss, after the manner of Show Biz, in which the kiss says: Who else is there but glamourosi like us, baby?

What is one to do? Get on his high horse over the

blatancy of the new etiquette, the boorishness of it all, the
cotillion-level snobbishness? Many worthwhile, secure, sincere, famous people try to pull out—but suddenly they
find they're not seeing *anybody* anymore. They can cut all
monkey dinners—but it almost means cutting out dinners
altogether. They are not going to put up with hopped-up
kids with Rudi Gernreich plastic breasties and vinyl thighs,
who come to dinner and say "Oh, fuck!" at the table, but
this soon means they are not putting up with social life,
period. So even the Worthwhile People go along with it—
just to have something, anything at all, to go along with.
They let themselves be used in monkey manners—they
give monkey parties for use by others—why fight it—the
only game in town! So for everybody, even these Nicies
everybody used to look to like lodestars of "true" civility,
manners take on a subconscious cynicism. No one feels a
sense of obligation toward the social gestures of others. Just
because Robin and Ellen invited Cork and Fan to their
dinner, to their place in the Hamptons, to their evening "at
the rock 'n' roll"—that wild evening when they reserved
thirty seats at this just too-Mafia roadhouse on Route 22
in New Jersey to hear—greasy little goslings!—a group
called The Sonic Booms—that does not mean Cork and
Fan will feel any special obligation to invite Robin and
Ellen to their dinner, their place in the Hamptons or their
"Big Lunch" at an Eighth Avenue pool hall where Brock
ripped up a table doing a *masse*—the sign *said* no *masses*,
Alva said—and everybody said Alva did it, and Alva was
humiliated by a large man eating a filthy sandwich, who
insinuated that Alva was a fairy, an East Side fairy. What a
time that was! Nobody feels obligated to *repay* social
favors because that is based on an old notion of simple,
naïve kindness. Simple naïve kindness! The truth is, today,
people are going to invite one *anyway* as long as one is
useful, decorative—*worth* it. And if one suddenly falls

from grace, they are *not* going to invite him, no matter how many social *debts* he has in his favor. So, why respond? Why bother to write thank-you notes, why call up after these fantastic, fat parties? So no one does and—miracle!—at last New York reaches the pure state where *it*—status—is laid right out on the line. Nirvana! Promised land! Sweet monkey universe.

11 The Life & Hard Times of a Teenage London Society Girl

ANY MOMENT NOW, little Sue, Chinless Wonder at the wheel here will pull to a stop and say one of two things to you. He will either say he has a terrible headache, or he will say—let's go to my flat. *With this supercool tomato-aspic look on his face;* let's go to my flat. Sue feels very *right* in the sense of *right people*. She is starved to near perfection. Her London fashionable chrome yellow straight hair hangs down to her shoulder blades and it looks . . . *right*. Which it should, since it is freshly ironed. She ironed it herself on an ironing board. But exactly!

Little Sue squints out between her new eyelashes like a camel and observes Chinless' nose, which sticks out above his lips like—well, one doesn't know what it is like, but his nose is large and sculptural and his lips are like a little sugarbud cherry-centered chocolate. All right? More perfection.

They are driving along Maida Avenue, W.2, in the so-called Little Venice section, and he cocks the wheel of the Mini-Cooper and sends it into a four-wheeled drift, London is full of such *fierce* Mini-aces, one understands, and they skid, drift, bump, bump, and the tapir leaves and iron pickets and decayed stucco of Little Venice go by in the dark like . . . oh, like something all scrambled up, like a brain salad.

Being exceptionally bright and alert at the party, Sue didn't catch his name, but he looks like a kind of Crispian Fetlock-Withers. One knows? But suppose he doesn't even ask her to his flat? Suppose she doesn't stir the slightest surge of concupiscence up into his soft sexless crispy chinless shanks. Too humiliating! Belinda will know about it. Nicki will know about it. Mary the Heathfield girl who was so . . . boring and condescending at the party, she will know about it.

Sue sinks back into the Mini-seat and closes her new eyelashes. Crunch. She feels anxious and defensive. She puts her fingers in her hair, like Belinda, and plays the harp in the air with her hair. Belinda is beginning to do some modeling, and all the successful models play the harp in the air with their hair. They also put their sunglasses on the tablecloth and admire themselves in the reflection.

Belinda—starved to near perfection . . . this "starved to near perfection" thing is from a poem Nicki started about Belinda, "Starved to near perfection, with her Kurdish clubfoot lover—" That is so great, Sue hates it. Nicki has a friend on *Queen* magazine and Sue dreads the day she picks up *Queen* and there will be Nicki's name: *a writer*. Belinda actually has a Kurdish clubfoot lover and a career, sort of. And Sue has . . . Crispy Chinless, per-haps. Of course, Belinda and Nicki are older than Sue. They are both 17. Sue is 16. Careers, kinky lovers, camel eyes, ironed hair, clubfoot love, status-and-sex, getting *planked* just to be sociable—oh christ, it gets to be a drag being a teenage Society girl in London today.

Crispy Chinless! He picked her up at this brainless Heathfield creature's deb cocktail party. Sue, like Nicki and Belinda and everybody, goes to these parties for the precise purpose of being picked up by the sort of boys Heathfields have around them, like him. Heathfields are the sort of girls who go, or went, to boarding schools like Heathfield, near Ascot, where Princess Alexandra went, or Benenden, where Princess Anne goes, or Cheltenham Ladies' School, which is to say, upper-class girls of good blood, good bone. Sue, and Belinda and Nicki, are . . . well—if it isn't too embarrassing to say so—middle-class, or upper bourgeois, girls who go, or went, to fashionable London day schools like Greycoats, St. Paul's, Town and Country, the French Lycée, and maybe even a couple from North London Collegiate School and Holland Park Comprehensive, where Anthony Wedgwood Benn's children go.

Anyway, the Heathfields speak of these middle-class Society girls as Dollies. That is supposed to be derisive, but it shows that they are worried. They ought to be worried. For the first time in the history of London, the Heathfield girls are slightly out of it. Sue means—well, she looked around at the party, and admittedly her new eyelashes were so heavy, she felt like she was a camel. All the Dollies look like camels, with their necks thrust forward, squinting out from between these huge false eyelashes. But that is better than the Heathfields. The Heathfields all go in for all this faky eye makeup, eye liners and everything and a lot of paint, just like a bunch of little mod shop girls on Oxford Street. It is very cheap and moddy looking. They also do a lot of very common things with their hair. They still go in for back-combing, just like the little mod girls. Everybody has picked up the *mod* thing, of course, but the Dollies are more . . . original. One means, one has a career, a kinky lover, a—

—oh, but let's admit it, my god, the Heathfields can still use the old snob business, and they are very good at it, Sue will admit that. There are these little things they know how to do, and no matter how many times one tells oneself they are brainless little nits, it gets one. At the party, for example, Sue runs into Mary, the Heathfield, and she says, "Hello, Mary! How are you!"

"Why, I'm absolutely *fi-i-i-i-ine!*" says Mary, without saying Sue's name, of course. Sue, the Dolly, says Mary's name, but Mary, the Heathfield, doesn't say Sue's. I'm absolutely fine. The way she said it! As if to say, of course I'm fine. What else did you think I'd be, a miserable, uncertain, hopeless little suck-up trying to suck up to people, like you are?

Then they close ranks and start talking to each other in these completely . . . Heathfield voices they have, kind of even, even, even, oiled-up voices with little lilts at the end of sentences, except when they throw in the Cockney, they like Cockney rhyming slang, they'll say "tit-fer" for "hat," which comes from the Cockney rhyming slang, "tit-fer-tat" equals "hat," they think "tit-fer" is especially funny, even though they are saying the same old things they said this afternoon at this place they go to, Luba's.

" . . . Jenny's got the curse and Jeremy's got the mini . . . "

" . . . one *can't* very well, *can* one, when one has to get Celia's present *and* go to the Viva ball . . ."

" . . . Celia! Too *spastic* . . ."

—they're always rushing to get some girl a wedding present, even though she is spastic, they use that word all the time, spastic, everyone and everything is spastic to the Heathfields, and the ball they're going to is always in Paris, or, rather, *one* is going to Paris, because one never says *I*, one says *one*, which makes it sound like whatever they do is being sanctioned by the whole community of . . . right people—

—talking, talking, talking, and they don't *listen* to *any*-thing, Mary was telling Sue she had found this absolutely super boutique on Carnaby Street, Lady Jane, and Sue said she didn't think it was so super, because she had gone in there and blah blah blah, and so forth, and Mary is obviously just waiting for Sue's lips to stop moving, because after all that she just says, "Yes, well, Lady Jane is a *super* place," she even says super the same way again, because why *should* she listen to Sue, who is Sue—

God! Sue has never been able to talk about any of this to her parents, inasmuch as they, of course . . . are the whole thing. The Heathfields always have these great parents, who are always either landed gentry or deceased. It's awful, but Sue once had this fantasy and it was a very curious feeling. In this fantasy her parents . . . were deceased. She was at a party and she was introduced to some people . . . "d'you know . . . *mumble* . . . how d'je do" . . . and then the conversation would get around to this and that and finally that . . . her parents . . . were deceased. She felt *right*. That's *horrible* to even reveal! Actually she loves her parents. Sometimes she practically cries over them, *sympathetically*. You know? They have *tried* so hard. Her father's family has been prominent in London, or, well, wealthy in London, for two generations, and he has made a great deal of money selling paper products in Europe and they have a, really, very large flat on Eaton Square and they have accumulated all the right things, these Tabriz and Bokhara rugs, Tilliard chairs, fruitwood sideboards, Grosvenor Street lamps, books, books, books, a Servant, a not bad collection of sort of School-of-Stubbs paintings, plus a Braque in the hall, which he got for 800 guineas in 1953, to show that they are *with it*, but they have all these second-rate friends in for dinner, these terribly correct Americans or these businessmen with processed accents that come to pieces when they get drunk, and Mother always comes on like overripe *switched-on* in a Pucci dress or something, why is it only old women wear Pucci, and after dinner Daddy has this really terrible *pipe* thing he goes through, bringing out this pipe and going through this hideously cozy, homey thing with a lot of sucking noises and tamping and tapping his teeth reflectively with the pipestem and Mother always brings up something like the Pinter plays with this voice of fruity cultural reverence that makes one want to vomit—*blegggh*—they don't have the slightest comprehension of what Sue's life is all about and why she really couldn't bring someone like Mary the Heathfield into the house.

She knows what *that* would be like! Sue happened to be on a train once with a lot of boarding-school girls who were coming back from an outing in the Lake Country. They all had on their little blue jackets. There were four of them in her compartment. One girl was the odd girl out, obviously. The other three kept doing things like forcing her to give her opinion on something and then ripping her to shreds for it. She couldn't cope with it. All she could figure out to do was to try to be correct, to give the right answers with the right accent, but of course they practically mocked her little pants off for that.

Finally she got off at Crewe. She left the compartment and the porter was helping her off with her things, and one of the three girls said, *"Let's look at the parents."* The poor girl's parents had come to the station to pick her up and there is the big family scene on the platform. So the three girls all press their faces against the window inside the compartment and go through this elaborate pantomime of waving and grinning as if they thought this girl was the greatest girl on the face of the earth and they were saying goodbye in a great big hearty chum-chum schoolgirl way. Actually, what they were saying were things like, "Oh, my god, look at *the mother*." And there was the girl's mother out there on the platform, a pleasant-looking woman, as they used to say of Mrs. Khrushchev, not exactly soignée, one understands, wearing a plain gray suit and a blouse that was obviously rayon and a kind of ratty department store coat and—"Ooo, look at *the father!* The mustache! The pipe! The trousers! He's dear!"—and the father looked all right except that he was one of those men with a pot belly who tries to cover it up by wearing his pants up high so that the belt seems to come up to about his chest, and the potty gut swells out under the fly front like he is pregnant or something, and he has this, well, one can't describe it, hopelessly Midlands middle-class mustache—and the pipe —the pipe seems to tell it all—and "Goodbye! Goodbye!"—and the Heathfields are faking all these waves and smiles through the window like maniacs, so that *the mother* and *the father* look over and wave back, it is so nice that their daughter has these wonderful, hearty schoolgirl friends on the train in their nice little school jackets—they wave at the nice little girls and smile—*the father* waves, *the mother* waves, and *the mother* is particularly carried away and does a little cutesy jiggle with her head as she waves— *Ooo!—Ooo!*—and oh god, *that* is *too much*, the three girls dissolve right there at the window, they start laughing their heads off—Oggggggggggggggh—wawwwwww—waw- wwwwww—and three upperclass English schoolgirls are all writhing in the window in this spastic laughing fit, and outside the platform, on the other side of the glass, *the mother* and *the father* can't figure out quite what has happened, their smiles and waves kind of freeze in mid-air, but the girl, she knows exactly what has happened, and the look on her face is pure humiliation and terror and desolation, and the train starts pulling off with the scene just like that —and Sue is not bringing Mary the Heathfield into *her* house. That *pipe,* for a start . . .

Sue's mother wants to have this big mother-daughter thing with her, but she doesn't understand anything. She gets upset, for example, when she finds Sue ironing her hair on the ironing board. Well, good Lord, it's nothing very extraordinary. Everybody she knows, or everybody with the hair, blond hair, does it. She kneels down on the floor and puts her head on the ironing board and lays her hair out on it and then *irons* it. She puts the iron on medium. The ironing straightens it out into that perfect London fashionable straight blond hair look, like Queen Guinevere drawn by Arthur Rackham or something, and it also gives it a shine. All right! It is weird to see some girl with her head on the ironing board, her cheek pressed down there, and her eyes are kind of glazed out at a weird angle and she is ironing her own hair—but who is there to watch? And it *looks great* afterward.

The Dollies will *do* things like that. The thing is, it isn't Sue's fault what London Society is like. The whole world is divided into four categories, the mods, the intellectuals, the Dollies and the Heathfields. The mods are working-class girls, shop girls, clerks and so forth. They started all the new styles, strangely enough, but they are totally brainless and *the voices*—they are not to be imagined. The intellectuals are girls the Dollies run into, chiefly. They are the daughters of intellectuals, these dowdy teachers and journalists and things, and they mock everything the Dollies do as "trendy," everything is "trendy," but they carry around books like *The Portable Gibbons* that their boyfriends told them to read—Gibbons!—and they go off to hear folk singers at the Albert Hall and they wear sandals and get in these stupid demonstrations. It's all too squalid, actually. So that leaves the Dollies and the Heathfields.

The thing is—there is this period in an English teenage Society girl's life from the time when she leaves school, at 16 or 17, to the time she gets married, and there has never been anything to do, really, except go to parties. In

America, these girls would all go off to college, but very few do in England. Some go off to finishing school in Switzerland, to Montesano or Gstaad or someplace like that. But mainly there is nothing to do but think about clothes, beauty and parties.

But then this whole *mod* thing started, all the styles and everything, and it was just like in the Regency Period, the upper classes suddenly adopting the styles of the lower orders, the pariah styles, for a kick—and this gave the Dollies their opening. They started going classless—or at least breaking rules the Heathfields had always imposed.

The Heathfields, for example, are absolutely committed to the idea of being anti-*cerebral*, anti-*earnest*, anti-*committed*, anti doing anything that involves looking like one is trying too hard. After a Heathfield leaves school, for example, the only kind of job she can take is something so mindless that it is perfectly obvious she is not serious about it. So Heathfields end up behind the soda fountain at Fortnum's or they are photographers' assistants, or, once in a while, secretaries, although that is already getting a bit *hearty* about it.

In the new era, being assistant to some socially tolerable photographer is just about it, although even then Heathfields do not feel altogether right. Once Belinda had a job modeling and the photographer took her out into Hyde Park for some pictures and this Heathfield was his assistant, and as they all trooped out into the park, the Heathfield kept . . . falling behind, walking in the most unconcerned, distracted way—so no one would think she was part of this sleazy commercial caravan.

The Dollies, meanwhile, discovered careers and business, all of it connected one way or another with the new styles. Belinda—starved to near perfection!—has started modeling, Nicki is going to have something in *Queen* probably— and she already has this business going, selling these fabu-

234 : *The Pump House Gang*

lous sweaters they knit on these Greek Islands. It is a big
thing among the Dollies to carry around invoice pads
instead of engagement books. The Heathfields all have
these leather engagement books that cost about a guinea,
and it really got to Mary once when she was making a date
with Nicki over something or other and she pulled out her
leather book with the gold tooling on it and Nicki pulled
out an invoice pad and wrote it down on the back. Mary
gave her such a look, of doubt and wonder. The thing is,
this is the kind of *déclassé* gesture Heathfields used to
specialize in.

The Dollies get *involved* in fashion, so they know how
to look. One can always tell a Heathfield. They try the
mod thing, but they are always too . . . matched up. A
Heathfield will go to Biba, the boutique, and get one of
these cheap coat-and-trousers suits in maroon and yellow
for about £5—and then go buy a pair of shoes to match it
for £10 and then go to Gucci's to get a yellow handbag to
match it for £40, and after it is all over, it all looks—well,
matched up.

Dollies are more original. This dress Sue has on—she
went to Portobello Road and bought it secondhand, in one
of those shops. It is made of mandarin-orange velvet, with
the hem about five inches above the knees and the bodice
low and cut straight across with just straps over the shoulder, sort of 1926 Tart, if one knows what she means, with
the upper parts of her breasts showing there like two
trembling servings of flan. The Heathfields would never
think of going to Portobello Road to find something like
that. They just go to Portobello Road to be on Portobello
Road. That one time Sue ran into three debs she knew on
Portobello Road and two of them had on black velvet
trousers and coats, all matched up, of course, completely
tacky looking, and she walked along with them and suddenly along came a whole group of girls from the school

they had gone to, in their blazers and the whole thing on a
school outing—and God, the three went into an absolute
orgy of nostalgia right there on the street, they threw their
arms around each other and said, "My God! remember
when we were like that! My God!"—and so forth and so
on, watching this parade of little girls all pallid from mashy
food, all squatty from sticky food, out on their outing—
"My God, remember when we were like that!"—it having
been all of one year or two years when they were like that,
this big orgy of nostalgia, we precious few, with Sue just
watching, poor Sue, she couldn't possibly understand what
this fantastic experience of having gone to this boarding
school and being on outings was like. They are always
talking about their outings. They won't go to museums,
plays, concerts, because they say they *did* all of that on
their outings at school. They won't go to foreign movies
because they are too peasant intellectual. Their idea of a
great movie is *Dr. Zhivago.* Sue once asked a Heathfield to
come see *Knife in the Water* with her, and the Heathfield
said, "Isn't that by some *Pole?*"

Of course, that is *stu*pid, *cret*inous, *brain*less—and yet
there they are, this procession of pallid, mashy, squatty,
sticky little girls, marching on, nevertheless, to victory, so
they can stand on the goddamned Portobello Road in tacky
black velvet and sob and clutch one another and say, My
God, remember when we were like that—because we *are* all
like one another, and we *cohere* like some cellular animal
from out the primordial ooze and we leave all the little
Sues, the poor Sues, out on the fringes, to watch and covet
and look away as if unconcerned, just writing captions in
the sky, counting flowers on the wall . . .

Anyway, Crispian Chinless, this boy, whatever his name
is, picked Sue up at the party. He said let's have dinner and
go to the Garrison Club. That would be absolutely fine.

Everybody leaving the party was going to the Garrison Club. Everybody was saying, See you at the Garrison, the Garrison, the Garrison and all of a sudden Sue was practically wearing Crispian Chinless like a medallion and she heard herself shrieking, See you at the Garrison. She could picture it. She would walk into the club with her certified Crispian Fetlock-Withers and there amid the blood-pudding plush and wax-my-filthy-military-mustache-brown leather and these faky lamps, which look like they were made of the Kaiser's old helmets with light bulbs screwed in—there will be Nicki and Belinda and Mary, the Heathfield girl, and they will see her walking in like that. That's it! They will *see* it. One understands?

The only thing is, Crispian Chinless didn't take her to dinner at the Garrison but at this sort of turtle-neck sweater restaurant, the 235, on King's Road—*the 235.* Then it became obvious that they weren't going to the Garrison at all. And now Crispy is doing all this faky ace driving around Little Venice, leading up to the point where he says let's go to my flat—or he dumps her.

Dumps her! God, and after all that See you at the Garrison thing. Already the middle-class Dollies, like Nicki and Belinda, and the Heathfields, like Mary, will be at the Garrison, only she won't be there, but *they* will be there, with the Heathfields being supercool and the Dollies shrieking too much with gaiety and excitement. Someone will be shrieking, "No, no, no, no, no"—the Dollies get excited and never say no or yes just once—it is always "No, no, no, no, no," five times, a predictable meter, "No, no, no, no, no! Here's the way she did it"—and then they always start in on how some poor girl, such as Sandy, a middle-class girl, never a Heathfield, somehow, made some ridiculous gesture, walked down the street moving her hips or something, although none of the Dollies has anything to brag about, not even Belinda or Nicki. The Dollies run the wrong way. Everything flops out to the sides like bird wings, their legs flop out like a rag doll's, as if they were hinged sideways, their little breasts flop out and they shriek and scream. The Heathfields—one can't even remember seeing a Heathfield run. They *don't* run. That is the whole thing.

The Heathfields don't run they don't shriek. Their whole thing is to remain . . . supercool. Bore bore bore bore bore bore. Sue was once in Mary the Heathfield's house and she found a piece of paper and Mary had been writing over and over again on the typewriter bore bore bore bore bore, just that, and Sue was—well, she wished she had typed that out herself on a piece of paper and casually left it lying around . . . but—

The Heathfields don't make faces while they talk, either. The Dollies make faces. They pull up their noses like a rabbit and they push out that little bag of skin with their tongues, whatever it is called, bag of skin, *bleggggh*—anyway, it runs from the lower lip to the chin and covers the lower teeth, oh christ, well, it is right there on one's face—anyway, they push it out to register general disapproval of whatever it is, such as Sandy's "funny shape."

They are all so paranoically concerned with the most minute things of style and acceptability, they go into incredible clinical detail about peoples' funny shapes, about how Sandy . . . *lumps out* at the hips and—shriek, scream —her legs don't . . . *move right*, and then Nicki makes a funny motion with her ischium to indicate how Sandy's trousers are always . . . *too tight*, which means they have . . . *too many creases*, and then everyone goes into this clinical orgy of telling just what creases and crevices they are talking about, such as the bottom ones where her buttocks meet her thighs, and another one at the top of the bikini panties—they talk about all this—and then these . . . *crevices*, fore and aft—one *means*, shriek, scream—

where the trousers practically disappear . . . *up her—* shriek! scream! oh! oh!

Sue shrieks, screams, laughs, mocks, reviles Sandy with the rest—but doesn't she remember the first pair of trousers she had made. Does she or doesn't she! Oh Lord. It was the most incredible mixture of sex and status. At first it was all status. She was almost 15 and she had to have a pair of tight trousers made. But then there was this funny moment. The tailor was a fairly old man, about 55 or something, and he had to measure along the inside of her thigh. It was strange! He was this old man, and he *was* a tailor, after all, it was his business, but he had to slide his horny old bellrope hand with the tape right up the inside of her thigh and measure, because the trousers have to be about this tight—and it . . . was sexual! Yes! Not in the usual way, but, well, one doesn't know how to put it, it was sexual.

And when she first put them on—this was a feeling she couldn't even tell Nicki and Belinda about in one of those clinical discussions where there is a great premium on talking about intimate things that *people don't talk about*, about heavy periods, for example, about how Nicki bets certain Negro singers with "soul" have very heavy periods, that sort of thing. Anyway, Sue put the trousers on and she could feel the trousers gripping her whole sacred ischial dark damp taboo wonderland of folds, flaps, integuments, tissues . . . just so. She felt sexually excited and at the same time . . . *with it*, a term, of course, she would never let pass her lips except sarcastically. It was sex but it was status and it was status but it was sex. And in a moment— her Crispy Fetlock-Withers is going to say either he has a headache or let's go to my flat.

Sex and status! The whole thing is that Crispy Chinless has got to *want* to take her to his flat, he has got to find her that attractive, and then she can report back to Nicki and

Belinda, if not Mary the Heathfield, and this bit of urgency
. . . *submerges* the whole prospect of what it is likely to
be like once they get to his flat. Like that awful thing that
happened to Sandy with the photographer, or whatever he
was, last fall. Sandy went to a deb party and got picked up
by a smashing-looking photographer-he-said. He was
dressed like Bill Travers playing Toulouse-Lautrec. His flat
was way out on Fulham Road and four flights up and he had
no electricity or gas and just a mattress on the floor. He lit
a Primus stove. It was horrid but Sandy did not want to
lose face. Afterward he barged into the flat downstairs to
use a towel. There was a lot of fetching and heaving about
down there, and yelling.

It was so squalid Sandy could hardly tell *that* to Sue and
Nicki and Belinda, either, but of course she did, finally,
leaving out the parts about the electricity, the Primus stove
and the towel. Also, she made fun of the photographer-he-
said when she told the story. The thing is, that is one way
the Dollies have of being superior to the Heathfields.
They are more worldy, more independent. They have
lovers. At 17, or certainly at 18, it is important to have a
lover—well, to be able to talk about a lover, at least. Old
randy yobbo photographers-he-said with filthy mattresses
and filthy Primus stoves and filthy towels and filthy lives are
not quite it. The point is to have someone like Belinda's
Kurdish clubfoot lover. He is a student in Paris and an
exile-he-says from Persia, and when he is in London, she
does wild things like go to Harrod's with him and steal
things, China cups with the Queen's beasts on them, a
stupid frozen crab from that big room on the first floor, all
sorts of crazy things, and then go tell everybody about it
at Grumbles, this restaurant place.

Oh christ, Nicki in Paris with her Kurdish clubfoot
lover. Cartridge belts, daggers, machine guns and Clubfoot
defying the Persian tyrant with Neo-Concrete verse. Sue

used to lie in bed and . . . *envision* Nicki and her Kurdish
clubfoot lover, she would close her eyes, a few wild
whippy rug designs would spin out behind her eyelids and
always the scene would not be Paris but someplace on a
beach, like on a Greek island, and Nicki and her Kurdish
clubfoot lover would be in a rowboat. Why!—but in a
rowboat all the same, with the sun going down, and Sue
could never see his clubfoot, she could just feel the fabulous . . . *idea* of it.

A 17-year-old English girl's lover can't just be an atten-
tive nicey, lapping her hand and rubbing against her shins.
He must be exciting to talk about. A successful photographer is all right, a real photographer, that is, oh christ,
photography is suddenly such a big thing, a boutique
owner is all right, even a man who has a hairdressing place
if he isn't *too* odious, actors, designers, nobody in television, but occasionally, *blegghh*, a journalist, if he is thin and
isn't baggy in the pants and hasn't got that sort of pulpy
Pablum pubby puddle in the jowls. One can't go out with a
boy one's own age at all, a student, one can't go out with
a . . . *boy*, period, unless it is some student from Paris or
something, a dark boy with a fashionable accent, something
of that sort. One must—well, one must have a lover one
can talk about, for godsake, and that makes it sexy, or
doesn't one understand that one hardly ever *feels* sex without status?

Sue would like to feel that the Heathfield debs have been
too sheltered or simply do not know about Kurdish delights,
filthy flats, Primus stoves, but she knows that is not true.
As a matter of fact, there are all those upper-class types
who go down to Italy in the summer as *au pair* girls and
work in resort discothèques and they make absolutely
nothing, but the whole thing is exquisite madness. They
call themselves The Witches and they drive these poor
Italian men absolutely wild. Italian men! They are so

quaint. In Rome, for example, *wicked Rome*. They have this quaint old notion about *seduction*, and if they sleep with a young, tender, blond English teenage Society girl, their little chicken chests puff out and they have accomplished *a seduction*. They haven't the faintest notion about English girls, Dollies or Heathfields. A girl just says, well, she is bored, she will take that one, bang bang, poor little puffy-breasted Italiano, always sneaking glances in the mirror, for a start, to try to look sexy, no, *romantic*, that is about the way they think, and they twitter in their throats while they—

—Well, sometimes it gets out of hand, however, one must admit. Sue was visiting a couple of—well, upper-class girls—in Paris—these girls were living in a funny little street, the rue de Savoie, way up in a kind of garrety building. Anyway, they were all balling Italian cats, as the Negroes say. One day an Englishman in an English suit turned up and announced that he had been asked by ———, who is the most utterly typical Devonshire squire-sort-of-thing, to come to Paris and retrieve his daughter, Mary. This is *another* Mary. Well, she hadn't been back in the flat for five days, for godsake, in fact, that was how it was that there was a bed for Sue in the first place, but this Englishman said, well, he would just wait there. He was a little prepossessing. He kept telling a boring theory he had about how it was easier to get around Paris if one didn't speak French, because the French spend all their time being irritable in small ways, which he had to enumerate, of course.

But every morning he would show up and wait, as if he had signed a bond of blood and honor with old Squire to bring Mary back, and sometimes there would be this awkward thing when Elizabeth, one of the girls, would come out from behind this big sheet they had thrown up as a screen with her Italian lover, a skinny little man, and go out and get some arty, picturesque fish or sausage thing for an arty, picturesque breakfast with her Italian lover, while the Englishman sat there in a striped shirt looking black in the tongue and the Italian sat there looking languid and O-desolate-youth and how-do-you-like-my-jawline-and-my-tight-pants and nobody said anything. Well, finally one morning Mary came dragging up there, *God,* she looked hideous. She had on these *cheap* sunglasses and a huge dirty raincoat and her hair looked like a clotty hall mop. She looked so bad it wasn't even funny. The Englishman could hardly say anything even after waiting all that time. It turned out she had gone the whole route. She had an . . . *operation* . . . on a back street in Naples—*Naples*—well, one *means* . . .

But the Heathfields don't talk about that. A Dolly might. What the Heathfields like to talk about is touring the South of France with someone like Prince Thing of Thing or the Earl of Thing or The Hon. Thing. It is very annoying, the whole thing about holidays. It is one of the places where class tells, as they say. The Heathfields always have summer holidays of weeks, months at a time in super places in France, Spain, Italy, Switzerland; Antibes, Biarritz, places like that. It is not just that it costs a great deal of money to have holidays like this, because plenty of Dollies' parents have the money, and they go to the South of France for the holidays or to some squalid place in Spain, God, Spain is squalid, and the South of France is a total drag, but anyway it is the whole . . . thing about the way the Heathfields do it. The whole thing is not to spend the holidays with one's parents and to travel around from one fabulous place to another, visiting fabulous friends in fabulous villas and palazzos and castellos and to do this, one has to be part of the . . . *réseau,* the network, and only the Heathfields have this network of families and friends, in Antibes, Biarritz, Venice, Capri, all established and waiting and casual, surrounded by servitors who seem to be happy about it—all set up and natural and . . . *right*.

The Dollies try to make the most of weekends in Paris or a week in Paris, and they all go to Paris and they all hit the circuit and they all go to the same places, Castel's, New Jimmy's, or Bilboquet if nobody has much money. And last summer, God, it was too much to see, everybody was wearing knit dresses last summer, very sexy, one understands, but so *god*damned hot, and there was everybody packed into these squatty little rooms doing the Frug or the Fat or the Two-backed Beast or something and sweating like a pig under all that knitted wool, all this expensive sweat pouring out of expensive skin and everyone keeps on grinning and showing teeth, drinking white lethal spirits and wrenching and bucking their little cupcakes and giblets about, until the onset of dawn or saline depletion, whichever.

Crispian Chinless turns his head, then does a lot of trick stuff with the steering wheel and his trick engine sounds and his little trick Crispian lips and comes hurtling to a stop like a centrifuge and turns to Sue—

—then his head oscillates back and then flops like a big fat eggplant into his hand, and he wipes his forehead with his palm and then he says in this terribly composed gassiness of agony!

"You know"—only he says "know" as if it were kneeee-ooooow, as if he had a polyhedron in his mouth and he just wrapped "know" around it, breaking it into 12 syllables—"I think I had a poisoned trout at lunch. D'you kneeeeeeeooooouuuuw? It's—"

A poi-soned trout?

Nicki! Belinda! And *you*, you . . . puce-faced little instrument of one's puce-faced little fate . . . Chinless Crispian's tomato aspic lips are moving and words are coming out. He is *very sorry*, but Sue doesn't hear it.

Humiliation is coming into her brain like steam, so that she cannot hear, her mind starts racing, she starts ransacking the evening, moment by moment, god, what was it she said when he said whatever it was just before they went to the *235—the 235—*could that have been it, what she said—oh christ, but she *isn't* Belinda, after all, she isn't.

Starved to near perfection, with her Kurdish clubfoot lover—

12 *The Private Game*

THE HELL with the American hormone-ointment magnates losing their hulking gourds at the chemin de fer table
at Aspinall's. The hell with the electric-blue Greeks playing it cool and black at Crockford's. The hell with the
yobbo punters—Yob-bo!—who keep falling off the curb
in front of Mr. Smith's and getting their arses broken. The
hell with George Raft's registered and copyrighted silver
grin at the Colony—

—just a little private game here. A little private game. I
took a cab and about midnight I pulled up in front of a
house on —— Street. There was a young man in his
shirtsleeves under the portico blowing ram-jam vapor trails
into the darkness. It was fairly cool out and he was having
a hell of a time blowing these tricky vapor trails into the
darkness.

I figured he was a lookout, so I got out of the cab and
walked up and introduced myself and stuck out my hand
to shake hands. This must have startled him, because he
gave me his hand like he was surrendering a packet of
contraband Jello. I guess nobody shakes hands with the
Tea Boy in England. That was what he turned out to be, a

tea boy, which is to say, somebody a club has around, usually a kid but sometimes some old guy, to go get tea, coffee, sandwiches, run errands, and so forth, for the punters at the game, check coats, or be a lookout, I suppose.

He motions for me to come on inside, into the foyer, or downstairs hall. I tell him who it is I am a friend of, and he says just a moment and goes into a room off the hall. It is absolutely quiet in here. There is just a lot of dark plaster on the walls and a couple of medieval chairs on the floor and a draft. It feels colder inside than out.

All of a sudden the tea boy is back, throwing a lot of sirs into the conversation and pointing to some stairs and telling me to go up such-and-such a number of flights and go to a certain door . . .

A certain door! Somewhere up there is the newest established permanent floating private illegal gambling casino in London. Even while I started up the stairs I thought about the irony of the situation. The thing is, gambling—in licensed clubs—has been legal in England ever since the Gaming Act of 1960. There are some twenty-five legal, full-scale casinos in London alone. Why would anybody want to go to a private illegal casino and risk the police, arrest, scandals, newspapers, ruination . . .

It is true that the legal casinos are set up as private clubs, and a few of them, such as the Clermont, or Aspinall's, as it is known, after John Aspinall, who runs it—more about him in a moment—a few of them such as Aspinall's are actually exclusive. But practically everybody in England has a friend who is a member of a club and can take him in to play. Hell, at many of the "clubs," if a man with money and his head on straight has to wait more than five minutes to become a "member," that is a damned rude situation. As for tourists with cash in their pockets—an American can go up to one of these clubs and the man at the door will

look down from under his overhanging eyebrows and say
with this formal drag in his voice, Are you a member, sir,
and the American says no, deferentially, probably, but then
suddenly the man's face changes and rearranges like Plastic
Man's and—Well, sir, yassuh, yassuh, yo smile is yo membership card with us any day in the week.

There was only a dim light on the stairway. I kept
climbing and finally I got to the door the tea boy talked
about and it was still just quiet, cold, dim and drafty in
somebody's old moldering townhouse. The door was
heavy and had a lot of crowded carving on it. I knocked,
but nobody answered, so I went ahead and turned the knob
and pushed it open and—
Santa Barranza!—
—inside, the scene was the way I always pictured it in
The Masque of the Red Death, the Edgar Allan Poe story,
when they go through all the rooms in the big old moldering castle or whatever it is, and finally they get to this last
room, where everybody is having one utterly final choking
red revel in a room suffocating with red velvet, gilt,
ormolu, heavy glass—inside, as soon as I open the door, this
great heaving fullness comes rolling over me, sherry-yellow
lights, florid browns, hunt-blood reds, smothers, smothers,
smothers of merino cloth, velvets, tapestry, swollen, swollen, swollen with gilt, covings, ogee and ovolo moldings,
all yeasting up with the heat of the gambling funk, the
smoldering armpits of the punters, a stagnant haze of cigarette smoke, and voices, a low burble of voices and clatter-
ing chips, and a woman with a low voice and a Central
European accent saying:
"... pos-see-bul   flush ... straight-y-ning ... no
help ..."
The room is a huge drawing room, filled with green-
baize gaming tables crowded with young men and a few

women, all florid and ripening amid fading Louis XVI needlework, old Sultanabad carpets with white ticks where the woof is coming up and the goddamnedest bunch of gilded tables, sideboards and commodes you ever laid eyes on, riots of rosewood and ormolu, every table leg in the form of a great swollen jaded baby hooker with blank eyes and gilded nipples rising up into a gush of acanthus leaves —perfect!

Curiously, up in front of the fireplace there is a young man in a plum-colored shirt sunken back into a wing-back chair, the back of it to the room and the wings out like blinders, and he is just sunk in there, reading a book in front of the fireplace. Up on the mantelpiece, or just above it, there are what look like some family portraits. There is a photograph of a young man in a lolly collar at Harrow and another of a good-looking woman in a party dress. This is a young man known as "Lord Jim." If you only looked at him sitting there reading a book, you would think that this was an ordinary evening in the old manse and any minute now a butler in black twill is going to appear with a cup of hot chocolate laced with Naval rum and a box of full Coronas with a lot of carbohydrate Havana houris on the box, wearing palm-leaf hats.

In fact, however, there is a big poker table right behind the chair, curved and covered in green, with seven punters around it and a thin dark woman, the woman with the low voice, dealing five-card stud poker and giving a running commentary as the face-up cards sail out.

". . . pos-see-bul flush . . . straight-y-ning . . . no help . . ."

Deeper into the room there is another big poker table with a Chinese dealer sitting there, and then a blackjack table with another Chinese dealing, both of them being kind of thin Hong Kong dandies in dinner jackets, major white shirts and some kind of Broadway cufflinks, like chrome-and-glass tile from the Metropole Café, New York City. Close by the fireplace and the wing-back chair there is a backgammon table and two men playing. One, like the Chinese dealers, has on a dinner jacket, and the other is a typical English Chinless Wonder who keeps leaning over the backgammon board and bobbing and sighing:

"You bahstad. You bahstad."

Over in the corner there is a bar, an Amboina-wood commode, actually, studded with Scotch bottles, gin, vodka, orange squash, glasses and Schweppes siphon decanters. There are a couple of creatures in short skirts and white stockings tending bar and giving people cigarettes out of a silver box. They are the tea girls. And there are young men all over the place, at the bar, at the tables, sitting down, standing up and watching, watching the poker, the blackjack, the backgammon game. Most of them are young Englishmen, but there are a couple of Hong Kong Chinese. One of them has long boho hair and a Byron shirt made of suède and he sits there flicking 10-shilling chips to the black-haired dealer whenever he wins a pot.

There are a couple of those young men you see in England who look middle-aged at 28, swollen with expensive fat, wearing layer upon layer of worsted, waistcoats with step collars, coats with solid jumbo lapels. But most have that much-prized look of offhand decadence, the 1966 rake, the Chelsea adventurer who went to a public school. Some have marvelous model girls in tow. They sit just back from the tables in Gourdin chairs with—fine era!—their legs crossed, showing a little alabaster thigh where the stockings end. All these dim burnt-orange, ocher and apricot lights play on the whole baroque scene, like flambeaux or something, throwing all the acanthus leaves and the palm carvings into gold highlights and black coves, glistening model girl legs, cream thighs—

"You bah-stad!"

This time the Chinless Wonder screams it out and stands up abruptly and wheels about and walks away from the table. The man in the dinner jacket stays seated at the backgammon table.

"Kissy," he says. "You owe me 60 pounds. Why don't you pay?"

"I don't have any checks."

"I'll give you a check, Kissy. I've got hundreds of checks."

"Well—Tony—put it on the tab," says Kissy. He keeps fading toward the door.

"They all knock me," says Tony. "Knocking" is the same as "flying the kite," meaning spinning the credit line out and out.

Tony runs the game. He is thin, has an upper-class accent and a fine face. He has on a tuxedo and a piqué shirt. Everybody has stories about who he really is. Tony fought with the Foreign Legion in Algeria. Tony fought with the Arabs. Tony is a pacifist. Tony abhors violence. Tony is strong as a bull. Tony—once some adrenal punter said something insulting to some girl at a game, a huge guy. Tony picked up a fire screen and didn't even look at the guy, he just took the screen in his hands and bent it and rolled it up into a ball of copper foil the size of a cricket ball. The guy fled in a cloud of funk. That is the way the stories go—

"Tony!"

A well-dressed Fat Boy comes hustling in through the door behind me and rushes past me over to Tony and says, "There's a police car out front!"

Tony just smiles and arches his eyebrows.

"I tell you, there's a police car!" says the Fat Boy. "Look. You know? I'm not worried, but just in case-sort-of-thing, I mean if there *are* questions, if it should ever *hap*pen-sort-of-thing, the police and so forth—well, I'm an Austrian milliner, that's what you tell them—just say that, I'm an Austrian milliner, and what do *I* know, and I'll say—well, I *won't* say—"

"Ffffffffft," says Tony.

"I tell you," the Fat Boy goes on, "there is a police car down front—"

All this time nobody, not even the Fat Boy, takes any particular notice of my presence, even though I am an American they don't know and I have on a go-to-hell necktie with some kind of silvery embroidery on it that I got in a 14th Street–Persian knickknack shop. So I go on over to Tony and start asking him about this and that and about the way the fellow named Kissy "knocked" him.

"What do you do when somebody won't pay?" I ask him.

"Nothing," he says. "What can I do?" Then he smiles. "This is a gentleman's game."

Amateur gentlemen! Then he says to me, somewhat earnestly:

"How do you think a game like this would go in New York?"

"I don't know."

"Is there anything like this in New York?"

I didn't know that either.

"I've been thinking about going to New York, but I think it's a tough place. Do you know—?" He mentions some Englishman I had met. "He was in New York. He said his English accent carried him for two months, but after that they stopped being impressed."

"Come to New York and go into public relations and it will carry you forever."

"I'm afraid I couldn't. I'm someone who lives by his wits."

"So are they."

"But do you think a game like this would go over in New York?"

I found out later why he was so interested in opening up in New York. It was the whole Aspinall thing.

This game here, in this great moldering old Regency drawing room, may not be the high life—but, goddamn it, it *is* the high life. The ingredients are here, the basic Aspinall atmosphere. John Aspinall is *the* great legendary figure of London's gambling boom. His whole point was to create an atmosphere where gentlemen are content to come and gamble and *be Regency*, upper-class bucks, even if that means losing one's bloody gourds in the process. Aspinall became the proprietor of the poshest gambling club in London, the Clermont, 44 Berkeley Square, where Prince Radziwill plays backgammon and Lord Derby plays chemin de fer and people lose £28,000 in 20 minutes at the chemmy table, it's not even unusual anymore—

—so Tony has started out on the long road to . . . Aspinalldom. He will pay somebody anywhere from £40 to £80 to use a flat or house for a gambling session. The session, however, may run twenty-four hours or longer. For a perfect Regency setting, like this place, Tony may go as high as £100. He brings in the green baize gaming tables, the backgammon board, high-class translucent amber chips, high-class decks of cards with marbled backs, high-class chip boxes, high-class liquor—and even a high-class tea girl. One of the tea girls is said to be a former deb. And the punters, mostly well-connected young men in their twenties or early thirties, pour in.

The main game at Tony's is five-card stud poker, with half-crown chips the smallest stake and £10 chips the largest, with up to £100 or, rarely, £150 to be won a hand. There is usually one blackjack table going, and one backgammon table and occasionally some chemin de fer.

Chemin de fer involves a lot of doubling and quadrupling
of bets, however, and not too many of the punters at
Tony's game have the resources to go through all that. So
he depends on poker. He takes five per cent out of each
winning pot. This has to cover all the expenses, including
something for the dealers and the tea girls and the tea boy.
They also get tips from the punters.

The biggest headache, however, is the perpetual, desperate search for some grand place to have the game in. The
trouble is that they can't use the same place too many times
in a row safely. Next week they can't use this place. The
game has to float. But if somebody has a place big enough
to set up the casino in, he probably has money, too, and
doesn't care to risk his hide for the 40 or 50 quid. He also
probably doesn't want his drawing rooms, rugs, curtains,
chairs, sofas cured like a side of Smithfield ham by the
smoke from about 900,000 cigarettes and cigars com-
pounded with sweat, funk, sebaceous oils, model girl makeup, god knows what.

So the game ends up in some crazy places. Some *au pair*
girl's employers go off to the Continent for a holiday—and
she wants to get her hands on £40 and go crazy at Biba, the
boutique, or she wants to get a little of the high life herself.
So she opens the place up to Tony and the young bucks, or
to one of the other private games now going in London,
and then spends twenty-four hours with guilt and fear running up and down her colonic track. Or maybe there is
somebody's young daughter who wants to be . . . *with-it—*
day tripper!—and she wants Tony around with his fine face
and thongy wrists and the Hong Kong croupiers with the
. . . *thin* look, suave as a mother-of-pearl inlay table underneath a big bladed ceiling fan—Hong Kong! Macao!
basketweave suits—oh god, the rake punters in *my house.*
So as soon as the family is off on a long weekend by the sea
at Norfolk with the clammy winds flapping their measly

old hair, she is giving the servants the long weekend off and
pulling the curtains . . . and jumping like a starling every
time the Fat Boy says, There's a police car down front—

Police! Scrog! Scandals! The troubles! A lot of narking
up. But exactly! One reason the young gambling bucks
welcomed a return of the illegal private game was that
they actually longed for the good old trembly-bowled
. . . *danger* of the game behind draped windows and
closed doors. More than that, however, they wanted to
recapture some of the social élan of the private game.

In England, unlike the United States, gambling has some
potent upper-class connotations. The aristocrat doesn't live
by the rules that keep those poor gray tea-bun plughorses
out there in line. The aristocrat is willing to have it out
with fate, which is what gambling amounts to. Legal gambling, in the clubs, started out okay socially. Crockford's,
Casanova's, A Pair of Shoes—these places, like the Clermont, were all done up in the height of Regency style.
Crockford's, in fact, was the most famous of the Regency
clubs. And they all had glittering crowds and all the slick
magazines took pictures. But, gradually, it became clear
that anyone with money could get to the tables one way or
the other, through friends who were members or otherwise.

Of course, who cares-sort-of-thing. Everyone knows
that everyone's a social equal around the gaming table, blah
blah blah. Life is reduced to a field of green baize and a
bunch of counters, blah blah. And yet—there was something . . . *not satisfying* about it when a good English
upper-class voice, coming up from out of a belly saddled in
a step-collared waistcoat, said, Well drawn, well drawn,
across the chemin de fer table to some Cypriot in a
petroleum-blue suit and the flashy little wog doesn't even
look up but just proceeds to skin the poor bastard clean.

"We don't let any Greeks in here," Tony tells me. "They would skin these punters in the first half hour."

Amateur gentlemen!

Then there is this whole thing about the dealers. There is a demi-aristocratic tradition of the gentleman dealer or croupier in England. Everybody knows ————, the croupier at the Clermont, because half of them went to school with him. The Casanova Club has even had a titled croupier . . . Somehow it is more . . . *graceful* to have a croupier in a dinner jacket that fits, a chap some friend of yours went to school with, saying, "Almost, Nigel," than to have some chrome-eyed little man with lubricated hair just rake in your £5 chips.

Man, those chrome-eyed little characters! That's another thing. Gambling in London has been getting a little gamy over the past year; a little of the old *aroma du mob*. There have been a series of shootings and beatings at clubs, some of them involving the fruit-machine racket, which is like the jukebox racket in the United States. Suddenly some much-vaunted "Corsican muscle men" are in town. People have been getting heavied up, as they say, outside the Victoria Sporting Club and Mr. Smith's. At Mr. Smith's, as they lie there in the gutter with their bloody arses broken, they are reluctant to say anything other than that they fell off the curb.

So far the British government has let the legal casino business grow into a huge thing with almost no controls. There are no inspectors. There are no taxes levied on the tremendous amount of money that moves through the casinos every night. Before 1960 the police used to have to keep up some kind of vigilance to stop the secret, private casinos, which was a nuisance. Once gambling was made legal, they just said thank god for that and ignored the irksome subject altogether. As a result—if the widespread reports are true—American and European gangster money, gangster thugs and gangster thuggery are pouring into London's—irony!—now-legal casinos.

Irony! One of the purposes of the 1960 Gaming Act was to make legal something that seemed widespread and ineradicable anyway, the gentlemen's game. The idea was, well, these are usually people who are friends or move in the same more or less genteel set and they play in a club or a clublike atmosphere, and it is not an underworld thing at all, so why not make it legal and license it. Out of these good intentions grew a situation that was tailor-made for the mobs. Legalized gambling! If gambling was going to become a big business, who was more primed to go into it in a big way than the mobs?

Irony! A private illegal permanent floating casino like Tony's—and there are several others going on in London today—has become, outside the law, much more like what the law had in mind in 1960. Namely, it is a game among people who are friends or move in the same more or less genteel set and they play in a clublike atmosphere and the underworld is not in on it. The underworld is only in on legal gambling, and the amateur gentlemen—gentlemen amateurs!—are all cloistered, exiled, behind draped windows, upstairs at—

—at Lord Jim's. Lord Jim stares into the fireplace, still sunk back in his winged chair. Tony rears back in the Gourdin chair at the backgammon table. The Abominable Honorable Kissy disappears out the door and down the stairs, just an hon. blur between the honeysuckle balusters. The tea girl smiles, the Fat Boy starts, the black-haired woman drones, the Hong Kong boho says, heh, the Hong Kong croupier is tired. He stands up and stretches and then shoots his cuffs and his City Lights cufflinks.

"Jim," says Tony.

Suddenly Lord Jim stands up. He smiles; he is refreshed. His plum-colored shirt doesn't have a wrinkle in it. He rubs his hands once, walks over to the poker table and smiles again, sits down behind the chip boot, and, ah, beautiful, how you do it, my boy! He puts those marble-back cards through a few hoops in the shuffle, and then—the voice of Lord Jim in the five-card stud deal, *possible flush . . . no help . . . pair of aces . . . straightening,* a public-school voice, under the aegis of the lolly collar. Some City type wins the pot and flicks Lord Jim a 10-shilling tip. A lolly tip! He scoops it up smartly, sitting up straight, and says:

"Then-kyou—"

Then-kyou. Yes. Then-kyou, indeed. Thank you, Harrow, thank you, Hong Kong, thank you, model girls, Hong Kong scions, hon. punters, men from the City, ex-deb tea girls and the agile bucks of this world. Somebody must be out there turned on at Dolly's tonight, sipping Nuit St. Georges and trying to get a word in edgewise between songs by screaming funk-rock Negroes. And somebody must be holding up the banner for the old fight, amid building-block chairs, Haitian rugs and nubby muslin curtains in Holland Park tonight, laughing at Quintin Hogg's laced-up boots and Ted Heath's processed-Tory accents and Midland vowels, in the name of Socialism. But the . . . sporting fellows happen to be here tonight, up in Lord Jim's drawing room, under the aegis of Harrow and the Empire, amid the waxy yellows, the ormolu, chiaroscuro, cream thighs, Prussian blues and red funks—the Fat Boy!—and if there is a police car down front tonight, the punterbucks say the hell with it and then-kyou, then-kyou, then-kyou, then-kyou, life is just a broken biscuit and a penny fade, life is just a . . . yes!—private game.

13 The Automated Hotel

DID ANYBODY here on the Fifteenth Floor Express in the New York Hilton Hotel ever hear the joke about the two nekkid colored men at the bar? Nobody's heard it, hunnh? None of you nice, docile, simpering, sober, captive punks on this automatic elevator ever heard the joke about the two colored men at the bar without so much as a Nehi lemon pop crate to cover up their gnarly shanks? Well, Mr. Charming Drunk is going to tell it to you now. Here, inside this fluorescent stainless-steel box. Charming Drunk's head sticks up out of his shirt and his alumicron suit like a squeeze of Ipana. He has eyes like the bubbles in a carpenter's level. Charming just walked into the elevator from the lobby with a glass full of iced brown whisky in his hand and a name card on his lapel. His name is Taylor and his card designates a convention, I forget which one, the Professional Budget Finance Dentists of America, something like that. Conventions carom around inside the New York Hilton, head on, haunch to paunch, with everybody wearing alumicron suits, striped ties, and name cards and drinking brown liquor and every now and then spinning off with the centrifugal force of a Hot Time in New York into the elevators. There are no attendants in the elevators, they are automatic, and they just lie there on the first floor with the doors open for a certain length of time before taking off, so everybody can stand around inside for a while and listen to Taylor tell about the two nekkid colored men.

"These two colored fellows are standing at the bar," he says, "you understand? Nice quiet boys, you know, drink a little, talk a little, tell a joke, talk about the ball game, the new car, you know, the usual—except for an *odd* thing. They're both nekkid as jaybirds! Not a stitch on! Nekkid as the day they were born! You know what I mean! All right. So one of them says, 'Fred, me boy, sure as you're born, sure, ol' Shorty's been comin' round to your house.' 'Ah, an' y'know,' says Fred, 'you're a dirty liar, too. There's no Shorty comin' 'round to my house, unless it's you that's bein' Shorty—' "

Unaccountably, Taylor gives everybody in the story an Irish accent. He has his face right in the face of some poor woman with upswept sunglasses on, breathing his hot Naples-yellow breath all over her, and the poor woman's husband is standing there mortified, trying to persuade himself that it's really not bad enough for him to have to do something.

The lively New York Hilton! The automated hotel! Automatic elevators! All of this came back clear as day to me today as I received a letter from Horwath & Horwath, accountants, representing the Hilton Corporation in the matter of $4.79 I am said to owe the New York Hilton Hotel. Two nekkid colored men at the bar! An enchanting story! Back to it in a moment! But just a second, Horwath, and you, too, Horwath, you may represent an automated hotel, the New York Hilton, but do you understand the automated hotel *style*? I don't think so. I don't think you know how to collect a bill the automated hotel way. I want you to listen to me a second. I *lived* at the New York Hilton for a week.

This came about because I was about five magazine stories behind, with people trying to get them out of me with jackhammers, and I kept procrastinating, walking all the way over to Stark's for applesauce, stupid things like that, and finally I figured the only way to get them done was to lock myself in a hotel somewhere and just write them. So I picked the New York Hilton. The place looked gorgeous, a great big brand-new slice of cake. Forty-six stories high on Sixth Avenue between 53rd and 54th Streets. My cab pulls up to the entrance amid a magnificent outlay of glass, architectural cedar bushes or something, some kind of Neo-Prehistoric stone sculpture and a lot of dramatic ceiling spotlight. There seemed to be about a thousand men in alumicron suits with name tags standing out there. Alumicron is a new wonder fabric made of aluminum and silicon. Its advantage is that it shimmers and bends rather than folds, so that it never wrinkles.

Anyway, I kept looking for a bellboy, but instead the doorman told me to put my bags down and gave me two red ticket stubs and told me to "take 'em inside." I took them inside, inside the Hilton's terrific lobby, full of shiny-topped counters, ceiling spots, and wall-to-wall, like a shopping-center savings and loan bank, only the greatest one in the history of the world. I walk in holding my two ticket stubs, and there seem to be thousands more people in there with alumicron suits and name tags. It finally works out that you give your red stubs to some man, a bell captain, I think, who turns them over to a bellboy, who goes outside and pairs them up with the tickets on your bags, and he brings your bags in. It is a small note, and I didn't think anything about it at the time, but it is a key to the automated hotel style. In an automated hotel, like any really efficient large organization, such as the U. S. Army, or the General Services Administration, you don't go around giving a lot of haphazard verbal instructions. You do it in writing. Or you say it into a tape recorder. You know how the world runs.

I had a lot of chances to see how this works. I will just give you a couple of examples. The first evening, I went up to my room, No. 1703, which was rather splendid. It had a terrific panoramic view, mainly of the backs of buildings on 55th and 56th Streets, but terrific all the same, and it had some splendid furniture and some terrific electric signs next to the wall. The signs gave instructions when they lit up—"DIAL 5, YOU HAVE A MESSAGE," "PRESS BUTTON TO TURN OFF ALARM," and so forth. I think these signs have terrific potential for home use. There are a few bugs to be worked out, as I will explain in a minute, but they are a terrific idea. But anyway, the first evening the main thing on my mind was to get a package off to my nephew for his birthday. I took the package down to the lobby to the desk marked "Mail," and the girl there referred me to a desk down the way, and the girl there opened a door behind her and talked to somebody inside and then came out and told me to go over and see the bell captain. He looked at the package and turned it this way and that, as if that might make it all come clear, and then he said: "I tell you what. Go back up to your room and call the mailing room."

So I went back up and called the mailing room and they told me they would send somebody up right away. Two and a half hours later there is a knock on the door, and there is a fellow with a kind of blond pompadour, whose name was Lightning. I may be wrong about that, but, anyway, Lightning was out there in a uniform puzzling over a slip of paper. Then he looks up and says,

"1703?"

"Yes."

"You're the one with the package for Australia, right?"

"No, mine's just going to—"

"You're 1703?"

"Well, yeah, this is room 1703."

"And the name's Howard, right?"

"No—"

"It says right here on this slip, '1703, Howard,' and you got a package for Australia."

"Wait a minute," I tell him, "I called about a package, yeah, but my name—"

"All right, all right," Lightning tells me, "let's start over. You're 1703, right?"

"Right," I tell him, "I'm 1703." And I meant it. I felt like 1703.

"All right. You're 1703," he says. Then he wraps his eyebrows around the bridge of his nose and stares down at the slip. He freezes that way.

"All right," he says, looking up, "if you ain't Howard, then where am I supposed to get the package for Australia?"

He had me there. I don't know what happened to Howard's package. All I know is, if I had had any sense, I would have given Lightning a slip of paper with 1703-Wolfe on it, and that would have been it. Put it in writing!

It's simple enough! They do the same thing at Monsanto Chemical. But I was a slow learner. I kept repeating the same mistakes. When I had checked into the hotel, I had said I would be leaving Sunday night. Sunday morning I had a fit of euphoria and decided to stay through the week. So I called the front desk. I would swear I talked to a human being down there, although later I was told that all automated hotels have a so-called "memory hole" they switch you onto for all verbal requests. You think you're talking to somebody but everything you say actually goes "down the memory hole." Anyway, this voice told me, "That's fine, that's fine," and then added, tonelessly, "1703." That was me! 1703! A warm feeling! You can't imagine! I didn't realize that none of this counted, it was all just so much wind down the memory hole, until Skinny and Hydrant, two of the Hilton's secret-service duns, came around four days later.

In the meantime, however, despite the fact that Lightning, the ace courier, had already thrown me off balance, I still might have gotten some writing done if it hadn't been for the automated electric signs. These signs were stacked up on top of the combination TV set-bureau-desk-dressing table counter up against one wall, a remarkable object designed in the style known as Two Guys From Harrison Danish. The bottom sign, "PRESS BUTTON TO TURN OFF ALARM," was connected to a complicated alarm system involving the telephone, a tape recorder, an IBM machine or something, an unbelievable buzzer, and the sign itself. This alarm system got to me very quickly. The first night I was there, I wanted to wake up at nine in the morning, so I did the usual thing, you know. I dialed the operator and asked her to ring me up at nine in the morning. She told me to "read the directions," then switched me onto "memory hole" if that is the right terminology for it. All right. There were some directions on the phone there, and they said that to get yourself waked up in the morning, you dial 1 and then dial the time you want to be waked up—nine o'clock was 9-0-0—then you start listening for instructions. A terrific woman—with a kind of detention-home matron's baritone—comes on and says, "This is a recording. For your nine o'clock call, wait for the tone, then repeat clearly your name and room number." Then came the big beep and I said, "This is Mr. Wolfe in Room 1703." Sure enough, at nine o'clock the next morning, all hell broke loose in the room. The alarm went off on the TV set-bureau-desk-etc., in shock waves like one of those incredible diesel claxons the New York Fire Department has now, and the big electric sign started flashing: "PRESS BUTTON TO TURN OFF ALARM," "PRESS BUTTON TO TURN OFF ALARM!" Pow! Flash! Pow! Flash! Get yo' mouldy shanks up on the flo'! Gawd, I roar up out of bed, throw my heart into fibrillation, and press button to turn off alarm. Relief! But then the whole thing began to bother me. There I had been, the night before, sitting down on the bed and talking into a set of machines and saying, "This is Mr. Wolfe." Mister! Massah! So the next night I dialed 9-0-8—and the voice came on and said, "For your 9:15 call . . ."—Gawdammit, I wanted to get up at 9:08, whathell was going on!—and then the beep sounded, and I said, "This is Mr. Wolfe in Room 1703 . . . a great human being!"—and then I hung up fast before they could catch me. The next morning, however, it was the same, the same madhouse alarm, that was all. The next couple of nights I made short speeches into the machine when the beep came, such as, "You! Slaves in the electronic bowels of the Hilton! This is Wolfe, the great organizer, in Room 1703. Cop out!" But nothing happened; same wildman alarm, with the electric sign flashing.

One afternoon, however, about 2 p.m., I came back into the room, and, boy, it was chaos in there. The alarm was going off like a diesel claxon, for no reason that I could think of, two o'clock in the afternoon, and the electric sign was running wild, "PRESS BUTTON TO TURN OFF ALARM!" flashing, pow, flash, pow, and reflecting off everything in the room, the coffee-table top, the glass that contained the water that melted from the ice from the automatic ice maker, everything. It was maddening. It got me. I threw myself at the TV set-desk-bureau-etc., and pressed the button. The thing turned off for about seven seconds and then—blam!—it was on again. Maniacal! I pressed the button, and it went off for seven seconds, and then came on again. There was no stopping the thing. I didn't know what to do. Then I saw the telephone book, a big heavy one with a Hilton binding on it, and I jammed it up against the button. Lawd; that took care of the alarm. Then all of a sudden—pow!—the electric sign right above it started going: "DIAL 5, YOU HAVE A MESSAGE!" "DIAL 5, YOU HAVE A MESSAGE!" Pow! Flash! The same stuff. This sign didn't make much noise, just a clicking, you know, but all that light and the urgent admonition—"YOU HAVE A MESSAGE!" —well, it was unnerving. Besides, I was in for it now. My crazy speeches had done something to the whole system. So the first thing I did was Dial 5.

"Is there a message for me?" I asked the woman.

"Who are you?"

"I'm 1703," I said brightly.

"1703," she said. "Nothing for you."

"Are you sure?" I said.

"Yes," she said. "Not a thing."

"Well," I said, "would you mind turning off my light."

"Your light's not turned on," she said, "you don't have any message. You're 1703, right?"

"That's me," I said.

"Well, there's nothing for you."

I didn't even have to turn around. I could see the light flashing in the glass over the Hilton Original Print over the bed. It was something by Marisol. That was all I needed, Pop Art, at that particular moment.

"I guess you're right," I said.

Then I dialed the operator and started to tell her—but she would tell me to "read the directions" and then switch me onto "memory hole." I read all the directions in the room, fire regulations, every damned thing, and there was nothing about berserk electric signs. And all the time this electric sign is flashing, pow, flash, pow, flash—"DIAL 5, YOU HAVE A MESSAGE." There was nothing to do about it, so I just put a shirt over the electric sign, with the tail dropping over the telephone book jammed up against the alarm button. Then I sat down and tried to do some work, but I was only kidding myself. I could hear this feverish clicking going on underneath the shirt, and I knew that down in there under the shirt, in that bank of electric signs, there was a pent-up explosion about to go off.

That night was terrible. When I turned out lights, I found out I could actually see the electric sign flashing underneath the shirt. I would doze off and wake up, and every time I woke up, I could see the electric sign lighting up underneath the cloth: "DIAL 5, YOU HAVE A MESSAGE." There I was, lying in the dark in a Formica cocoon, with two layers of fabric over the picture window, one curtain like theatrical gauze and the other all lavender, purple, Damson plum and green-sap, seventeen stories up over Manhattan, flanked by New Jersey, Queens, continental America, the Atlantic Ocean, insulated from the world, with even the air preprocessed there in the air conditioner, in absolute quiet, except for the clicking that went along with the warning that was beaming out from under my own shirt in electric letters amid a Worldgloom packed in absorbent cotton: "YOU HAVE A MESSAGE."

When dawn came, I knew I couldn't stay in that room, so I went out and walked around, all over the place, and came back to the hotel about 4 p.m. The lobby was packed as usual, and I threaded my way through the alumicron suits to the elevator, and it was then that Charming Drunk, also known as Taylor, showed up. Naturally, the elevator was automatic and was going to ascend from the first floor at some predetermined time and not before, and so every-

272 : *The Pump House Gang*

body stands in there impaled by Charming and his joke about the two nekkid colored men.

He keeps bobbing his squeezed-out head toward the poor woman with the upswept eyeglasses, while her husband dies a few deaths, and he goes on:

"Shorty is, you know, when you're away from home, Shorty comes around to see your wife, and you know he's been there, but you look all around"—Taylor looks around in an exaggerated bug-eye above everybody's head —"and you never see him. He's Shorty! Hey, old sport!" Taylor says to the poor woman's husband. "You're an old sport! No, no, wait a minute, let me finish. These two nekkid colored men—nekkid as a jaybird, you know?— these two nekkid colored men are about to have a fight over Shorty sneaking around with Fred's wife, you know? A terrible fight. So Fred takes off his hat and puts it on the bar and then he takes off his coat and he undoes his tie and rolls up his sleeves and he hitches up his pants, and the other guy takes off his coat and takes a huge fishknife out of his pocket and taps his shoes together and takes off his belt and wraps it around his fist with the buckle out, you know, vicious—" Suddenly he stops talking and his eyes light up to about 150 watts and his mouth opens in a grin, but nobody says anything, and the lights go out. "Old sport," says Taylor, "you're supposed to say, 'But I thought these were two *nekkid* colored men.' Right? Memory! Memory! All right? And then I come back with, 'What are you trying to do, be smart—or pick a fight!'" Then he breaks into a laugh and lurches around . . . and . . . I don't know. What got me, in the long run, was not the fact that everybody stood there and listened to a drunk tell this stupid story that had nothing to do with colored men, nudity, bars, or anything, for that matter. What got me was that by that time it seemed inevitable, a random catastrophe, like a shove in the back and a blast of garlic

and armpit in the subway. It was Taylor who was right.
Taylor had on his alumicron suit and his name card. He
was plugged into the System. He was down in writing.

It seemed like that ride took forever, but finally I got off
at 17 and walked through the chilled mothball tunnels to
1703. I didn't know it, but Skinny and Hydrant, the Hilton
secret-service men, were hiding in the wings. I went into
the room. Skinny and Hydrant waited a decent interval
before coming in, about seven and a half seconds, I would
say. There was a knock on the door, and when I opened it,
there was Skinny, saying—Hydrant never did utter a word
—saying, "1703?"
"Yes," I said.
"We want to talk to you, Mr., eh, Wolfe," said Skinny.
He pronounced "Wolfe" as if he were playing along with
some kind of elaborate but foiled incognito I was trying to
pull off.
"Who are you?" I said.
"Security," he said.
"Well, come on in," I said.
All I could think of was that they were coming in to
liquidate me for making speeches into the alarm apparatus
and making the System go wild. What could I do? There
was no stopping them. I wasn't going to call the operator
and go through that "read the directions" again.
They walked in like John Ireland used to do as lieutenant
surveying the premises for concealed automatic weapons.
Skinny had on an alumicron suit and a striped tie with a
Windsor knot and was carrying a clipboard and papers. He
had a face like the neat guy in the "after" photo in the
toupee ads, sort of grateful to the Mo-Hair Co. and at the
same time all miffed about the whole thing. Hydrant was
much shorter and looked like—well, the only way I can

describe it is, he looked like a 1935 Michigan Valve fire hydrant.

"Have a seat," I said.

"What's that?" said Skinny, swinging around. Then he said to Hydrant out of the corner of his mouth: "Over there!"

Hydrant scuttled over to the door. This, I took it, was to make sure I didn't "make a break for it."

"The Beretta's in the closet," I said. It was the last good line I got in.

"What's that?" said Skinny. "Now look here, Mr., eh, Wolfe, let's see some identification."

"What for?" I said.

Skinny shot a look at Hydrant: Hydrant braced.

"All right, Mr., eh, Wolfe," said Skinny. "Let's just suppose we tell you that you gave us a phony address when you registered here."

"I'd say you had bad information."

"Then suppose we tell you we checked, and you're not registered where you say you live. Your name's not on the mailbox."

"I don't know. I suppose I'd have to tell you there aren't any mailboxes in the building. It's a co-operative. You know?"

"Yeah?" said Skinny. All this time Hydrant was ready for anything. Skinny stood there for a while with the room's various electric glows reflecting off his alumicron suit a little, and finally he said:

"Well, that doesn't change the basic facts. Your bill is four days overdue."

"Overdue?" I said.

"Yeah," he said. "You were supposed to be out of here Sunday."

"Well, you know, I called down to the desk Sunday morning."

Skinny said, "The Card—" he produced a card from the clipboard, "—the card says you were supposed to leave Sunday."

"They never let me speak to the card," I said.

"I don't care about that! I go by the card, and the card says your bill is overdue," he said.

Later on, "on the stairs," as they say, I had a vision of what should have happened next. In this vision, cleverly, behind my back, I edged the telephone book away from the alarm button and yanked the shirt off the bank of electric lights, and—pow—flash—the whole fireworks started, bam "DIAL 5, YOU HAVE A MESSAGE!" "PUSH BUTTON TO TURN OFF ALARM," the diesel claxon. Everything in the arsenal. It went crazy in there. Skinny collided with Hydrant at the door.

Actually all that happened was, I said to Skinny, "By the way, what's your name?"

But that produced an odd effect. Skinny got a blank look on his face. Then he took out his billfold and began rummaging through, and finally he handed me a card.

It said, "Kenneth Morgan, Assistant Credit Manager."

"You're Kenneth Morgan?" I said.

"It's on the card," he said.

But, of course. Perfect! Thank God, the man was down in writing.

Then he looked up with his Mo-Hair Co. toupee ad look and said: "I hope you realize, sir, this is a very tricky business."

I gave Asst. Credit Mgr. a check for $133.65, and then he and Hydrant ducked out. Which brings me to the subject of the aforementioned $4.79, Horwath & Horwath. The next morning I called up the front desk and told them to get my bill ready, I was checking out at 3 p.m.

There was almost an open laugh on the other end, I want you to know, Horwath, and you too, Horwath.

"Oh, don't you worry," this voice told me. "It will be

ready as soon as you check out. We have instantaneous billing. Yes, sir."

All right. About twenty minutes to three that afternoon, I rang up the bell captain to send a bellboy up to the room, but nobody ever showed up. It was my fault, of course, but I couldn't think of any convenient way to get something down to the bell captain in writing. Anyway, I carried the bags on down to the lobby, where the scene was some kind of modern Bosch or Brueghel. The Hilton is bedlam every afternoon at checkout time, and all the alumicron suits are caroming off one another. I didn't have to wait more than twenty minutes to get my instantaneous bill. Finally, a girl took my punch card out of a file—I got a look at it, and it was old 1703 all over—and she disappeared into the electronic bowels of the Hilton and finally came up with my last day's bill, another $24.17, which I paid.

So, Horwath, and you, too, Horwath, I don't know what that $4.79 represents, or how it could have been lost between the Hilton secret service and the electronic bowels, but that is not even the point. The point is that you are not going about the thing in the right way, the automated hotel way. I hope you have learned a few lessons in the course of this story. God knows I've tried my best.

All I'm trying to say is, if you go about it the right way, I'll pay the $4.79 immediately, even though I don't know what it's for. It's *style* I'm concerned with. So I hereby, publicly, openly, right now, herewith, pledge to you and to the Hilton Corporation my word: if you will do this thing the true automated hotel way, and send two assistant credit managers around to my front door, I'll pay up to-morrow, on the spot. They'll be able to recognize me. I'll be just inside the door with a baseball bat.

14 The Shockkkkkk of Recognition

THIS could be so perfect. Clarence, or "Clancy," as he wants to be called, a 23-year-old boy from Woodhaven, Queens, with tractor-tread shoes on and a charcoal raincoat that shines and an unsqueezed purple goober on his chin and a mother who gives him such a look when he comes home at night from wherever it is he goes—he, Clancy, will have Natalie Wood all to himself. *Shock*—the real Natalie Wood will be . . . *his in the dark*. None of those idiots like Penner, with his Leica, what a joke, $400 for a camera when what he needs is a complete brain job—but Penner and none of them are out here and Clancy will have Natalie Wood all to himself, if she will only come out of the hotel. Make her come out!

Because this could be so perfect! There were six photograph hounds out here in front of the Sherry-Netherlands waiting for Natalie Wood. The photograph hound is the new version of the autograph hound. Instead of getting autographs of the stars, they take pictures. Clarence, and all of them, they read the newspapers in *such a way*, like an old man picking around in the bottom of a Ritz cracker box, to find out who is in town. Pretty soon one learns that

Natalie Wood always stays at the Sherry-Netherlands, Fifth Avenue and 59th Street. One waits and waits with a Nikon around his neck and finally this little, girlish figure will come out of that great burst of brass facings at the revolving door—*Natalie!*—it will be the *actual, real Natalie Wood*, and one will have her in the viewer and—*shock*—suddenly, in that instant, one will *have* her. Nobody understands this, it's comical, they don't get the point—you have your face all pressed into the back of the camera and your eye, your . . . *self*, engulfs her like a lava-Jello amoeba, her marvelous great huge eyes open—little girl!—like they did in *West Side Story* and *Splendor in the Grass*, and when you press the button it makes this sound in your head, *shock*, and with a flashgun it is even better, the whole . . . *feeling* runs down your body like electricity, so that Clancy keeps the flashgun on even in the daytime—*shockkkkkk*—that *feeling!* Make her come out here.

Natalie Wood and some magazine writer in a striped green suit leave all the people in her suite on the 12th floor and get on the elevator. One floor down a man gets on and stares straight ahead and then he cuts a glance at Natalie Wood, and that's Natalie Wood, all right, that same trim little figure that turned everybody on in *Rebel Without a Cause* eleven years ago, the great big marvelous huge mothering brown eyes, looking a little more mature, of course, but very lively looking in this pink plaid suit and white textured stockings, it's Natalie Wood, all right—so he looks away and a runny smile starts to work its way over his face and then he turns to her, beaming, and says, "I saw you on television in Montreal last night."

Natalie Wood smiles, but she doesn't say anything. Uh, yes, TV, Montreal—man, this elevator moves slow. Ten, 9, 8, 7, 6—Silence is blowing up in here like a balloon. "Well, you see," he says, "I was in Montreal on business, and I happened to be in my room, usually I'm not up in my room much, but I was in my room, and I turned on the television set." Whew, boy, they make it to the bottom. Green Suit and Natalie Wood head through the lobby toward the revolving door.

I saw you on TV in Montreal. The thing is, Natalie Wood has been through the whole course in Hollywood, even more thoroughly than Elizabeth Taylor or Marilyn Monroe or any of them. She started in the movies at the age of six. She was a child star at eight in *Miracle on 34th Street*, an adult star at 16 in *Rebel Without a Cause*. She went through a highly publicized Hollywood marriage, to Robert Wagner, from 1957 to 1961, had the full Holly-wood movie queen treatment, including a marble bathtub on the second floor of her home that was so heavy the ceiling below started collapsing about the time her marriage did. By the end of 1961, when she was 23, she had made 33 movies, including two great ones that year, *West Side Story* and *Splendor in the Grass*. She had pushed the publicity mill as hard as it would go, then had withdrawn from it almost like Garbo. She was known as one of the better actresses in Hollywood, was ambitious and aggres-sive about her career but was well liked, cooperative—and today, at 27, is a rather natural, thoughtful person emerg-ing from twenty-one solid years inside of the Hollywood Petri dish.

One thing she has discovered is the Restrained Polite solution for responding to strangers who saw her on TV in Montreal. To be aloof is to have everybody hate you as an egomaniac. To be too responsive, especially for a female actress, is to egg on the kind of fan who hangs on, *waiting* for something, God knows what. So Natalie Wood smiles.

She made this trip east for a kind of medley of things, the TV show the man saw, *What's My Line*, a trip to Harvard to confound everyone and accept, in person, the Harvard *Lampoon*'s "Worst Actress" award, to get some clothes at Scaasi—and to see about buying a . . . yes, great work of art at the Wildenstein Gallery. This is very much on her mind, Monet, Bonnard, Courbet, and Mr. E. J. Rousuck.

Green Suit and Natalie Wood head through the lobby and out the revolving door, all those brass facings, shaped shrubs in great pots, the doorman, under the canopy, old Fifth Avenue—and suddenly, out there on the sidewalk some kid who has been lollygagging up against the brass rods that hold up one side of the canopy—he spins around, she gets a glimpse of his face and the nice fat pustule on his chin before he jams his face behind this camera he has, a camera with a flashgun, even though it is daytime—

"Natalie!" his voice says, "Natalie! One shot, Natalie, one shot!"

At first she thinks it must be some magazine photographer or some New York version of a paparazzo, whatever that might be, and she snaps into one of those big-eye sidewalk poses to accommodate him, but this guy is really a compulsive maniac, he keeps jerking into jungle-cat crouches, batting all over the sidewalk, emitting groans, gurgles, directions, supplications—"That's it! That's it, Natalie, one more!"—all the time operating the flip-roll mechanism on his Nikon like eighteen versions of Horst Faas, Vietnam photographer, rolled into one—"Just one more!"—bat, rocket, lurch, crouch, the flash just kind of winks in the daylight—"Heeeeeee!"—"Oooooonh!"—"Natalie!" Natalie, Natalie, per-fection . . .

Inside the Cadillac, as it cruises off, Natalie Wood says to Green Suit, "I always wonder who they are. There are about five or ten of them, I think. I see the same faces everywhere."

The Cadillac heads on over to the Wildenstein Gallery, 19 East 64th Street, and on the way over people in other cars keep peering into the limousine to see who is in there, they are still that way about limousines in New York, and a few spot Natalie Wood, who is almost like a perfect little Eloise doll in the back of this huge car, and then begins the funny thing with the floating heads. There will be a car full of people and someone in there spots Natalie Wood, and then there is a lot of agitation, but all behind glass, soundless, like something out of *8½*, and then the car is forced, by the traffic, to pull ahead of the limousine, and all these agitated heads behind glass float out of one's field of vision, and then the limousine catches up, and these agitated heads float back toward it, all soundless, a lot of silent shouting, Natalie Wood, Natalie Wood . . .

Green Suit asks her about her art collecting.

"Oh, I've been buying things for some time," she says, "but not by big names, just things I liked. I bought one recently by a Sacramento artist, Silva—come to think of it, practically everything I've bought has had children in it. The Silva has a child and sort of a beach ball, it's very impressionistic, but there's a child."

The Silva is over the mantelpiece in her house in Bel Air, but something else is going up there. Natalie Wood is moving up, to Old Masters, or fairly Old Masters, Monet, Bonnard or perhaps a Courbet that she especially likes.

"I like the impressionists, Monet, I love his water lilies," she says, and then, "What do you think of pop art?"

"Well — —"

"That's the way I feel about it. I don't think much of art that is just a *comment* on art. You know? And that's what I think pop art is, just a comment on art."

A few agitated heads float by, screaming soundlessly.

"George Axelrod and his wife collected pop art," she says, "and they can tell you why it's art and why it's good, but it's not for me."

George Axelrod. She has gotten to know several . . . rather more intellectual types from the East and even

Europe, Axelrod, Mike Nichols, Adolph Green, Tony Newley. There was a time when nobody paid much attention to Eastern intellectuals in Hollywood. They were bright and all, but they were . . . *shabby*. One means, some great critic or something turns out to be a poor old bastard who lives in a two-room apartment in a brownstone and gets down on his knees at night to leave a poisoned slice of raw potato under the drainboard to annihilate the cockroaches. But people like Axelrod and Nichols are not only bright, they have the money, too, on the Hollywood scale. When Axelrod is in New York and is strolling along the sidewalk, window-shopping, he has his driver tagging along, five paces behind, out in the street, in the Cadillac, because he feels like having it there. That is what they say. So who can knock Axelrod? Anyway, Axelrod collects pop art, and Mike Nichols likes Vuillard, and Joe Levine just bought a Monet for $100,000, *Charing Cross Bridge*, and Hal Wallis has his eye on a Bonnard, *La Femme au Chien*, and Natalie Wood's old friend William Goetz, the producer who changed her name from Natasha Gurdin to Natalie Wood, as a matter of fact, is one of the big collectors in the country—and suddenly *she*, like just a handful of the major collectors like Goetz, is in on the great moment in Hollywood art collecting: Jay Rousuck of the Wildenstein Gallery, New York City, holds a private showing at the Beverly Hills Hotel.

He flies out to Hollywood with a whole shipment of masterpieces, all crated just for this. All of a sudden there in the rubbery greenery and hot concrete of Beverly Hills is . . . real art. It really is. Such as the last time, when Rousuck brought about twenty paintings, about ten Bonnards, a Pissarro, an early Gauguin, a small Degas, a Sisley, a Courbet and, it is hard to remember them all, some transparencies of a couple of Monets. It's great—someone like Natalie or Hal Wallis the producer or Edward G. Robinson walks in the suite, and there are these masterpieces, right there, in the Beverly Hills Hotel, while the rest of the Hollywood world is still tooling around outside on the concrete with upholstered anti-whiplash bolsters sticking up on top of the car seats, beating time on the steering wheel to the music "Magnificent" Montague plays. All the while, up in the suite, Mr. Rousuck is putting one of these great, great Bonnards up on a little easel he has brought along. Well, it is called an easel, but it actually is a velvet-covered stand about the size of those trunks with rollers on the bottom that door-to-door salesmen carry around. Mr. Rousuck puts a painting up on the stand near a window, the daylight hits it and—*shock* . . . it's a *Bonnard*, in Beverly Hills—and one begins to emerge . . .

Wildenstein! The limousine pulls up; look at it. This place could be so perfect. Natalie Wood, or "Nat," as her close friends call her, a 27-year-old movie star from Bel Air, with a pink plaid suit on and white stockings, tucked back into the nether reaches of a Cadillac limousine— Natalie Wood will be in this palace of art greatness with the work of Monet, Bonnard, Courbet, the others. *Shock*— there will be the brush strokes they made at some actual moment in history, *right there*. Greatness captured—

It could be so perfect. One means, nobody in or out of Hollywood ever thought up a more perfect High Culture gallery than the Wildenstein. The Wildensteins built it as a gallery in 1932 at 19 East 64th Street. Five stories of pink stone in the C. A. Busby townhouse manner, with a blue banner flying high, saying "Wildenstein." Natalie Wood and Green Suit walk in, and here they are in Wildenstein's archetypical townhouse with soaring ceilings and pink and white squares of marble, a kind of Nash interior styling, arches, vaults, busts, tapestries, and two retainers who pop to attention out of an anteroom and say, "Miss Wood!"

Joseph Duveen used to keep the men in his gallery in striped pants. At the Wildenstein they dress in dark blue or gray.

"They are ready for you upstairs. Mr. Rousuck will be out in a moment."

Mr. Rousuck turns out to be a tall, large man, dignified, stately, as one might say, with a custom-made set of British worsteds on. He and Natalie Wood meet like good friends by this time. He shows her Mr. Wildenstein's office, which is like something out of the Musée Camando, quite Louis ornate.

And—the velvet rooms! The Wildenstein has velvet that just won't quit. There is an exhibition of French romantics and realists, Corot, Courbet, Daumier, Delacroix, Géricault, Millet and so forth, loaned by a lot of museums and big league collectors, such as Averell Harriman, Mary Lasker, Benno Schmidt, Robert Lehman, William Coxe Wright. The exhibition is on the first two floors, the public galleries, but even they are all velvet, the walls being completely lined, floor to ceiling, with pale gray velvet, with the floor covered in anthracite blue wall-to-wall and the baseboard, all around, made of marble. Rousuck takes Natalie Wood over and shows her a Millet and says, "He had a great influence on Van Gogh," which is kind of a tough way for old Millet to be remembered, but that is about the size of it.

Then a Corot.

"Once an art student asked Corot to tell him how to paint leaves like that, and he told him, 'Always paint leaves so a bird could fly through.' See those leaves? A bird could fly through."

They leave that gallery and just out in the hall is a Courbet, *View of Entretat*, with the sun setting over the sea.

"I'm really hung up on sunsets," says Natalie Wood.

Rousuck summons the elevator, which means they are going up into the private upper reaches of the Wildenstein. Up on the fourth floor, Rousuck opens the doors to a private gallery, and the three of them, Rousuck, Natalie Wood and Green Suit, step inside, and Rousuck flips on the lights, a whole set of ceiling lights go on—

"Ohhhhhh," says Natalie Wood. Suddenly here is an entire gallery, a private velvet room—*shock*—lined with Bonnards. This whole exhibit is for Natalie Wood. Oh god—across the room, opposite the door, is the Bonnard both she and Hal Wallis like. A beam of light is on it, a picture of a woman in yellow seated at a table covered with a checked tablecloth with a dog opposite her perched up on a chair or something. It is sketchy.

"God, it's . . . beautiful," says Natalie Wood.

"It is a magnificent Bonnard," says Rousuck. "It has everything you expect to find in a Bonnard. And of course that is his wife and that is his home."

"God, it's really lovely."

"It's a magnificent Bonnard. It has a very unusual composition. You see the way the table shoots up out of the top—"

They go down to the third floor, and this is the place. Mr. Rousuck opens the door, and here it is, *The* Velvet Room. It is like a cascade of velvet. Port-colored velvet, in Château de la Malmaison folds, seems to be pouring down from a great height. Four huge upholstered velvet armchairs face one wall. The wall to the side is one huge port velvet drapery, pulled back just enough to let in a shaft of daylight. Mr. Rousuck seats Natalie Wood in the chair nearest the light, and suddenly here is a trim little girl in pink plaid sunk into a huge port velvet chair with her legs in the white stockings crossed and sticking out from the chair like some kind of petite Spode *objets*.

Rousuck walks out the door and says to somebody in the

hall, "Philip, bring the Courbet." Out in the hall they have opened two more doors, which concealed what amounts to a safe the size of a storage loft. Inside is rack after rack of paintings in great gilded and ochre frames. Philip, who turns out to be a younger man in gray, comes in carrying a painting. He puts it on the velvet easel ledge, then steps away and the light hits the Courbet, nestled in the red velvet, with a sunset and wild ocean, and god, the way it lights up as the shaft of daylight hits it on the easel and—*shockkkkkk*—this is it. Natalie Wood leans forward from the great nest of port velvet she is in. This is The Moment, the great velvet moment in American art collecting, in *The Velvet Room* of velvet rooms, with a *masterwork* on the velvet easel, an actual Courbet, the actual canvas he put his hands and his brush to in some place almost a hundred years ago—*shockkkkkk*—frozen greatness!

"God, it really is beautiful," says Natalie Wood.

"Oh, it's a magnificent painting," says Rousuck. "Magnificent."

They have a discussion about how the red of the sunset is repeated daringly on the tops of the waves, and then Natalie Wood's head emerges from out of the velvet deeps:

"How . . . what did you say the . . . *value* of this painting is?"

"It's 40," says Rousuck.

"God, it's beautiful," says Natalie Wood. She sinks back into the velvet deeps.

"Philip! Bring the Monets!"—a magnificent, wondrous procession starts, Philip bringing in the Monets, bringing in the Courbets, bringing in the Vuillards, the Pissarros, the Sisleys, Corots, Toulouse-Lautrecs, up on the easel—*shock*—Natalie Wood's head bobs forward, then sinks back, god's own daylight hits god's own divinely inspired paintings, the actual, real paintings these demi-gods did, one can—*shock*—feel it, it is a *feeling* as the daylight hits these . . . *masterpieces*—god—

"God, that's lovely—"

"It is a magnificent painting—"

" . . . beautiful . . . "

" . . . magnificent . . . "

"God, it's really lovely—"

"It is a wondrous painting—"

" . . . lovely . . . "

" . . . wondrous . . . Philip! Bring the Lautrecs!"

Philip brings in the Lautrecs, two small ones, and one has only to—light—God—José Ferrer down on his knees —one picture has a red-headed woman's head and a few sketchy lines. The other one has a few lines of blue indicating a body and an arm and the beginning of a white background. They seem to be something the artist started and gave up on.

"God, that's really beautiful. What is their . . . value?"

"This one is 85. The other is 90."

Rousuck gives the figures, 40, 85, 90, in a matter-of-fact way. He is talking about $40,000, $85,000 and $90,000— but of course!—in this velvet cascade, in this . . . *moment* in art collecting, the figures are . . . *counters.*

Next, a Corot, a big one of a girl, nude to the waist, standing by a stream. "It's expensive," says Rousuck, "250 . . . She is half nude but she is carefree. See the leaves—a bird could fly through."

"Philip! Pull the curtain on the Manet!"

Philip pulls the cord and the whole wall on the other side seems to fall away, the whole velvet drapery slides back like a stage curtain and—*shockkkkkkkkkk!*—yes. Here is a huge Manet, about seven feet high and five feet wide, it has been back here behind the port velvet *all the time*—35 square feet of frozen greatness, a ceiling spot hits it, floods it, a picture of what appears to be a tramp with a broken wine bottle or something at his feet. It looks like the cosmic ideal of the whole genre of paintings of lovable . . . disadvantageds.

"How much is that one?" says Green Suit, speaking up for the first time.

"About a million," says Rousuck.

Downstairs Rousuck takes Nat Wood into his office and she says she will be back in two days to make up her mind, and he says he wants her to have something, and he goes to a bookcase and pulls down a huge creamy frondose art book, on Turner. Nat Wood looks up at Rousuck, then puts her arm on his shoulder and kisses him on the cheek.

Outside she says to Green Suit, "You know, I really envy Mr. Rousuck."

"Why?"

"Just think, every day he is with those"—*shockkk*—"great works of art."

About dusk the limousine gets back to the Sherry-Netherlands. Natalie Wood gets out and, boy, from out of the potted plants or somewhere, here come five photograph hounds, only instead of their usual state of ecstasy and exhilaration, they are almost belligerent.

"Hey, Natalie! What about it!"

"Yeah, we heard about it!"

"That guy Clarence says you gave him a nice little session this afternoon!"

" . . . a nice little session . . . "

"What about it! When do we get ours!"

"Yeah—"

" . . . one little session . . . "

" . . . Yah! . . . "

Natalie Wood and Green Suit hurry in through the revolving door.

In Clarence's—Clancy's—darkroom, there is not a sound, except for the water running into the zinc pans and just a little shuddering when a train goes by the elevated on

Woodhaven Boulevard and his grandfather goes into a fit of asthmatic phlegm snorts in front of the TV set two rooms away. Old men have this secret language or something. There is no light except a black light, just enough to look down into the pearling fluid and watch . . . the body of Natalie Wood start to take place—*shockkk*—oh christ, it will really be her, in Clancy's own darkroom, the actual Natalie Wood, still just a little girl, barely five feet tall, 100 pounds, just the . . . *joint* of a fructuous adolescent hip beginning to shimmer in his hypo, coming out, getting darker, oh god, those marvelous huge eyes will come out, right here, like a deer's, real, spread open at Clancy, like a surrender, sweet, a child, Natalie here in the dark in Woodhaven, Queens, opening, oh God, come out now, Natalie—*shock*—a celebrity *autograph* . . . no! a goddess captured . . .

Two days later—well, Natalie Wood wanted to get back to the Wildenstein, but so many things got in the way. All of a sudden there wasn't a minute left in the day, fittings at Scaasi, the picture for the cover of the *Sunday News Color Roto*—the man pushes up Nat's chin with his thumb and forefinger and says, "That's it, honey, chin up, and put your hands like this, that's cute," and there is a huge gilded shell as a backdrop. Pictures! But in time it all came to pass: she returned to Wildenstein's and bought them . . . and had them . . . a Bonnard, a Courbet, a Pasternak—Old Masters' *autographs* . . . no! Culture captured . . .

I JUST SPENT two days with Edward T. Hall, an anthropologist, watching thousands of my fellow New Yorkers short-circuiting themselves into hot little twitching death balls with jolts of their own adrenalin. Dr. Hall says it is overcrowding that does it. Overcrowding gets the adrenalin going, and the adrenalin gets them hyped up. And here they are, hyped up, turning bilious, nephritic, queer, autistic, sadistic, barren, batty, sloppy, hot-in-the-pants, chancred-on-the-flankers, leering, puling, numb—the usual in New York, in other words, and God knows what else. Dr. Hall has the theory that overcrowding has already thrown New York into a state of behavioral sink. Behavioral sink is a term from ethology, which is the study of how animals relate to their environment. Among animals, the sink winds up with a "population collapse" or "massive die-off." O rotten Gotham.

It got to be easy to look at New Yorkers as animals, especially looking down from some place like a balcony at Grand Central at the rush hour Friday afternoon. The floor was filled with the poor white humans, running around, dodging, blinking their eyes, making a sound like a pen full of starlings or rats or something.

"Listen to them skid," says Dr. Hall.

He was right. The poor old etiolate animals were out there skidding on their rubber soles. You could hear it once he pointed it out. They stop short to keep from hitting somebody or because they are disoriented and they suddenly stop and look around, and they skid on their rubber-sole shoes, and a screech goes up. They pour out onto the floor down the escalators from the Pan-Am Building, from 42nd Street, from Lexington Avenue, up out of subways, down into subways, railroad trains, up into helicopters—

"You can also hear the helicopters all the way down here," says Dr. Hall. The sound of the helicopters using the roof of the Pan-Am Building nearly fifty stories up beats right through. "If it weren't for this ceiling"—he is referring to the very high ceiling in Grand Central—"this place would be unbearable with this kind of crowding. And yet they'll probably never 'waste' space like this again."

They screech! And the adrenal glands in all those poor white animals enlarge, micrometer by micrometer, to the size of cantaloupes. Dr. Hall pulls a Minox camera out of a holster he has on his belt and starts shooting away at the human scurry. The Sink!

Dr. Hall has the Minox up to his eye—he is a slender man, calm, 52 years old, young-looking, an anthropologist who has worked with Navajos, Hopis, Spanish-Americans, Negroes, Trukese. He was the most important anthropologist in the government during the crucial years of the foreign aid program, the 1950's. He directed both the Point Four training program and the Human Relations Area Files. He wrote *The Silent Language* and *The Hidden Dimension*, two books that are picking up the kind of "underground" following his friend Marshall McLuhan started picking up about five years ago. He teaches at the Illinois Institute of Technology, lives with his wife, Mildred, in a high-ceilinged town house on one of the last great residential streets in downtown Chicago, Astor Street; has a grown son and daughter, loves good food, good wine, the relaxed, civilized life—but comes to New York with a Minox at his eye to record—perfect!—The Sink.

We really got down in there by walking down into the Lexington Avenue line subway stop under Grand Central. We inhaled those nice big fluffy fumes of human sweat, urine, effluvia, and sebaceous secretions. One old female human was already stroked out on the upper level, on a stretcher, with two policemen standing by. The other humans barely looked at her. They rushed into line. They bellied each other, haunch to paunch, down the stairs. Human heads shone through the gratings. The species North European tried to create bubbles of space around themselves, about a foot and a half in diameter—

"See, he's reacting against the line," says Dr. Hall.

—but the species Mediterranean presses on in. The hell with bubbles of space. The species North European resents that, this male human behind him presses forward toward the booth . . . *breathing* on him, he's disgusted, he pulls out of the line entirely, the species Mediterranean resents him for resenting it, and neither of them realizes what the hell they are getting irritable about exactly. And in all of them the old adrenals grow another micrometer.

Dr. Hall whips out the Minox. Too perfect! The bottom of The Sink.

It is the sheer overcrowding, such as occurs in the business sections of Manhattan five days a week and in Harlem, Bedford-Stuyvesant, southeast Bronx every day—sheer overcrowding is converting New Yorkers into animals in a sink pen. Dr. Hall's argument runs as follows: all animals, including birds, seem to have a built-in, inherited requirement to have a certain amount of territory, space, to lead their lives in. Even if they have all the food they need, and there are no predatory animals threatening them, they cannot tolerate crowding beyond a certain point. No more than two hundred wild Norway rats can survive on a quarter acre of ground, for example, even when they are given all the food they can eat. They just die off.

But why? To find out, ethologists have run experiments on all sorts of animals, from stickleback crabs to Sika deer. In one major experiment, an ethologist named John Calhoun put some domesticated white Norway rats in a pen with four sections to it, connected by ramps. Calhoun knew from previous experiments that the rats tend to split up into groups of ten to twelve and that the pen, therefore, would hold forty to forty-eight rats comfortably, assuming they formed four equal groups. He allowed them to reproduce until there were eighty rats, balanced between male and female, but did not let it get any more crowded. He kept them supplied with plenty of food, water, and nesting materials. In other words, all their more obvious needs were taken care of. A less obvious need—space—was not. To the human eye, the pen did not even look especially crowded. But to the rats, it was crowded beyond endurance.

The entire colony was soon plunged into a profound behavioral sink. "The sink," said Calhoun, "is the outcome of any behavioral process that collects animals together in unusually great numbers. The unhealthy connotations of the term are not accidental: a behavioral sink does act to aggravate all forms of pathology that can be found within a group."

For a start, long before the rat population reached eighty, a status hierarchy had developed in the pen. Two dominant male rats took over the two end sections, acquired harems of eight to ten females each, and forced the rest of the rats into the two middle pens. All the over-crowding took place in the middle pens. That was where the "sink" hit. The aristocrat rats at the ends grew bigger, sleeker, healthier, and more secure the whole time.

In The Sink, meanwhile, nest building, courting, sex behavior, reproduction, social organization, health—all of it went to pieces. Normally, Norway rats have a mating ritual in which the male chases the female, the female ducks down into a burrow and sticks her head up to watch the male. He performs a little dance outside the burrow, then she comes out, and he mounts her, usually for a few seconds. When The Sink set in, however, no more than three males—the dominant males in the middle sections— kept up the old customs. The rest tried everything from satyrism to homosexuality or else gave up on sex altogether. Some of the subordinate males spent all their time chasing females. Three or four might chase one female at the same time, and instead of stopping at the burrow entrance for the ritual, they would charge right in. Once mounted, they would hold on for minutes instead of the usual seconds.

Homosexuality rose sharply. So did bisexuality. Some males would mount anything—males, females, babies, senescent rats, anything. Still other males dropped sexual activity altogether, wouldn't fight and, in fact, would hardly move except when the other rats slept. Occasionally a female from the aristocrat rats' harems would come over the ramps and into the middle sections to sample life in The Sink. When she had had enough, she would run back up the ramp. Sink males would give chase up to the top of the ramp, which is to say, to the very edge of the aristocratic preserve. But one glance from one of the king rats would stop them cold and they would return to The Sink.

The slumming females from the harems had their adventures and then returned to a placid, healthy life. Females in The Sink, however, were ravaged, physically and psychologically. Pregnant rats had trouble continuing pregnancy. The rate of miscarriages increased significantly, and females started dying from tumors and other disorders of the mammary glands, sex organs, uterus, ovaries, and Fallopian tubes. Typically, their kidneys, livers, and adrenals were also enlarged or diseased or showed other signs associated with stress.

Child-rearing became totally disorganized. The females lost the interest or the stamina to build nests and did not keep them up if they did build them. In the general filth and confusion, they would not put themselves out to save offspring they were momentarily separated from. Frantic, even sadistic competition among the males was going on all around them and rendering their lives chaotic. The males began unprovoked and senseless assaults upon one another, often in the form of tail-biting. Ordinarily, rats will suppress this kind of behavior when it crops up. In The Sink, male rats gave up all policing and just looked out for themselves. The "pecking order" among males in The Sink was never stable. Normally, male rats set up a three-class structure. Under the pressure of overcrowding, however, they broke up into all sorts of unstable subclasses, cliques, packs—and constantly pushed, probed, explored, tested one another's power. Anyone was fair game, except for the aristocrats in the end pens.

Calhoun kept the population down to eighty, so that the next stage, "population collapse" or "massive die-off," did not occur. But the autopsies showed that the pattern—as in the diseases among the female rats—was already there.

The classic study of die-off was John J. Christian's study of Sika deer on James Island in the Chesapeake Bay, west of Cambridge, Maryland. Four or five of the deer had been released on the island, which was 280 acres and uninhabited, in 1916. By 1955 they had bred freely into a herd of 280 to 300. The population density was only about one deer per acre at this point, but Christian knew that this was already too high for the Sikas' inborn space requirements, and something would give before long. For two years the number of deer remained 280 to 300. But suddenly, in 1958, over half the deer died; 161 carcasses were recovered.

In 1959 more deer died and the population steadied at about 80.

In two years, two-thirds of the herd had died. Why? It was not starvation. In fact, all the deer collected were in excellent condition, with well-developed muscles, shining coats, and fat deposits between the muscles. In practically all the deer, however, the adrenal glands had enlarged by 50 percent. Christian concluded that the die-off was due to "shock following severe metabolic disturbance, probably as a result of prolonged adrenocortical hyperactivity. . . . There was no evidence of infection, starvation, or other obvious cause to explain the mass mortality." In other words, the constant stress of overpopulation, plus the normal stress of the cold of the winter, had kept the adrenalin flowing so constantly in the deer that their systems were depleted of blood sugar and they died of shock.

Well, the white humans are still skidding and darting across the floor of Grand Central. Dr. Hall listens a moment longer to the skidding and the darting noises, and then says, "You know, I've been on commuter trains here after everyone has been through one of these rushes, and I'll tell you, there is enough acid flowing in the stomachs in every car to dissolve the rails underneath."

Just a little invisible acid bath for the linings to round off the day. The ulcers the acids cause, of course, are the one disease people have already been taught to associate with the stress of city life. But overcrowding, as Dr. Hall sees it, raises a lot more hell with the body than just ulcers. In everyday life in New York—just the usual, getting to work, working in massively congested areas like 42nd Street between Fifth Avenue and Lexington, especially now that the Pan-Am Building is set in there, working in cubicles such as those in the editorial offices at Time-Life, Inc., which Dr. Hall cites as typical of New York's poor handling of space, working in cubicles with low ceilings and, often, no access to a window, while construction crews all over Manhattan drive everybody up the Masonite wall with air-pressure generators with noises up to the boil-a-brain decibel levels, then rushing to get home, piling into subways and trains, fighting for time and for space, the usual day in New York—the whole now-normal thing keeps shooting jolts of adrenalin into the body, breaking down the body's defenses and winding up with the work-a-daddy human animal stroked out at the breakfast table with his head apoplexed like a cauliflower out of his $6.95 semi-spread Pima-cotton shirt, and nosed over into a plate of No-Kloresto egg substitute, signing off with the black thrombosis, cancer, kidney, liver, or stomach failure, and the adrenals ooze to a halt, the size of eggplants in July.

One of the people whose work Dr. Hall is interested in on this score is Rene Dubos at the Rockefeller Institute. Dubos's work indicates that specific organisms, such as the tuberculosis bacillus or a pneumonia virus, can seldom be considered "the cause" of a disease. The germ or virus, apparently, has to work in combination with other things that have already broken the body down in some way—such as the old adrenal hyperactivity. Dr. Hall would like to see some autopsy studies made to record the size of adrenal glands in New York, especially of people crowded into slums and people who go through the full rush-hour-work-rush-hour cycle every day. He is afraid that until there is some clinical, statistical data on how overcrowding actually ravages the human body, no one will be willing to do anything about it. Even in so obvious a thing as air pollution, the pattern is familiar. Until people can actually see the smoke or smell the sulphur or feel the sting in their eyes, politicians will not get excited about it, even though it is well known that many of the lethal substances polluting the air are invisible and odorless. For one thing, most politicians are like the aristocrat rats. They are insulated from

The Sink by practically sultanic buffers—limousines, chauffeurs, secretaries, aides-de-camp, doormen, shuttered houses, high-floor apartments. They almost never ride subways, fight rush hours, much less live in the slums or work in the Pan-Am Building.

We took a cab from Grand Central to go up to Harlem, and by 48th Street we were already socked into one of those great, total traffic jams on First Avenue on Friday afternoon. Dr. Hall motions for me to survey the scene, and there they all are, humans, male and female, behind the glass of their automobile windows, soundlessly going through the torture of their own adrenalin jolts. This male over here contracts his jaw muscles so hard that they bunch up into a great cheese Danish pattern. He twists his lips, he bleeds from the eyeballs, he shouts . . . soundlessly behind glass . . . the fat corrugates on the back of his neck, his whole body shakes as he pounds the heel of his hand into the steering wheel. The female human in the car ahead of him whips her head around, she bares her teeth, she screams . . . soundlessly behind glass . . . she throws her hands up in the air, Whaddya expect me—Yah, yuh stupid —and they all sit there, trapped in their own congestion, bleeding hate all over each other, shorting out the ganglia and—goddam it—

Dr. Hall sits back and watches it all. This is it! The Sink! And where is everybody's wandering boy?

Dr. Hall says, "We need a study in which drivers who go through these rush hours every day would wear GSR bands."

GSR?

"Galvanic skin response. It measures the electric potential of the skin, which is a function of sweating. If a person gets highly nervous, his palms begin to sweat. It is an index of tension. There are some other fairly simple devices that would record respiration and pulse. I think everybody who goes through this kind of experience all the time should take his own pulse—not literally—but just be aware of what's happening to him. You can usually tell when stress is beginning to get you physically."

In testing people crowded into New York's slums, Dr. Hall would like to take it one step further—gather information on the plasma hydrocortisone level in the blood or the corticosteroids in the urine. Both have been demonstrated to be reliable indicators of stress, and testing procedures are simple.

The slums—we finally made it up to East Harlem. We drove into 101st Street, and there was a new, avant-garde little church building, the Church of the Epiphany, which Dr. Hall liked—and, next to it, a pile of rubble where a row of buildings had been torn down, and from the back windows of the tenements beyond several people were busy "airmailing," throwing garbage out the window, into the rubble, beer cans, red shreds, the No-Money-Down Eames roller stand for a TV set, all flying through the air onto the scaggy sump. We drove around some more in Harlem, and a sequence was repeated, trash, buildings falling down, buildings torn down, rubble, scaggy sumps or, suddenly, a cluster of high-rise apartment projects, with fences around the grass.

"You know what this city looks like?" Dr. Hall said. "It looks bombed out. I used to live at Broadway and 124th Street back in 1946 when I was studying at Columbia. I can't tell you how much Harlem has changed in twenty years. It looks bombed out. It's broken down. People who live in New York get used to it and don't realize how filthy the city has become. The whole thing is typical of a behaviorial sink. So is something like the Kitty Genovese case—a girl raped and murdered in the courtyard of an apartment complex and forty or fifty people look on from their apartments and nobody even calls the police. That kind of apathy and anomie is typical of the general psychological deterioration of The Sink."

He looked at the high-rise housing projects and found them mainly testimony to how little planners know about humans' basic animal requirements for space.

"Even on the simplest terms," he said, "it is pointless to build one of these blocks much over five stories high. Suppose a family lives on the fifteenth floor. The mother will be completely cut off from her children if they are playing down below, because the elevators are constantly broken in these projects, and it often takes half an hour, literally half an hour, to get the elevator if it is running. That's very common. A mother in that situation is just as much a victim of overcrowding as if she were back in the tenement block. Some Negro leaders have a bitter joke about how the white man is solving the slum problem by stacking Negroes up vertically, and there is a lot to that."

For one thing, says Dr. Hall, planners have no idea of the different space requirements of people from different cultures, such as Negroes and Puerto Ricans. They are all treated as if they were minute, compact middle-class whites. As with the Sika deer, who are overcrowded at one per acre, overcrowding is a relative thing for the human animal, as well. Each species has its own feeling for space. The feeling may be "subjective," but it is quite real.

Dr. Hall's theories on space and territory are based on the same information, gathered by biologists, ethologists, and anthropologists, chiefly, as Robert Ardrey's. Ardrey has written two well-publicized books, *African Genesis* and *The Territorial Imperative*. *Life* magazine ran big excerpts from *The Territorial Imperative*, all about how the drive to acquire territory and property and add to it and achieve status is built into all animals, including man, over thousands of centuries of genetic history, etc., and is a more powerful drive than sex. *Life's* big

306 : *The Pump House Gang*

display prompted Marshall McLuhan to crack, "They see this as a great historic justification for free enterprise and Republicanism. If the birds do it and the stickleback crabs do it, then it's right for man." To people like Hall and McLuhan, and Ardrey, for that matter, the right or wrong of it is irrelevant. The only thing they find inexcusable is the kind of thinking, by influential people, that isn't even aware of all this. Such as the thinking of most city planners.

"The planners always show you a bird's-eye view of what they are doing," he said. "You've seen those scale models. Everyone stands around the table and looks down and says that's great. It never occurs to anyone that they are taking a bird's-eye view. In the end, these projects do turn out fine, when viewed from an airplane."

As an anthropologist, Dr. Hall has to shake his head every time he hears planners talking about fully integrated housing projects for the year 1980 or 1990, as if by then all cultural groups will have the same feeling for space and will live placidly side by side, happy as the happy burghers who plan all the good clean bird's-eye views. According to his findings, the very fact that every cultural group does have its own peculiar, unspoken feeling for space is what is responsible for much of the uneasiness one group feels around the other.

It is like the North European and the Mediterranean in the subway line. The North European, without ever realizing it, tries to keep a bubble of space around himself, and the moment a stranger invades that sphere, he feels threatened. Mediterranean peoples tend to come from cultures where everyone is much more involved physically, publicly, with one another on a day-to-day basis and feels no uneasiness about mixing it up in public, but may have very different ideas about space inside the home. Even Negroes brought up in America have a different vocabulary of space and gesture from the North European Americans who, historically, have been their models, according to Dr. Hall. The failure of Negroes and whites to communicate well often boils down to things like this: some white will be interviewing a Negro for a job; the Negro's culture has taught him to show somebody you are interested by looking right at him and listening intently to what he has to say. But the species North European requires something more. He expects his listener to nod from time to time, as if to say, "Yes, keep going." If he doesn't get this nodding, he feels anxious, for fear the listener doesn't agree with him or has switched off. The Negro may learn that the white expects this sort of thing, but he isn't used to the precise kind of nodding that is customary, and so he may start overresponding, nodding like mad, and at this point the North European is liable to think he has some kind of stupid Uncle Tom on his hands, and the guy still doesn't get the job.

The whole handling of space in New York is so chaotic, says Dr. Hall, that even middle-class housing now seems to be based on the bird's-eye models for slum projects. He took a look at the big Park West Village development, set up originally to provide housing in Manhattan for families in the middle-income range, and found its handling of space very much like a slum project with slightly larger balconies. He felt the time has come to start subsidizing the middle class in New York on its own terms—namely, the kind of truly "human" spaces that still remain in brownstones.

"I think New York City should seriously consider a program of encouraging the middle-class development of an area like Chelsea, which is already starting to come up. People are beginning to renovate houses there on their own, and I think if the city would subsidize that sort of thing with tax reliefs and so forth, you would be amazed at what would result. What New York needs is a string of minor successes in the housing field, just to show everyone that it can be done, and I think the middle class can still do that for you. The alternative is to keep on doing what you're doing now, trying to lift a very large lower class up by main force almost and finding it a very slow and discouraging process."

"But before deciding how to redesign space in New York," he said, "people must first simply realize how severe the problem already is. And the handwriting is already on the wall."

"A study published in 1962," he said, "surveyed a representative sample of people living in New York slums and found only 18 percent of them free from emotional symptoms. Thirty-eight percent were in need of psychiatric help, and 23 percent were seriously disturbed or incapacitated. Now, this study was published in 1962, which means the work probably went on from 1955 to 1960. There is no telling how bad it is now. In a behavioral sink, crises can develop rapidly."

Dr. Hall would like to see a large-scale study similar to that undertaken by two sociopsychologists, Chombart de Lauwe and his wife, in a French working-class town. They found a direct relationship between crowding and general breakdown. In families where people were crowded into the apartment so that there was less than 86 to 108 square feet per person, social and physical disorders doubled. That would mean that for four people the smallest floor space they could tolerate would be an apartment, say, 12 by 30 feet.

What would one find in Harlem? "It is fairly obvious," Dr. Hall wrote in *The Hidden Dimension*, "that the American Negroes and people of Spanish culture who are flocking to our cities are being very seriously stressed. Not only are they in a setting that does not fit them, but they have passed the limits of their own tolerance of stress. The

United States is faced with the fact that two of its creative and sensitive peoples are in the process of being destroyed and like Samson could bring down the structure that houses us all."

Dr. Hall goes out to the airport, to go back to Chicago, and I am coming back in a cab, along the East River Drive. It is four in the afternoon, but already the damned drive is clogging up. There is a 1959 Oldsmobile just to the right of me. There are about eight people in there, a lot of popeyed silhouettes against a leopard-skin dashboard, leopard-skin seats—and the driver is classic. He has a mustache, sideburns down to his jaw socket, and a tattoo on his forearm like a Rossetti painting of Jane Burden Morris with her hair long. All right; it is even touching, like a postcard photo of the main drag in San Pedro, California. But suddenly Sideburns guns it and cuts in front of my cab so that my driver has to hit the brakes, and then hardly 100 feet ahead Sideburns hits a wall of traffic himself and has to hit his brakes, and then it happens. A stuffed white Angora animal, a dog, no, it's a Pekingese cat, is mounted in his rear window—as soon as he hits the brakes its *eyes* light up, Nighttown pink. To keep from ramming him, my driver has to hit the brakes again, too, and so here I am, out in an insane, jammed-up expressway at four in the afternoon, shuddering to a stop while a stuffed Pekingese grows bigger and bigger and brighter in the eyeballs directly in front of me. Jolt! Nighttown pink! Hey—that's me the adrenalin is hitting, *I* am this white human sitting in a projectile heading amid a mass of clotted humans toward a white Angora stuffed goddam leopard-dash Pekingese freaking cat—kill that damned Angora—Jolt!—got me—another micrometer on the old adrenals—